# SHAME

||||||||||||||||||||||||||||||||||||||||||||||||||||

## America's Failed Prison System

### RaeLynn Ricarte

Fulton Books, Inc.
Meadville, PA

Published by Fulton Books 2021

ISBN 978-1-64952-183-5 (paperback)
ISBN 978-1-64952-184-2 (digital)

Printed in the United States of America

*To those on the inside: The winds of change are blowing. Never lose hope.*

# Contents

# Introduction

America's prison system is failing on every level—public safety, economics, and humanitarianism—and this book was written to expose the heartbreaking truth about what is happening behind the wall, as told by those who are being warehoused instead of rehabilitated.

As you read *Shame*, I ask that you picture your loved one in prison. Would it be okay with you if that person was caged twenty-three hours a day, year after year, in a six-foot-by-nine-foot cell?

Would you have a problem if they were raped (or sexually abused) by corrupt prison guards or other inmates?

How would you feel if your loved one suffered from a life-threatening medical condition yet was denied treatment by bureaucratic snarls and an apathetic system?

Could you rest easy knowing that the potential for violence was always present and even the smallest misstep could land your son or daughter, husband or wife, or sister or brother in mortal danger?

Would it upset you to watch your loved one be debased, demeaned, and subjected to calculated humiliation at the whim of the very guards tasked with their care?

What would your response be to knowing someone you cherished would forever be treated as a "throwaway," stigmatized long after their debt to society had been repaid? What if they were labeled "irredeemable" at the age of nineteen or twenty-five and locked up the rest of their life?

Only when you contemplate and comprehend these harsh realities and so many other atrocities happening to someone's friend, lover, or family member will you internalize the desperate need to reform America's criminal justice system.

Like many people, I once held the "lock 'em up and throw away the key" mentality. My heart was fundamentally changed when a young man I adopted as a Marine mom suffered a mental health meltdown after returning from combat in the Middle East. In the throes of his breakdown, he committed a violent act in 2014, which put him behind bars for a dozen years.

It was horrifying to watch this child of my heart have his dignity repeatedly stripped away in dozens of different ways by a system that flexed its muscles simply because it could.

My concern about the dehumanization process of inmates I was witnessing firsthand led me to befriend other prisoners. Each has been inside for more than twenty years. They have taught me much about our menacing, bleak, and unforgiving system.

I began to ask, "How does anyone go through this and come out an undamaged person?" My sobering research shows they don't.

The idea of writing this book came from my anger and pain. As a journalist, I wish to give a voice to those without one. I asked Keith Ward, an inmate without family support, and Kevin Young, another incarcerated veteran, to help me put the project together, and they have given it their all.

You will meet Ward and Young, as well as two former prison residents, Trevor Walraven and Kathleen Blankenship, in a series of chapters anchoring this work. These main subjects helped gather answers from prisoners to a questionnaire. Some prisoners expanded on the questions by writing essays to further explain their experiences, and some provided art that reflects their plight.

Also anchoring the book are three chapters exploring the inequities in death row sentencing and botched executions. These are troubling and another indicator of major systemic problems.

I started writing this book in Oregon, so there is a greater focus on that state's inmates because I had easier access to its people. However, with Ward in Nevada, I was able to get help from prisoners there, too. As word spread about my project, I had the opportunity to gather information from North Dakota, Washington, California, and Florida. This book truly reflects what is taking place across the nation.

Nowhere in these pages will you find even a hint that crime victims do not deserve justice; people must be held accountable for the harm they cause. The other harsh truth is that there are those who are truly beyond rehabilitation, who can never be released.

Yet that is not the reality for the vast majority of incarcerated men and women, especially those who have committed crimes to support a drug addiction, those who have serious mental health issues, or those who grew up on the streets with few options for survival.

America's prisons are a national shame and we can, and must, be better. It is my firm belief that prisons are full of untapped potential waiting to be realized if we can change our punitive mindset and instead offer opportunities for redemption.

"Civil Death" by Francisco Hernandez, a former
resident of Oregon State Penitentiary

# Bye-Bye, Mama

*How do I tell the woman who carried me within for nine months, birthed me, raised me, loved and cared for me, loved me totally and unconditionally—whether she liked me or not, whether she liked what I was doing or who I had become—the one woman whose love has never failed me or faltered, who loved me beyond any other; how do I tell her goodbye?*

*Not because she is old and ailing, riddled with sickness and death, or taking her last breath. Not because of accidental death or something like a car wreck.*

*No, not her—me!*

*How do I tell my mother goodbye? Because I'm alive but not living—a man in a cage.*

*Because I'm sad, depressed, and so very tired of sleepless nights, nightmares, and voices in my head that are making more sense than the so-called doctors and mental health meds.*

*Hours upon hours lying in the dark with my head under the blanket, wishing darkness was death. That death was now.*

*How do I tell her that my greatest want, need, wish, and desire is death? Oh, Lord, how?*

Travell "Paycheck" Holmes
Serving life at California State Prison, Lancaster

||||||||||||||||||||||||||||||||||||||||||||||||||||||||||||||||||||||||

# Major Flaws In The System

"The question is who we are as a society. That's a hard one to take on," says Rob Raschio, lead defense attorney in Grant County, Oregon.

"Most people don't give a damn about prisoners. And when they do, it's too late. They think they are all just animals and then, one day, their kid becomes one of those animals and it gets personal."

On the wall of Raschio's office in the community of John Day hangs a forensic artist sketch of the trial of Charles Manson, a notorious leader of a cult in California who was convicted of masterminding seven murders.

He obtained the sketch from a friend and hung it in his office as a reminder that every defendant, no matter how horrific the alleged crime, must be given the right of due process under the Fifth and Fourteenth Amendments to the US Constitution.

For almost two decades, Raschio has been representing defendants facing jail or prison time on criminal charges. He says the core principles behind "reasonable doubt" and "presumption of innocence" are really just the golden rule—treat others as you would like to be treated.

"Justice is about making sure that all people are treated fairly," he says.

With clear evidence that America's prison system is failing, Raschio says it is time to factor the golden rule into our treatment of human beings who have been incarcerated.

Raschio gives an interesting history lesson on the American criminal justice system. First of all, the burden of proving an accused's guilt has been laid by the founding fathers at the feet of the prosecutor, who is acting on behalf of the government. In order to achieve a guilty verdict, the prosecutor must convince a jury of the accused's peers that the facts of each particular case support no other logical conclusion than that the accused committed the crime as alleged.

Perhaps aware of fallible human nature, the founding fathers took special care to guard against the unfair imprisonment of citizens, yet our system as it currently operates is heavily stacked on the side of the government, Raschio argues.

In Oregon, the process to decide if a case should move forward takes place behind closed doors. Grand juries are convened to hear evidence on proposed indictments to determine whether formal charges are warranted for each case.

The problem, as Raschio sees it, is that these procedures are handled in secret, so no one outside the prosecutor's office knows how each grand jury decision has been reached.

The defense counsel representing the accused is granted no chance to argue opposing, potentially extenuating evidence, so the grand juries only hear one side.

This is an enormous advantage to prosecutors and a "fundamental flaw," says Raschio.

But there's more to it than that. It has become clear to Raschio in his time representing the accused that humans tend to look at things from a worst-case scenario, and there is nothing in our system to alleviate that prejudice.

He has found it common for prospective jurors to enter the jury box automatically believing the accused must have done something wrong if he or she was arrested in the first place.

"Defendants are supposed to be innocent until proven guilty, but that is not really the way people see them," says Raschio.

He suspects that many people don't understand the importance of the power and responsibility they are given, as jurors, to protect their fellow citizens from overzealous law enforcement officers and prosecutors.

In 2016, Raschio went to Trial Lawyer College in Wyoming to learn tips and tactics on how to talk to juries. The end goal was to teach him how to discern between a jury ready to convict the defendant before the facts have even been presented and a juror who is open-minded enough to weigh all the evidence fairly and without prejudice.

"I think most people altruistically believe in the golden rule," says Raschio. "We each have the capacity to care about other people and to hold true to the notion that a person can be innocent, and that is what we ask the jury to do."

The deck may even be stacked against jurors these days, too, Raschio believes. Numerous obstacles stand in the way of truly fair and unbiased juries. One such problem is the fact that citizens who are selected to serve are often frustrated by experiencing setbacks in their own lives simply by their being chosen. Jurors are given only a small stipend for their time, so for the vast majority of Americans who live on the brink of poverty, service can be a devastating blow to their livelihoods. This problem is compounded by difficulties jurors face in obtaining child care or handling their own business during trials.

It is easy to understand why a juror would take every opportunity to vent their frustration on an alleged criminal unfairly, says Raschio.

To make matters worse, jurors are often frightened to learn from the judge about hung juries, those difficult cases where they are unable to reach a unanimous verdict. The results of a hung jury can weigh heavily on jurors' minds, especially when faced with the prospect of forcing the parties to try the case all over again at the expense of taxpayers. The specter of a hung jury can sway weaker jurors to succumb to more powerful personalities in the deliberation room simply to avoid the shame of a hung jury.

Once you get past the unfairness of the hidden grand jury and biases of jurors, there are even more problems with the system at the sentencing stage, says Raschio.

Unfortunately, Oregon voters approved Measure 11 (M11) in November 1994. That law requires mandatory minimum prison sentences for violent crimes and sex offenses, yet allows no reductions for time served or good behavior.

Sadly, more and more states have adopted similar laws.

Of the many arguments made in favor of M11 was the belief that judges had historically been too lenient when sentencing violent offenders, so voters thought harsher sentences would lower crime rates, which it seemed to do for a time. However, a comparison of Oregon's crime patterns and recidivism rates after a decade had passed showed that other states had achieved even better results with more flexible sentences at much lower costs.

Raschio opposed the "one size fits all" approach to sentencing because it deprives judges of the ability to rule based on each case and each defendant's unique or extenuating circumstances.

"People are individuals, they have a lot of different motivations for the things they do, and those factors need to be considered," he says.

Raschio's clients often choose to plead guilty—even when he advises them they are likely to win the case—simply because of the risk of much more time behind bars if they lose.

"The matrix we use just strips away choice. You don't think that could be you?" asks Raschio. "Let me tell you a story…"

Maryanne (name changed to protect her identity) was a certified nursing assistant but was off work and trying to settle issues with her estranged husband. Word came to her husband that his sister's child was very sick and had been used as "collateral" and left with a drug dealer in Idaho.

When the sister did not return to claim the child, the drug dealer turned the girl over to her grandparents, who refused to accept responsibility for the care of an infant.

Maryanne and her husband took it upon themselves to drive all the way to Idaho Falls to pick up the child, even spending their own money to buy a car seat so they could transport the girl safely.

Unfortunately, because of head trauma and complications from pneumonia, the child died in the couple's custody ten days later. Maryanne was charged with her murder.

"We could have presented all kinds of reasons why the girl died, all tied to her prior treatment and abuse, but my client chose not to take the risk of going before a jury and facing life in prison," says Raschio.

Instead, Maryanne pleaded guilty to the lesser charge of criminally negligent homicide, opting not to fight and risk the loss of her own child, age four at the time.

Despite Raschio's firm belief that he could win in the end and prove her innocence, the mother accepted a plea deal because she would be released in two years.

"We moved from a system compassionate in nature, where the judge made a decision based on a number of factors—evidence of guilt, nature of crime and harm created by the crime, who the person was and what type of a life structure he or she had to achieve a successful life moving forward—to one that doesn't consider the individual at all, but assigns and executes a number for the crime."

Raschio does not disagree with the fact that some prisoners are truly beyond redemption, but he wishes to point out that those cases are outliers and represent only a small percent of the total inmate population.

He is frustrated that M11 superseded felony sentencing guidelines that had already been adopted by the Oregon Legislature a few years earlier, which were supposed to make sentences more predictable and uniform. "The guidelines were sort of the middle of the road, but we never really had a chance to see how effective they could be," he laments. "The judge would have been allowed to use a grid that factored in criminal history and both mitigating and aggravating circumstances so that a person could be given more time or less based on those factors."

Today, Oregon has extended M11 mandatory minimums to encompass a variety of lesser property and drug crimes, which has made the system very complicated and more difficult to comprehend.

The result has been much higher incarceration rates, with Oregon ranking near the top in terms of prisoner population growth. There are now nearly fifteen thousand inmates in fourteen prisons and Oregon is one of four states that spend more on corrections than it does on higher education.

Even so, Raschio says our prison system is so expensive that there is still not enough money for decent programs that have the opportunity of changing inmates' lives for the better.

Instead, people are locked away in a violent environment where they are subjected to abuse at every turn by predatory inmates and corrupt guards.

"Prison is a gladiator sport," according to Raschio, which does nothing to set the stage for inmates to emerge into society as better citizens when they are eventually released.

"Retributive justice sets the stage for people to suffer, but it does not restore them," he concludes. "It is a system of oppression and works as such."

With the government now paying to house one out of every 108 Americans in one prison or another, Raschio says it is time for people to open their minds to the need to modernize and humanize an archaic and cruel structure.

To prove the point about our criminal justice system's failures, Raschio points to the fact that 90–95 percent of inmates are eventually released and more than 76 percent of those people will reoffend and be reimprisoned within five years.

The US has 2.3 million people in prison—more than any other country in the world—and that number has increased by 500 percent in the last forty years, according to the Sentencing Project, a Washington, DC, nonprofit.

It is difficult to effect any sweeping change to our system since the vast majority of inmates are held at the state level. In 2018, according to the US Department of Justice, almost 90 percent of America's inmates were held in state-run prisons, and only about two hundred thousand of the 2.3 million were in federal custody.

As such, true national oversight, or true accountability for the way each state handles inmates, is almost impossible to achieve, says Raschio.

However, the Eighth Amendment protects the rights of prisoners from "cruel and unusual punishment," and Raschio questions whether mass incarceration meets that test.

When asked what America should do to fix its broken prison system, Raschio leaned back in his chair and took a deep breath to gather his thoughts before answering.

"If you commit a crime, you should pay a price. Unfortunately, we don't seem to know how to calibrate what the punishment ought to be. All we seem to succeed at doing is making the person worse."

He continued: "We don't even recognize the old saw, 'You did your time.' Instead, we make them register as sex offenders, we leave them as felons—drastically curbing the work they can get—we leave their mental health problems unchecked, so they walk with pain every day. We do not forgive, we do not forget, we lack compassion. Until we show empathy, I fail to see how we can expect empathy."

Raschio had one more thought to add: "This is a very human system and it has all the fallibility of humans in it."

# Part I
# Kat: Journalistic Crucifixion

*When you drop that rock in the water, you watch
the ripples go out and you do not know whose life
they are going to touch.*
—Kathleen Blankenship

Walter Blankenship was the cop who rescued Kathleen (Kat) and her
two sons from an abusive twelve-year marriage, so she couldn't help
but see him as their hero.

When this hero began to court her, Kat felt on top of the world.
She had finally found a man who would love and protect his family.

In 1997, a year after finalizing her divorce from the boys' father, Kat, thirty-four, walked down the aisle again.

"I always had to be in a relationship, so codependency ran my life," she remembers.

The stone thrown in her life pond seemed destined to send out ripples of positive energy, but such was not to be.

As soon as the ink was dry on their marriage certificate, Walter's behavior changed. Kat recalls that he became controlling with their finances and monitored her whereabouts, even going so far as to track the mileage on her vehicle.

"I could have no friends at all," she says. "An abuser is good at finding an emotionally vulnerable person and building a web of deceit to slowly gain control. One day you wake up and say, 'How in the hell did I get here?'"

Kat, who had worked at the Stanfield city hall in Eastern Oregon, was required to give up her job after the marriage. It was considered a conflict of interest to have both spouses working for the same public agency, so Walter, on the city police force, had the priority as the family breadwinner.

Completely under Walter's thumb for financial survival, Kat was unhappy but managed to find ways to cope with her situation.

Then another ripple changed the course of her life.

One day, a high-speed pursuit ended with bullets riddling Walter's patrol car. The adrenaline-filled experience exposed a heart condition, which required surgery.

"He came out of the operating room a totally different individual, and everything he had been hiding became exposed," says Kat.

Walter went on disability and left the police force. The Blankenships paid too much to buy a stove and spa business, which soon started failing.

By their second wedding anniversary, Walter no longer pretended to be a loving husband. Later, Kat would determine by evidence that he was a pedophile and had married her only to gain access to her young sons.

"He really taught me what domestic violence was," she says. "I had been afraid of my boy's father, but I was terrified of Walter."

She started noticing changes in her boys' behavior, especially when Walter was around, but she initially attributed their withdrawal from family life as stress caused by the tension in the household.

Her suspicions deepened when she learned that Walter had lied about the age of a nephew who had committed suicide. Her husband had claimed the teen was eighteen or nineteen, but she learned the boy was actually much younger.

"It was a mother's instinct. I just knew something wasn't right with him, that he was a predator," said Kat. "I started getting my resistance back. I started to challenge him. I became a threat to him, and he started trying to control that threat."

The arguing and bickering between them escalated, and Kat began walking on eggshells so as not to trigger Walter's wrath. He would often say, "You don't have to like me, but you *will fear me.*"

There were always paybacks whenever she defied Walter or didn't live up to his expectations.

"My life was lived in dual appearances," says Kat. "The face I showed to the public, peers, and family—and the truth of the reality that existed behind closed doors."

Walter began threatening not only Kat's life but the lives of her children and mother if she tried to leave.

As desperate as she became, Kat could not think of an exit strategy because Walter would inevitably be able to track her down through his contacts in law enforcement.

"Breaking up with a volatile man is not like other breakups," says Kat. "You have to extract yourself carefully, gingerly, and then, even if you do everything right, you can still end up seriously hurt.

"Leaving an abuser can trigger so much disruption and danger that freezing in place may feel more like a logical choice. Staying is not just an act of victimhood. In some cases, it's also an act of survival. I often describe leaving a volatile relationship as being similar to a bomb technician—pull the wrong wire and an irreparable explosion may occur."

On April 6, 2001, the ripple in her turbulent life became a tsunami.

Kat had risen that morning to a quiet household. Her boys were with their grandmother. Later, they would pick Kat up for a bowling tournament.

Kat decided to delve into spring cleaning to ward off her depression. She flipped on the TV to provide some background noise. What she saw turned her world inside out.

"Walter had left this tape in the VCR, and I couldn't believe what I was seeing," she says. "There were three officers in the interrogation room at the police station and they had a woman handcuffed to the table and were taking turns having sex with her."

Kat felt like she was emotionally drowning as she watched the footage. This was proof that her husband was a sexual deviant.

"I don't think that my finding that tape was an accident," she says.

Kat popped the video out of the machine and marched upstairs to the bedroom where Walter still slept.

"I rapped him on the head with the tape and told him that I was going to expose him," she says.

She wanted to safeguard the video, so she ran to her car and locked it inside.

By that time, Walter was up and chasing her. He intended to make sure she couldn't use the evidence against him.

"I didn't realize what I had done," says Kat.

Somehow, during the fight that ensued, they ended up back in the bedroom. Walter threw Kat onto the bed and sat on her. He put a .40 caliber handgun to her head and threatened to lodge a bullet in her brain.

"He gave an enraged scream and yelled, 'I'm going to kill your kids and you're going to watch me do it, and then I'm going to kill you,'" she says. "The only thing I was focusing on was how to get the gun out of his hands so he couldn't shoot us."

Kat went still. The boys were due home any minute. She finally managed to calm Walter down enough that he put the gun in his bedside drawer.

She wrestled free of his grip and grabbed the gun.

Kat kept a wary eye on Walter, once again enraged by her action.

Standing with her back to the wall, Kat knew she was in trouble, and as Walter began to turn toward her, she shot him.

"To this day, I swear I never pulled the trigger," she says. "I think the safety may have been off and I bumped the trigger while I was aiming the gun."

Walter continued to lunge in her direction, and Kat fired again, this time intentionally to protect herself.

She backed out of the room and into the hallway, Walter still coming. Kat fired a third round. It hit him in the face, and he finally went down.

"I was faced with a life-changing split decision moment. Live or die. I chose to survive," she says.

In shock, Kat ran from the house and jumped into her vehicle, roaring away in search of her mom and children. She knew Walter kept a loaded rifle in the house by the balcony, and she was terrified that he was still capable of using it to snipe them if they showed up at the residence.

"I was totally out of it by then. I disassociated myself from reality and stayed that way for months," says Kat.

She intercepted her mother, who was headed toward the house. She had her follow until they found a place to leave one car so they could travel together.

Their plan for the day had been to go to the state bowling tournament. Kat showed no sign that something horrific had just happened while at the event.

Back at the house, Walter lived long enough to place a 911 call. Two friends from the department responded to the scene and found him dead. Much later, when Kat remembered the video, it could not be found.

On the following morning, Kat was arrested and charged with murder. By then, she was mentally and emotionally incapable of comprehending what was happening around her.

"I wasn't there," she says. "I went to a place in my head that was normal, in the middle of a bubble. It was too much for me to handle."

When Kat did later start recalling the events of that day more clearly, she knew that she was in serious trouble because the prosecutor and investigators had been Walter's friends.

"They planted females with me [in jail] who found a way to talk about the tape and ask me if there was a second copy—and I hadn't said one word about that," she says.

Much, much later—after the ripple of her life turned into a tidal wave—Kat learned the same fateful recording had been seen by others.

She would also find out—too late for her defense—that complaints had been filed against Walter for inappropriate sexual contact with other juveniles and had been covered up by authorities. Family members of other victims spoke out about how Walter used his cover as a cop to prey upon their children.

In one incident, a teen killed himself after suffering from sexual abuse by Walter.

"There's your ripple effect again," says Kat. "Walter worked diligently to control the web of his environment to ensnare his next victim. He perfected control using his police training and authority to exert his position and enforce submission."

Kat was tried by the media during the buildup to her criminal trial. Prosecutors fed information to reporters, who ran stories without verifying facts or even attempting to learn "the other side." She was referred to in the local newspaper as a "black widow," and suggestions were made that she had killed Walter for life insurance money.

(In reality, she and Walter had each been required to maintain an insurance policy to secure their business, with the previous owner the beneficiary of each policy.)

"I wasn't even the beneficiary, but they never bothered to check the facts," says Kat. "It was journalistic crucifixion. Articles sensationalized what the district attorney wanted the public to believe. These articles were printed without substantiation, only assumptions and theories."

Kat's attorney refused to allow her to plead self-defense or even take the stand. Instead, the lawyer tried out a new mental health theory, catathymia, which is similar to battered woman syndrome.

Dr. Reid Meloy, an expert from Los Angeles, took the stand to testify about this phenomenon, whereby an offender believes she can resolve inner conflict with a person she is emotionally bonded with by committing an act of extreme violence. The state moved to strike Meloy's testimony as he had not personally evaluated Kat, and that motion was granted.

Next, Kat's defender filed a notice of intent to provide evidence that Kat suffered from extreme emotional disturbance at the time of the crime. Toward that end, she was evaluated by Dr. Scott Recklind at the Oregon State Hospital. However, he ruled out this defense, testifying he did not believe Kat's version of events and there was no corroboration for her story.

In 2003, Kat was convicted of murder by the jury and given a mandatory twenty-five-year sentence. The Oregon Court of Appeals upheld her conviction without opinion, and the state Supreme Court denied review, as did the United States Supreme Court.

Kat's life had turned into a sea of despair, and it would be ten years before the ripples began carrying her back toward a safe harbor.

"I Am Human" by Jorge Cabrera from Oregon State Penitentiary

# When I Quietly Slipped Away

*I arrived at the Nevada State Prison in September 1975. My name is Frank DePalma and I was sentenced to ten years for grand larceny (auto), of which I had to serve about two years, but I spent forty-four years in prison.*

*How can that be, you ask? I was nineteen years old when I was incarcerated on a plea deal. To survive, you typically had to join a prison gang. Such insured, to a degree, your safety. Those who were independents, as we called ourselves, were those who sooner or later had to decide whether we would become a sheep (victim) or wolf (someone to fear or respect). My path was to become a lone wolf.*

*I was approached by heavyweights within the white gang and asked if I wanted to prospect for them. I must have surprised them when I said, "Thanks, but no." They asked again, and I reiterated my "No." That bothered them, and it also put me on my own.*

*In those days, prison guards did not involve themselves in convict issues, and we didn't bother the guards. So help from them was not an option.*

*I had been in a couple of fights in my first year, but aside from that, I kept to myself and was low profile. One night, while in my cell, four prisoners came in and asked me if I had chosen yet.*

*I didn't know what they were asking, so I surmised it was some gang crap. They quickly made it clear that they found me "pretty" and were going to have their way with me, either easy (willingly) or hard (forced).*

*I was born and raised in Brooklyn, New York, until I was thirteen years old, and growing up there, in what most call the ghetto, I learned never to hesitate in a situation. I didn't that night either.*

I hurt two of the four, one pretty badly, and he turned out to be number two in command of one of the gangs in the prison. Well, a hit went out on me, which meant I was to be killed.

Being on my own and having an entire group of people in a confined environment gunning for me made my future somewhat bleak and possibly short.

In the years that passed, I fought and stayed alive. I was convicted of one murder and numerous violent acts, which added a lot of time to my sentence.

In 1989, I was sent to Ely, and I was in the general population for, well, until the first week of February 1992. I was locked up for no reason except that there were lots of young gangbangers coming in and the director thought some of us violent old-timers were going to end up killing some young idiot. So he started locking us up and I was number one on the list.

I argued to no avail. I stayed in lockup, and as one often does in prison, I had a few encounters with guards and caught some new charges—attempted murder, assault with a deadly weapon, and battery.

I spent from 1992 until March 2014 in solitary confinement. No TV, no radio, most often no books. I fought until something inside, deep inside me, grew tired, lost all hope, and simply gave up.

I wrote on the wall. There was nothing more to think, nothing more to say, so I thought that I'd just quietly slip away. I did. I shut off, and little by little, my brain also shut off. Memories faded, I couldn't come out of the cell without freaking out (they say I developed agoraphobia).

I couldn't speak as I had hardly spoken to anyone for years, and my vocal cords were very weak.

I had OCD terribly bad, and by 2007, I stopped coming out of the cell completely. Time had no meaning.

My window was covered, so I had no sense of day and night. I only have fleeting glimpses of memory, vague as if "I think this took place," but I can't be sure. It's all a cloud to me.

Then in 2014, after twenty-two years in solitary confinement, I was taken from Ely to Northern Nevada Correctional Center for a psych evaluation because I had been observed pulling out my teeth, which took *hours, when they got infected. I chose the pain over the horror of coming out of the cell.*

*For nearly seven years, I didn't come out of my cell, and the guards didn't come in. I was just waiting to die.*

*This prison system took so much from me. It took my soul for a time, but I got it back; it was given back to me by an assistant warden who refused to give up on me (that is a story for another time).*

*This place might have taken much, but it taught me what needs to be done, and now I must give back so my life will count for something. I believe in myself and I hope again—real hope. I am ready to stand on my own and go out to a world I know nothing about.*

*I intend to fight for change. It's what I must do, and it's what I want and need to do. And I'll be heard, I promise you.*

# Warehousing Humans Doesn't Work

"When someone has broken a law in America, we say, 'Bad human!' and then we put them in a literal cage. We strip them of all their rights, including dignity and respect," says Oregon Representative Duane Stark.

"Then after we've caged people, we expect them to come out as better humans. Is it any wonder that we have the recidivism rates we do?"

Stark, a Republican, has added his voice to the growing call for prison reform after touring Norway's prisons and seeing the effectiveness of restorative justice.

As a pastor at River Valley Church in Grants Pass, Stark has always believed the Christian faith requires mercy and grace—and that all people are redeemable in God's eyes.

He resides in Grants Pass, a former logging community that is largely politically conservative, a segment of the population that tends to hold to the old saw "lock 'em up and throw away the key."

Stark says that mindset is changing among GOP leaders because it has become clear that America's public safety needs are not being met by the current system.

Not only do taxpayers fail to get a return on their investment, Stark says the cruel, dangerous, and inhumane living conditions of US prisons have grown increasingly troubling to people of all political stripes.

There are 1,945 state and federal prisons operating within the US, more than four times the number of second-place Russia.

"Despite how much we've tried here, our model of punishment just isn't working," says Stark.

He believes the huge prison population in the US can be tied to a series of harsh sentencing policies adopted during the "tough on crime" era of the 1980s and 1990s. This philosophy put more people behind bars for longer periods of time as "just deserts" punishment.

Following implementation of these laws, the US saw a huge spike in the number of life sentences that were imposed—one in nine inmates is now serving life, nearly a third without the possibility of parole, according to a report by the Sentencing Project. The nonprofit group advocating for change reports there are more people behind bars for a drug offense than the entire prison population for any crime in 1980.

It will take a while to turn things around, says Stark. However, there is a growing push among states, including Oregon, to adopt evidence-based practices for incarceration. This new movement involves a "criminogenic" needs assessment that determines factors in an offender's life that contributed to his or her breaking the law. It asks questions such as "Was the individual part of an antisocial peer group?" "Was he or she addicted to drugs or alcohol?" and "Did the person have a lack of impulse control? "A dysfunctional belief system?"

The assessment also looks at causal factors that may have led the person into crime, such as whether his or her basic needs for food and shelter were met, or if there was a lack of a job or a sustainable income.

The next step in evidence-based sentencing is to determine what would motivate the offender to change and what types of incentives would be effective. The goal is to rewire the mindset of inmates through repetitive practice of pro-social behaviors, thereby reducing occurrences of recidivism.

Matching inmates with a customized treatment program instead of using a one-size-fits-all approach is another component, says Stark.

He believes that an effective recidivism reduction plan for inmates would necessitate collaboration with nonprofits, faith or community organizations, and job training services. All these groups would be involved in preparing the person behind bars for successful reentry into society.

A vital part of the program to rehabilitate inmates, says Stark, is making sure positive actions in prison are recognized and reinforced. This has been shown in numerous studies to be more effective than sanctions at bringing about change. Years of studies show that sanctions can quickly become meaningless because humans have the capacity to rapidly adapt to even the most miserable conditions.

Evidence-based practices are being used on a widespread basis in Canada, Australia, and the United Kingdom. Stark had the opportunity to view these procedures in action when he visited Norway in 2017. The trip was sponsored by the Prison Law Office, a California-based public-interest law firm.

"Norway opened my eyes to what incarceration should be about," he says. "I now look at inmates from a different viewpoint."

Like most Americans who do not know someone on the inside, he didn't care one way or the other about how prisoners lived.

Colette Peters, head of Oregon's Department of Corrections and several Democratic legislators, accompanied Stark. They witnessed a justice system that focused not only on healing victims but also on those who had caused harm.

They learned Norway's prisons generate hope instead of the despair that permeates America's institutions.

At the heart of Norway's justice model is the knowledge that stripping someone of freedom is enough of a punishment for a crime. Time behind bars is spent helping inmates acquire job and life skills so they can return to the free world as good neighbors.

Even the most violent criminals are given an original sentence of not more than twenty-one years in Norway. The twenty-one-year sentence applies even to Andrews Breivik, who killed seventy-seven people in July 2011 in Norway's worst act of violence since the Second World War.

If Norway officials deem someone still poses a threat to society after being incarcerated for two decades, five-year increments are tacked onto their sentence, but there is always the possibility for them to earn freedom.

"You can take someone and put them in a room at a luxury hotel and give them room service, but despite the great living conditions, it is only going to take about a week before they feel they are in a cage if they are given no freedom," says Stark. "People are not wired to have no liberty—the comfort will only satisfy them for a short time if they are not free."

In Norway, he found normalization of inmate lives is considered essential to helping them learn the value of stability. Toward that end, inmates are given privacy, with individual bathrooms instead of having to use the toilet in the open. There are even mini fridges in each cell. They are able to check out for work and school on the outside. Many can earn home leave with good behavior, strengthening their connection with families.

Inmates in each unit work together to pack lunches and pool resources to plan a menu, shop for groceries, and cook meals. Tables are set with metal silverware and glass plates, all of which are considered as potential weapons in the US.

"Their whole program is designed around individual responsibility," says Stark.

In Norway, conjugal visits are another way to help keep family bonds strong. These visits are regarded as a right rather than a privilege that has to be earned.

In US prisons, inmates are even prohibited from releasing sexual tension through masturbation. Conjugal visits are only allowed in four states—Washington, New York, California, and Connecticut—but there is little money for these programs. Stark said these states do at least recognize that a prisoner who has maintained close spousal ties will have a stronger relationship to come home to, making the likelihood of a successful return to society far greater and the draw of further criminal activity less powerful. Studies have also shown that prisoners allowed conjugal visits are less prone to violence and other misconduct while incarcerated.

The Bureau of Justice Statistics reports that around eighty thousand women and men a year get sexually abused in America's prisons.

Reform groups believe the actual number of rapes is much higher because subjects are unlikely to report abuse due to shame or fear of retaliation.

The overwhelming majority of these cases are men raped by other men. To deal with the problem, Congress passed the Prison Rape Elimination Act in 2003. The purpose of the act is to "provide for the analysis of the incidence and effects of prison rape in federal, state and local institutions and to provide information resources, recommendations and funding to protect individuals from prison rape," according to elected leaders.

"People might not like the idea of conjugal visits because it seems to be rewarding people who we think should be suffering, but Norway does not have the problem of prison rapes that we do," says Stark.

Another aspect of Norway's humanitarianism, he says, is that corrections officers are trained social workers. Guard stations are designed to be tiny and cramped, which encourages officers to be out on the floor interacting more with inmates.

Prisons in Norway, said Stark, are modern and cheerful and there are plenty of green spaces, a direct contrast to the colorless, bleak institutions of the US. The conventional security devices of America's prisons, such as barbed wire, electric fences, and towers manned with snipers, are missing in Norway.

Despite not having a paramilitary approach to security, Stark says little violence is reported at Norway prisons—most occurs in the unit where inmates with psychological disorders are housed. Normally, when inmates have a dispute, they engage in a mediation session under staff supervision.

"When we were looking around, we were like deer in the headlights—you just don't see anything like that here," says Stark.

One inmate, who served as their tour guide, told the Americans, "We are treated so respectfully that I have no choice but to reflect and become a better human."

Stark returned from Norway with a passion to change the way Oregon deals with inmates. He is now meeting with other legislators to draft reform proposals to bring before the assembly.

Stark cochairs the Public Safety Ways and Means Committee that oversees the DOC budget, which gives him an ability to influence change. He says reforms for the immediate future might be small, such as hanging shower curtains around toilets for privacy or adding greenery to prison settings, but he is aiming for big long-term changes.

"You tend to do what you know but now we know something different, so we need to do things differently," he says.

To pave the way for change, Stark says there was an exchange of corrections officers between Norway and Oregon so people who work in our facilities could witness the difference between the two systems.

"How do we find the balance between justice and even punitive satisfaction for the victim and still offer rehabilitation?" he asks. "I'm just getting started, so right now I'm trying to figure out what we need to do to start that conversation."

The bottom line, says Stark, is that the US has a lot to learn about how to do prisons right, and he urges people to check out how Norway and other nations are succeeding in their rehabilitation of those who commit even heinous crimes.

"We're making some great attempts but we're far from where they are," Stark says.

||||||||||||||||||||||||||||||||||||||||||||||||||||||||||||||||||||||

# Part I
# Keith: Neglected And Suffering

*The State of Oregon almost killed me, and it would
be nice if the State of Nevada didn't finish the job.*
—Keith Ward

Keith Ward, sixty-four, has been in and out of jail and prisons since
his teenage years for crimes he committed to feed a heroin addiction.
A judge in Nevada ultimately sentenced him to life with the possibility of parole for being a habitual offender, and he is incarcerated at
Warm Springs Correctional Center in Carson City, Nevada.

Keith will admit that being incarcerated the first time did no good.
He exited prison after that thirteen-year stint still an addict because "you

can get anything you want in here." Five years later, in 2001, he committed another armed robbery in Las Vegas and fled the state.

After several months on the run, Keith turned himself in to federal authorities on the East Coast. He was extradited from Virginia back to Nevada and found guilty by a jury of the robbery. He has served twenty years of his life sentence. Keith eagerly awaits his next parole hearing in 2023 and is hopeful of being released.

He kicked his drug habit shortly after being locked up the final time and long ago completed all the available rehabilitation programming.

"I am hoping that I live long enough with what's going on in here to get my freedom back," he says.

In early 2018, Keith received a settlement from his medical neglect lawsuit against the Oregon Department of Corrections and Dr. John Vargo, the physician he accused of malpractice.

Despite having committed his crimes in Nevada, Keith was housed for nine years in Oregon due to security concerns tied to a case he declined to discuss.

Keith's lawsuit for medical neglect was based on a forty-year-old landmark ruling by the US Supreme Court that ignoring a prisoner's serious medical needs amounts to cruel and unusual punishment, which is prohibited by the Eighth Amendment of the US Constitution.

The high court noted in *Estelle v. Gamble* that inmates are forced to rely on prison authorities for care, and if those officials fail to meet that responsibility, they can be held liable for the harm that is done. In the worst cases, the Supreme Court determined that such a failure may constitute physical torture or even cause a lingering death. They held that the denial of medical care resulting in pain and suffering serves no penological purpose.

Keith's story exemplifies a violation of such constitutionally mandated care, but sadly his one case is among thousands demonstrating the apathetic and abusive attitude of prison healthcare workers.

"I'm not a weak person, I grew up in the streets, and I didn't have shit handed to me," he says. "But dealing with this system has taken all the strength I have because it will break you down."

In January 2011, Dr. Alan Hay of Willamette Urology in Salem, Oregon, noted Keith's PSA (prostate-specific antigen) level was elevated and needed monitoring. Hay recommended that testing be done every six months to watch for any emerging health problem.

Hay wanted to watch Keith's PSA, a protein produced exclusively by prostate cells. Higher levels of PSA often indicate cancer.

Vargo, who worked at the prison, did not tell Keith about Hay's recommendation and more than four years passed before another PSA was done. That followed Keith's trip to an outside hospital for treatment of a blood clot that passed through a lung.

"It seems like the only time you get help is if you can get to an outside doctor—and they make that pretty difficult," says Keith.

When he returned to prison, a new doctor looked over his medical records and noted the comment written by Hays. She asked Keith if he had received regular tests and he was surprised. That was the first time he had ever been told of Hay's recommendation.

At that point, prison staff finally ran a PSA test. It showed an elevated protein level.

In July 2015, Keith returned to Willamette Urology for a biopsy that revealed stage three prostate cancer.

Keith had been told he would never return to Nevada, but Oregon didn't want to pay for his cancer surgery and treatments, so he was transported back to that state.

By the time he underwent radical surgery to remove his prostate gland, Keith had dropped more than fifty pounds and was in such poor health he feared not being able to survive treatment.

Every day, for more than a month, Keith was shackled and transported into Carson City for radiation therapy. Suffering from fatigue and energy loss, he became focused on making Oregon pay for its callous disregard of his health.

He followed through on that plan in the spring of 2017 by filing a civil rights lawsuit against Vargo and the Oregon Department of Corrections. He asked for $300,000 in compensatory and punitive damages, plus attorney fees.

With help from an outside advocate, Keith obtained the services of Michelle Burrows, an attorney specializing in prison abuse and neglect cases who primarily practices in Idaho and Oregon.

Burrows knew she was in for a fight. The Oregon Department of Justice defends state employees in cases such as Keith's. Attorneys from the ODOJ immediately challenged Keith for not exhausting his available remedies through the standard grievance process.

Burrows countered with a detailed summary of Keith's attempts to go through the proper "chain of command" in spite of his debilitating physical condition. This is the timeline Burrows presented:

- On July 27, 2016, Nevada denied Keith's request to grieve the issues in Oregon because "you may only grieve issues that fall under Nevada Department of Corrections jurisdiction."
- Despite that denial, Keith requested that his advocate send an email (August 29, 2016) to Carissa Casper of ODOC asking for a grievance form. Casper replied to that request by stating, "Once an inmate leaves ODOC custody, grievance and appeals can't be accepted for processing." However, she agreed to send the form.
- On October 19, 2016, Keith finally submitted his grievance against Oregon on the proper form, and it was denied.
- Keith appealed that denial on November 2, 2016. He argued that it had been impossible to submit a grievance within thirty days as required by ODOC because he had been ill and fighting for his life. He also pointed out that he did not discover the "injury" in the case (the system ignoring Dr. Hay's recommendation) until he was undergoing other, unrelated medical care and afforded the opportunity to see his records.
- Keith relied on Oregon's rule that the clock did not begin ticking on the two-year statute of limitations until the plaintiff became aware of the injury or wrongdoing. He argued that ODOC officials intentionally manipulated the grievance process to avoid liability.
- On December 22, 2016, ODOC returned Keith's paperwork, stating, "No further appeals will be accepted for processing once the inmate is released from the custody of ODOC."

"I went through every available process," says Keith. "It is not an easy thing to get all of this paperwork together when you are in prison and have limited resources or contact with the outside world."

As it turned out, Keith had unknowingly missed a federal deadline for filing a suit by twenty-one days. Under the Prison Litigation Reform Act enacted by Congress in 1996, there are stringent timelines and conditions to move inmate cases forward. The purpose of the act was to reduce the number of prisoner court lawsuits in the system.

Despite the strength of its case, the ODOJ agreed to pay $20,000 to settle Keith's case.

"They knew they had messed up," believes Keith.

He remains angry about being treated like his life had no value.

"They took something from me that I can never get back," he says.

Cancer was not the end of his health problems. In early 2017, Keith began having pain in his groin. He sought medical attention, fearing that his cancer was back. A Nevada medical staffer told him that his discomfort around the incision of his prostate surgery was "probably gas," but Keith insisted something was wrong. He was then informed that the pain was likely just a buildup of scar tissue from the operation.

Doctors offered Keith opioids to relieve pain, which he refused because of his past addiction.

"They don't tell you exactly what's going on," he says. "If you ask, they say something like 'I'm not sure.'"

Several months later, in such agony that he could hardly move, Keith began to drop weight again. He was finally transported to an outside physician for tests that revealed three kidney stones hung up in scar tissue. Two of the stones were too large to dissolve with medication.

The solution prescribed was a laser lithotripsy procedure, which would pulverize the stones, but it did not happen. Keith finally asked his advocate to intervene and she complained to prison officials and, when that did not produce results, called the Nevada governor's office to request an investigation.

Shortly after that call, Keith finally underwent the procedure.

"No one should have to be suffering all the time. It shouldn't be like that," he says.

According to Keith, inmates without an advocate on the outside suffer and sometimes die of neglect.

Few inmates earn compassionate release as they age and get sick in prison. At the end of their days behind bars, their families are prohibited from being with them, so it falls on their fellow prisoners to provide comfort and care.

In both Oregon and Nevada, Keith has worked in a hospice unit, which he sees as a ministry because he is able to be present at the moment an inmate meets God.

Nevada has allowed inmates to paint murals of the four seasons on the wall of the hospice area, giving color and warmth instead of the usual bleak and cold look.

Inmates also make afghans and hats so the dying prisoner stays warm and feels valued. A journal is kept by the bedside so the dying can write thoughts to his loved ones, and medical staff and volunteers can also preserve final words. The journal and handcrafted items are sent to the family after the death to help provide closure.

"No one should die in prison, but if they have to, they should not be alone," says Keith. "I do this because one day it could be my turn and I'd want someone to do the same for me."

There is a growing call for compassionate release for terminally ill inmates, which Keith says would be the humane way to end a life already full of deprivation and suffering.

"Inmates have no more control over their dying experience than their everyday life," he says.

Respect for the end of an inmate's life must begin by treating each inmate as carefully, as compassionately, and as thoroughly as we treat the unincarcerated, and it should start the very first day they enter their cell, says Keith.

"Can't Shake My Shadow" by Jorge Cabrera

III

# Institutionalization

*Some researchers put five gorillas in a cage. They hung a banana some dozen feet from the ground and put a set of stairs underneath. Immediately, the boldest gorilla (or merely the one who figured it out first) began climbing the stairs to get at the banana. But as soon as he touched the staircase, all of the gorillas were hit with water from a fire hose for several long, stinging, howling seconds.*

*When the water stopped, the gorillas shook themselves off, grumbling, "What was that about?" Then a moment later: "Banana!" And off they raced to the stairs. But as soon as the first touched the stairs, it was the super-sharp water all over again.*

*Well, that was all it took; none of the five approached the stairs again. So what happened when one of them was replaced by a newcomer who didn't know the rules? He was taught—not by the fire hoses but by the other four—that even though the stairs obviously led to a banana, no one could touch them.*

*The gorillas were, as one might guess, unable to explain about the sharp-water that would strike, as if from a God angry at the violation of his express taboo.*

*The gorillas had a simpler but certainly no less effective manner of controlling behavior: They beat up the new gorilla when he touched the stairs.*

*Then another gorilla was replaced, and the same thing happened, with the first new gorilla taking part in the initiation of the second to the special rule of the cage: no one touches the stairs.*

*Three more substitutions and as many more after: gorillas ten gen-erations removed from those who felt the sharp water still beat up new-comers who touched the stairs that led to the banana.*

*At the end of the day, the name of the game is survival.*

Patrick Bacon, thirty-six
Serving time for assault
US Penitentiary Coleman in Florida

# Juvenile Reforms Will Have A Ripple Effect

Early prisons in the US were established to lock people up only long enough for them to "get right with God" and change their ways. Marc Brown, the lawyer giving this history lesson, is chief deputy defender for the Office of Public Defense Services, Criminal Appeals Section, in Oregon.

He believes the American justice system went wrong somewhere in the shift from a restorative to punitive model, and he studies the early origins of our penal system to find clues on how to correct this problem.

"The Quakers built the first prison in Philadelphia in 1829 out of the belief that people weren't really bad, that they had just lost their connection to God and needed help to reconnect," says Brown.

The Quakers put early prisoners in solitary confinement with a Bible to spend time thinking about the evils that had led them down their dark path.

"When you were in prison back then, there was no interaction with the person who brought your meals, but you were given work to do because the sentiment at the time was 'Idle hands are the devil's workshop,'" says Brown.

Despite the prisoner being isolated, Brown learned the system was not entirely cruel. Every cell was heated and had indoor plumbing, and a skylight to focus the inmate's view on the heavens.

"Ultimately, you were to have some kind of great enlightenment, and then you were good to go," he says.

Prior to the establishment of these earliest prisons in Pennsylvania and New York, criminals were jailed only long enough to be tried for a crime, which Brown says normally happened within weeks.

"If you were convicted of a murder, you might be executed or you might be sentenced as an indentured servant to the family of the one you killed so you could provide the labor they lost."

For lesser crimes, sentences usually meant flogging or hard labor, punishment in the form of physical injury or discomfort.

The Supreme Court has since interpreted the Eighth Amendment to limit the government's ability to inflict certain types of punishment.

America has gradually acquired a more punitive mindset over the decades, explains Brown. As a result, the prison population began to grow, but there was still restorative thinking in the parole system.

Through most of the nineteenth and twentieth centuries, people seated on the parole board had the discretion to decide whether someone sentenced to thirty years would spend that entire time behind bars or be released early due to a good rehabilitative track record and positive psychological evaluations. These parole boards reviewed each case and talked directly with the inmate in an attempt to assess his or her thinking and intentions.

"The thought was that you only needed to be in prison as long as necessary and the intent was to release as early as possible under the right circumstances," says Brown.

In the 1980s, victim groups decried shortened sentences, and politicians eager for votes took up the call. They began winning campaigns with a "tough on crime" stance.

Sentence reductions became even rarer in the 1990s when the "you do the crime, you do the time" mindset led legislators to establish mandatory minimums, says Brown.

"By that time, we had swung entirely over to the punitive point of the continuum and that really increased the prison population."

America became so vengeful that the age at which a juvenile could be tried as an adult was lowered to twelve and children who killed were sentenced to life in prison, he says.

"The minute we started putting juveniles in adult prisons the recidivism rate skyrocketed."

Brown believes that our system is now as far from a restorative model of justice as you can get.

His strong focus for the past fourteen years has been working to reform juvenile justice because he believes that will be the start of real change that will reduce the prison population.

Toward that end, he has taken on the state for its hard stance on youth crimes. "If you are representing a juvenile who has been waived to adult court, you are not representing an adult," he argues. "Even if your seventeen-year-old client looks like an adult, his brain is still a juvenile's brain."

Unfortunately, Brown explains that Oregon still has a legal loophole that allows juveniles to be given life sentences without the possibility of parole.

Historically, Oregon had no juvenile delinquency laws from statehood to the late 1880s. During this period, the law held that children younger than seven lacked criminal capacity, and children seven to fourteen were presumed to lack criminal capacity. However, an argument could be made against this presumption under the right circumstances.

If a juvenile was deemed to have capacity, he or she was treated as an adult in the criminal justice system.

In 1887, Oregon passed a new statute permitting a judge to sentence a convicted juvenile under the age of sixteen to reform school instead of prison, although the juvenile could still be subject to capital punishment.

Oregon then created the first juvenile court in 1907, which functioned until 1995 on a rehabilitative model, says Brown.

In 1959, the legislature enacted the first comprehensive juvenile delinquency code, which allowed youth to be tried in adult court. In 1985, the legislature lowered the age a juvenile could be treated as an adult defendant to 14.

Ten years later, Brown says the legislature made significant changes to the criminal code that lowered the age a juvenile could be sent to adult court to twelve and allowed teens fifteen or older to be given a life sentence for aggravated murder.

By the mid-1990s, Oregon had abandoned any sort of juvenile rehabilitative system and had become purely punitive. In an attempt to reconstruct the rehabilitation model, Brown says the state established the Oregon Youth Authority to oversee facilities where juveniles were sheltered until they turned twenty-five, at which time they entered the adult system.

Starting in 2005, the US Supreme Court issued a series of opinions that juveniles were not to be treated as adults in sentencing due to their "lack of maturity and underdeveloped sense of responsibility."

States were directed to only apply a life without parole sentence to a "rare juvenile offender whose crime reflects irreparable corruption."

Brown says that, unfortunately, Oregon has not recognized that distinction because the presumptive sentence for a juvenile convicted of aggravated murder still includes the possibility of life without parole.

He explains that circumstance as follows: If a juvenile gets a thirty-year minimum sentence, he or she is not automatically eligible and must still go before a parole board to plead a case for release. The inmate must present sufficient evidence that they are likely to be rehabilitated within a reasonable period of time to qualify for the shorter sentence.

"Therefore, even with a thirty-year minimum, the original sentence must be life without the possibility of parole, which is unconstitutional," argues Brown, who is pursuing a higher court judgment on the issue. "Because of this weird quirk in the system, the only difference between a juvenile over fifteen and an adult is that the juvenile cannot be given the death penalty."

Sentencing reforms are difficult because victim rights groups usually strongly and vocally oppose any leniency, he says. Even if there is a general societal acknowledgment that the current criminal justice system is not working well, too much political pressure is put on politicians to get real changes made.

"I think people are swayed by emotions and that overcomes their rational minds. Victims have powerful stories and they are very persuasive."

He believes that eventually America will have to deal with its prison problem because the current system is unsustainable.

If America focuses more on reforms for the juvenile system, Brown says all of society will benefit. With fewer juveniles reoffending, he said the adult prison population will decline, so more money can be invested in rehabilitation and treatment programs.

"A reformation model at the juvenile level makes sense because it will have a ripple effect in the adult system," Brown says.

# Part I
# Trevor: Growing Up
# Behind The Wall

*I was once asked when to give up on someone, and
I responded that everyone is capable of change, and
while not everyone will change, who is anyone to
judge when someone no longer holds value?*

*—Trevor Walraven*

Sitting across the restaurant booth from Trevor Walraven, it is difficult to believe he was sentenced to life in prison at the age of fourteen for aggravated murder.

He said the decision to carjack the victim's Chevrolet Suburban was made to impress his brother's peers. Trevor has admitted to shooting Bill Hull, a business owner in the town of Wolf Creek, Oregon, and dumping his body over an embankment so there would be no witness to his crime.

Now thirty-five, he is clean-cut and articulate, free of jailhouse tattoos or the hard, bitter expression of a man who has spent almost two decades behind bars.

Trevor has been in the free world for more than a year—as free as a man can be while wearing a GPS tracking device on his ankle and subjected to a curfew and travel restrictions.

"It's important to live in ways that are meaningful, and I have found that can be done regardless of my environment."

He is in a legal battle with the Oregon Department of Justice to keep what freedom he now enjoys. Trevor was released early under the Second Look program available to juvenile offenders.

Second Look allows some juveniles convicted as adults to seek early release after they have served half their sentence.

Trevor sought release through Second Look in 2014, but the state successfully fought that request on grounds that his original sentence provided no opportunity for participation in the program.

"They were just emphatic that I had nothing coming."

In 2016, technical problems with jury instructions from the Josephine County district attorney led a judge to toss out Trevor's conviction. Instead of going through the ordeal of another trial, he pleaded guilty to aggravated murder.

This time, the judge wrote the prospect for a Second Look into Trevor's life sentence.

"The judge stated his belief that I was the poster child for reformation. He did a great job securing a legally sound sentence," says Trevor.

His legal team brought another Second Look request before the court and a judge granted his release.

Taken into consideration was the fact that Trevor had zero infractions or violations on his prison record and a psychological evaluation had determined he posed no threat to public safety.

A dozen or so witnesses—prison staff, psychologists, and professors—described him as respectful and trustworthy.

Although a judge determined that Trevor was reformed enough not to pose a threat to society, the state wants him back in a cell out of the belief he does not qualify for Second Look. His original sentence granted the possibility of parole only when he had been behind bars for thirty years and prosecutors want him to finish out that time.

The state, having lost its bid to keep Trevor incarcerated, used a series of stall tactics to keep him locked up nearly eighteen months after the judge ordered his release.

His legal team finally succeeded in getting the state supreme court to set a fourteen-day deadline for prosecutors to provide written reasoning for not complying with the judge's decision.

"I have been engaged in litigation since I was fourteen," says Trevor. "It has been a suspended state of existence."

Last year, he succeeded in getting his conviction vacated and was released. However, the state then rearrested him on the original indictment, and he found himself back in custody for nearly four months while his legal team fought to free him.

After returning to Oregon State Penitentiary, he was reunited with his half-brother, Josh Cain, who is four years older. Cain was sentenced to twenty-five years as an accomplice in the same 1998 murder but was an adult and so has to serve out his mandatory sentence.

Trevor's insistence that Cain had been home asleep at the time of the murder has fallen on deaf ears.

Although Trevor admitted in court that he and Cain had discussed the attack, he insists that he acted alone.

"My brother is serving time for something that I did," says Trevor. "He should not be in there."

Witnesses saw Josh and Trevor driving the stolen vehicle and they were later arrested. They claimed they had only found the Suburban with the keys inside.

Trevor had been using methamphetamine and drinking since the age of twelve, which he believes influenced his mindset so that killing someone to take his vehicle actually seemed like a viable plan.

"I was not going to let myself start shooting up meth or heroin until I was fifteen, that was the age where I thought I would be mature enough for it to be appropriate," he says. "That's just an example of how I was thinking."

Being a teenage killer is a difficult subject for Trevor to discuss, and he still struggles when he speaks of taking a man's life all those years ago.

"I don't really believe I can ever be redeemed—I can't undo what I did—but what I can do is live a redeeming life," he says.

Part of his redeeming life is fighting relentlessly for his brother's release. He is also pushing hard to undo Oregon's one-size-fits-all approach for punishing young offenders.

Oregon currently incarcerates more youth than forty-seven other states.

On any given week, Trevor can be found speaking in criminology classes at Oregon's universities or public venues. He takes advantage of any opportunity to educate people about the differences between restorative justice and America's punitive laws.

If Trevor had been tried in Oregon as a juvenile instead of an adult, he would have been automatically released at age twenty-five. He describes what the difference would have meant: "The biggest cultural difference between juvenile and adult prisons is that staff for younger offenders are more likely role models and they largely set a good example. There is much more contact in the adult prison and the mindset is much different—more hard lines and an 'us against them' mentality. The staff are cops and you are not going to have conversations with them. Counseling is a joke on the adult side because the caseload is too high, and you might see yours once every six months—they are usually only seeing people in crisis."

Even though he was a teenager sentenced as an adult, Trevor was not sent directly to the adult penitentiary because he would have been at greater risk of being victimized by older inmates. Instead, he was housed in MacLaren Youth Correctional Facility in Woodburn, Oregon, until he turned eighteen.

"I was fortunate because my brother was already established at OSP, so I had people looking out for me after I arrived."

Trevor earned his high school diploma inside and took college sociology courses. He demonstrated leadership abilities as president of the 150-member Lifers Club at OSP and supervisor of a work crew in the laundry facilities.

"Even when I was in prison, I wanted to learn, I wanted to grow. It either breaks you or makes you stronger. I don't think there's a lot of in-between."

Trevor coauthored a book of essays compiled by lifers titled *Wisdom Within the Pen* as a fundraiser for Angels in the Outfield, a nonprofit organization that seeks to brighten the lives of children impacted by crime or abuse.

"Ultimately, what is important to me is that an awareness of our continued existence as human beings be recognized and that, although we've made horrible decisions in our lives, we are not lost and forever worthless," wrote Trevor in the introduction to that work.

"There are individuals incarcerated with me who are the smartest and more caring people I have ever engaged with. Second chances are paramount! Hope is paramount!"

His Second Look case has been charged with political overtones; one judge was the brother of the victim and another the prosecutor who brought charges against him. One more judge recused herself from overseeing hearings after three of her rulings were overturned by a higher court.

In all, Trevor has prevailed in eight or nine challenges brought by the state. He is confident that the state's top court will ultimately support his release.

If he remains free, Trevor will transition off the stringent Second Look conditions of release in five to ten years, but he will remain on post-prison supervision for the rest of his life.

He believes that people should care about what happens to juvenile offenders on humanitarian grounds. But if they can't muster that, they should be concerned about the high cost of locking kids up. A life sentence for a teenager requires decades of taxpayer expenditures. The cost to house an inmate runs about $34,000 per year and roughly doubles when that inmate is over fifty. Adding this all up, a life sentence for a sixteen-year-old will top $2.25 million in taxpayer funds.

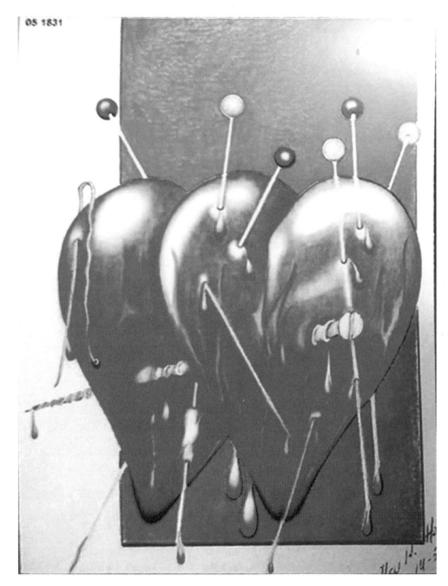

Untitled by Allen Howard from Oregon State Penitentiary

||||||||||||||||||||||||||||||||||||||||||||||||||||||||||||||||||||||||||||

# A Deal With The Devil
# Led To Murder

*My name is Chad Hamlin and I was convicted of murder on June 26, 2000, and the length of my sentence is twenty-five years to life. I am now forty-five years old.*

*Let's explore the events that led me to this life in a cage:*

*In 1994, I fell deeply in love with my high school sweetheart. After dating only six months, she suggested that we make a lifelong commitment to each other. The girl of my dreams had just asked me to marry her, so of course, I said "Yes!"*

*Marriage is something I took very seriously, so when I made a vow to stay loyal to the love of my life, I meant it.*

*We were married in 1995, and it was a very exciting time in my life. Not only was I a newlywed, I was also playing bass guitar for a fairly successful band in Texas, and we had just been offered a steady line of gigs to keep us busy.*

*My wife and I were inseparable. She traveled everywhere with me, even on tour, and people were always comparing us to John Lennon and Yoko Ono. My bandmates and the other bands we toured with were always asking, "Chad, can't you go anywhere without your wife? It's like you two are attached at the hip."*

*In 1998, my son was born, and life was like a fairy tale. I had a beautiful wife and a healthy baby boy, and to top it off, I was becoming a legitimate rock star.*

*Then just when I thought I had it all, tragedy descended upon my life like an apocalyptic storm.*

*My band self-destructed, succumbing to the typical issues that wreck bands, such as members getting arrested, quitting, or having nervous breakdowns from the pressures of the rock-and-roll lifestyle.*

*I was heartbroken about the band splitting up, but I had a family who loved me, so life was good.*

*Later that year, my wife and I decided to start our lives over, so we packed up everything and moved from Texas to Eugene, Oregon. I enrolled in school to study sound engineering and audio production. Money was tight, so I was forced to work two jobs to make ends meet, and my wife was depressed because she missed our old life.*

*I was no longer the rock star she had fallen in love with. I was just a guy working sixty hours a week and going to school full-time. Unfortunately, I was too busy to notice her unhappiness at the time, and that was the beginning of the end of our marriage.*

*She started having an affair, and I had no idea because I was always at work or school. There would be no happily ever after in our story, no fairy tale ending in our lives.*

*On April 1 (yeah, April Fool's Day) two years after moving to Oregon, my wife cleaned out our bank account, including all my college money. She took the car that I had just finished paying off, emptied our house of everything that we owned—all while I was gone for the day.*

*Honestly, none of this matters compared to her running off with the most important person in my life, my son. My little boy was only two years old, and he had vanished from my life.*

*No one seemed to know where my wife had gone. Both of our families were extremely worried, so we looked into the possibility of a private investigator to locate my wife and son.*

*After three months with no leads, her disappearance became too much for me to handle and I decided to take my own life. I sat in our empty house with a gun in my mouth ready to pull the trigger. I pleaded with God to bring them back to me, but my prayers fell upon deaf ears. At the last moment, right before I squeezed the trigger and ended my life, I decided to make one last plea. This time, however, I didn't ask for God's help in a moment that still haunts me to this day—I made a deal with the devil (I didn't really believe in that sort of thing, but I was desperate).*

*Love can make you do stupid things. I asked to have my wife brought back to me, and in exchange, I would give anything. I struck this crazy bargain on June 8, 2000. My plan was simple: if she didn't come home by June 16, my twenty-fifth birthday, I would go forward with my suicide.*

*On June 11, 2000, the unthinkable happened. My wife showed up at my house but not to rekindle our love and not to work things out. No, she came back to extort me. She threatened to never let me see my son again unless I met her demands. She told me that she had found out that I had come into some money and that I was to give her everything.*

*The heartbreak I felt crushed my sense of reasoning, and I lost touch with reality just long enough to snap. Something inside me went rogue from the devastating anguish I felt from her betrayal. I crossed over into a dark place, like flipping a switch that led to utter madness. I didn't think I was capable of doing something as horrific as taking someone's life, but once I started down the path into the darkness, I couldn't seem to return, and I lost myself in that horrible moment.*

*On June 11, 2000, I committed murder. Now here I sit, rotting in prison for taking her life.*

*That dreadful event not only took her life, it destroyed our families' lives. Now my son will never know his mother or his father. He lives in Texas with my wife's family.*

*I have no excuses. All I can say is that I wish I could take it back and make the outcome of that day turn out completely different. It was absolutely the biggest, most horrible mistake of my life, and I will never forgive myself for my actions.*

*I was raised by a single mom, and she has always been there for me through this entire nightmare, but unfortunately, she lives in Texas, so I haven't been able to have face-to-face visits with her. I'm her only child, so I know how incredibly hard this has been on her.*

*I would have to say one of the worst parts of this experience is that I haven't been able to be there for her when she's needed me.*

*I also feel horrible that my son had to grow up not knowing his parents. I haven't seen him since he was two, and he is now twenty-two. Sadly, I'll never know the joys of being his father, and my son will probably never forgive me for the pain I have caused him and our family.*

*Although my son and I don't know each other, he's still an extremely important person in my life. I think about him every day. I hope one day he'll know how much he means to me and how sorry I am.*

*I had never been in trouble before, so getting locked away in a maximum-security prison (Oregon State Penitentiary) was horrifying. I was basically just a kid when I came to prison, and honestly, all I really knew about prison was what I had seen on TV and in movies.*

*Prison made me realize that I'm very adaptable when presented with a challenging situation.*

*I quickly found my niche in the prison music program. I used my talents as a musician to gain respect from the other inmates, and I've never had a problem with anybody in here. Thankfully, I'm a very liked person, so my fears of all the horrible things I had seen happen in movies were never issues that I had to deal with during my incarceration.*

*I'm not candy-coating the prison experience, because sometimes it can be crazy in here, but it's like anywhere else—stay away from the drama and be a good person to others and you can survive with a relatively peaceful existence.*

*I went to the hole the first year I was here for seven days. The write-up was ridiculous—I helped someone less fortunate by giving him some items that I had bought from canteen. The guy had just arrived and didn't have any supplies, and I didn't want him to go without.*

*I was charged with "disobedience of a direct order" for buying the supplies. I learned the hard way—don't give anything to anyone, even if it is meant as a kind gesture.*

*Other than that one episode, I've never been in real trouble. One visit to the hole was enough to let me know that I didn't want to go back.*

*These days, between teaching music and taking a heavy load of college classes, I stay so busy that I don't mind being locked in my cell. When I'm in there, I read and I am constantly writing songs and composing new music. I guess I've gotten used to being locked in a cage. It has become my normal existence.*

*What scares me now? Well, I'm a bit worried about the future because I have no savings. I currently only make $60 a month from my job as the prison music teacher.*

When I stop and ponder about what comes after the prison sentence, that's when the worry kicks in, and it's always about money. When it's all said and done, I'll be spending at least twenty-five years in this place, and that's twenty-five years that I haven't paid into Social Security.

No retirement is probably what scares me the most. I'll probably be getting out sometime in 2025—that is, if the parole board decides they want to release me. I'll be a fifty-year-old man with no savings and no retirement plan. There is no possible way to save money with the little bit I earn.

It feels like prison is all about slave labor. It's a place that overcharges for everything they sell yet pays us just a few dollars a day for the labor we provide. That forces us to depend upon our families for help, but unfortunately, not all families can help with money issues even if they wanted to, and not everyone has a family to call upon for support.

Sadly, most people have to sacrifice their canteen needs so that they can afford to spend the funds on phone calls.

There are some programs available to teach job and life skills but not enough. The opportunities are very limited—the prison industry is more about slave labor than they are training programs.

I thought incarceration would be the death of my musical career, but in a twist of fate, it has led to an amazing opportunity for me as a recording artist.

I was afforded a wonderful privilege in 2009 when I was approved to purchase, at my own expense, some music equipment and recording gear to keep in my cell. This led to the creation of two recording projects: LooNurGooSe and Element66, both of which have grown into something much bigger than I could ever have imagined, thanks to social media.

In 2013, one of my good friends was paroled and asked if he could take with him the fourteen-song Element66 demo, Drukis Blah.

A few months after the album was made available for digital download, my friend contacted me with some great news. He said, "I gave your demo to a radio station and they loved it. They were astonished to discover that all the music was recorded, mixed, mastered, and fully produced from inside a prison cell."

*I knew that we were onto something with what we were creating, so I remixed the original fourteen songs demo and added eleven new bonus songs to create our second release from* Element66, *titled* The Dysprosium Collection. *This twenty-five-song album opened up an entirely new world for us and gave me my start as a professional recording artist.*

*Within six months of releasing the collection, I did a radio interview and had three songs featured on several different stations.*

*Thanks to social media,* Element66 *started to build a solid fan base, and in 2014, I was introduced to the friend of a friend who helped us emerge onto the worldwide music scene.*

LooNurGooSe *(pronounced "lunar goose") is a project that continues further down the path of experimental music, picking up where* Element66 *left off. Through a collaboration with my good friend, Erik Libbert, we have created six mini albums containing almost forty songs. Find out more about* Element66 *at* www.esixsix.com *and* LooNurGooSe *at* www.loonurgoose.com.

*Looking back on my time in prison, I've seen myself grow into someone who's not afraid to make bold suggestions to help shape a greater outcome, someone who wants to help change lives for the better.*

*But at the same time, I can identify that, no matter how much I don't want to admit it, I can feel the gravitational pull of institutionalization trying to drag me under with that little voice in the back of my head getting louder and louder, telling me that maybe it's better in here than it is out there. I question my thinking sometimes, wondering if this is some delusional Stockholm syndrome.*

*As a first-time offender, I would have liked the opportunity to not be stuck with a life sentence. And as someone who made a huge mistake in my twenties, I feel that twenty-five years in prison is not the healthiest way to spend my entire adult life, only to be thrown back out into the world at age fifty. Society in the real world seems completely strange and alien to me now, but even though so much has changed out there, I know that I'll learn to adapt back into that environment, just as I adopted to this prison environment when I first got here almost twenty-one years ago.*

||||||||||||||||||||||||||||||||||||||||||||||||||||||||||||||||||||||||

# The Barbarism Of Life
# Without Parole

Much like the way Prohibition tried to solve alcohol problems with a nationwide ban, life sentences without parole try to solve our society's violence problem.

Bobbin Singh, the man behind this mindset, currently serves as the executive director of the Oregon Justice Resource Center.

Prohibition, in force between 1920 and 1933, was an attempt by pious Protestants and social progressives to fight crime and corruption and cure other societal ills that were blamed on alcohol abuse.

It appeared at first that Prohibition was working because alcohol consumption declined, yet crime increased and became "organized." Court and prison systems became stretched to the breaking point. Ultimately, the costly ban failed.

"The fundamental response in our society to alcohol then or drugs now is that if we make it illegal or criminal, we can fix and control it," says Singh. "This is the same conceptual framework we have towards violence in our country—that, somehow, if we lock people away forever, it will never happen again or that somehow we can incarcerate our way through this problem."

Singh believes that America's vengeance has done nothing to stop violent acts and has instead created a major moral crisis. Politics of fear and anger dominate our culture and make it difficult to have a rational conversation about the failures in our system.

"Violence will always exist and we all want to see people held accountable for the harm they do, but life-without or a death-in-prison sentence is not going to stop our society from experiencing some levels of harm committed by individuals," he says. "Through incarceration, we forward a value system that people can be disposed of, treating individuals with a lack of dignity and compassion."

Life without mercy, a life sentence without the possibility of parole, is seen by many proponents as a "humane alternative" to an outright death penalty. Nothing could be further from the truth, says Singh.

Prisoners, told by society they are so irredeemable they must never walk the streets again, are stripped of hope, motivation, and inspiration. They are forced to spend the rest of their lives within an acre or two of concrete buildings and, at the end of a bleak existence, to die alone in a cell.

"There is no possibility for rehabilitation, no recognition that people can change."

In many ways, a life sentence without parole is crueler than the death penalty. These prisoners do not have access to the unlimited appeals and state-funded legal support of those on death row. They have no hope and no ability to fight.

Most lifers disappear into the background noise of society. Their issue is never as pressing or emergent as that of an inmate sentenced to die at midnight. They can rarely convince lawyers to examine their cases or prove their innocence.

As the late Supreme Court Justice Antonin Scalia said in a 2015 opinion: "The reality is that any innocent defendant is infinitely better off appealing a death sentence than a sentence of life imprisonment."

According to Singh, no-parole life sentences are considered so cruel by the European Court of Human Rights that they are outlawed. As a result, life-without is rare in the rest of the free world. Being forced to exist with the absence of hope is seen as barbaric.

The Sentencing Project reports there are currently fifty-three thousand Americans serving life with no possibility of parole in the US. This number has quadrupled since 1992 and is now at an all-time high. In the rest of the free world, there are about two hundred prisoners serving this sentence.

"In many cases, these prisoners are there because of the complex realities they have faced, whether it be mental health issues, substance abuse, or poverty," says Singh. "They may be broken for a variety of reasons, they couldn't break away from a toxic culture that, in part, is created and sustained by us."

The harsh reality is that defendants who can afford to hire a criminal defense attorney who specializes in capital cases rarely end up on death row or serving life sentences. "If you look at who is serving, it's arbitrary," says Singh. "Poverty is the greatest indicator of how you are going to get treated in the criminal justice system."

About 56 percent of "life without" inmates are black.

As a result of the hopelessness among this prisoner population, the suicide rate of lifers is incredibly high. With no chance of parole to live for, there is a constant internal struggle against hopelessness and despair.

Still, many lifers are able to develop coping skills and still find purpose in such a bleak existence. For Singh, this speaks to the resiliency of the human soul—and makes the case for restorative justice. "That people are able to find meaning in that severe and trauma-filled place is a signal that they have the ability to change, be different than they were at the time of the crime. It's not anything in the prison system that's allowed them to be who they are, which only suggests that if we were able to give them the proper support, they could be very successful."

Singh believes there is a place for life sentences. Serial killers and murderers who have committed particularly horrific crimes might need to be locked away forever, but there should still be a periodic review of all sentences.

There needs to be accountability for violent acts or there is no justice for the families of victims, says Singh. However, he believes if America is going to be a nation that espouses a belief in redemption and the ability of people to turn their lives around, then Americans need to walk their talk.

"Life-without is imposed without any thought of true accountability, without real consideration of public safety. It is purely about punishment," he says.

A study by the Justice Policy Institute, a Washington, DC-based nonprofit dedicated to reducing incarceration levels, found that those who commit violent crimes mature out of lawbreaking by middle age. In fact, the recidivism rate of lifers who are able to parole out is markedly less than other released prisoners. The study found that lifers had a reoffense rate of just 3 percent, making them the safest of all prisoners released.

Singh explores why this might be. Taking a life is a terribly heavy burden to come to terms with. It is a terrible pain, he says.

"Many come to understand very well what it is they have done, and they will carry that with them the rest of their lives. They also know they will never harm anyone again because of the pain they have to live with."

The Sentencing Project and other reform groups contend that we should return to viable alternatives to life-without, which worked well prior to 1984 and the inception of mandatory minimum sentencing. Singh agrees.

Indeterminate sentences of twenty-five years to life would grant the inmate access to a parole board, which would not necessarily always lead to parole but would provide at least the possibility. The inmate would need to convince the parole board, a body of trained professionals, or a judge, in front of the public that they warrant release and pose no danger to the community.

In some countries, such as Norway, Singh knows that everyone is given the opportunity to earn their way out of prison. Communities help with rehabilitation efforts, and the system provides hope that motivates people to change. In juxtaposition, America throws a person in prison for life with a clear message that even thirty or forty years later, they can't have changed enough to no longer be deemed a threat. Singh finds this approach far from sensible.

It is not fair to ask a victim's family to forgive a killer. That journey they must travel as individuals, and their feelings should be respected.

However, Singh says the judicial system must be disconnected from emotion and able to impose sentences that are fair but treat the defendant with dignity and provide opportunities for rehabilitation. "The system should be bigger and stronger than an individual and able to give that forgiveness."

Since 2011, when Singh cofounded the Oregon Justice Resource Center in Portland, Oregon, he has worked tirelessly to help women in prison successfully rejoin their communities, and to advocate for an overall system that is fairer. He also works to expose civil rights abuses by authorities.

In addition, his organization runs the Oregon Innocence Project, whose goal is unearthing factual evidence to free the wrongly convicted.

Singh gives an example of how the system protects itself: The Innocence Project has been fighting for four years to get DNA testing for a death row inmate they believe has a compelling case of innocence. Inexplicably, the state is fighting this testing even though it could prove that the person condemned to death did not commit the crime. Singh believes the state does not want it proven that a wrongful conviction took place.

The root of America's punitive mindset toward prisoners has to be examined before true change can happen.

"We have to have a very honest conversation about how this country was founded," Singh says.

Colonists were willing to commit genocide on Native American tribes to take their land and shape the New World as they saw fit. Then plantation owners used slave labor to build wealth, relying on racism that determined some people disposable.

"Without confronting our origins and the role white supremacy has played in our history, we will never be able to change the culture to value all people," he says. "I think that's a hard dot for people to connect, but true change can't happen unless we do, and hopefully, we'll get there."

# Part I
# Kevin: An End Run
# Around Voters

*Being sentenced to life-without is the ultimate cruelty. It's like society sees you as a wounded animal but will not put you out of your misery by executing you, nor will it heal you. Instead, you are put in a cage and left there to suffer and die.*

—Kevin Young

Oregon legislators debated allowing life sentences with no possibility of parole for aggravated murder without asking voters for permission to amend the state constitution, in what Kevin Young believes was an abuse of their power.

"Anytime elected officials are in doubt of their powers, they should defer to the will of the people," says Young, fifty-six, who has served twenty-eight years at Oregon State Penitentiary and devoted much of his time to understanding how our system has failed him and so many others.

Kevin vowed never to give up his fight for freedom after being convicted by a jury for the death of Stanley Bernard Norris, which occurred on April 22, 1991. Kevin insists he was only trying to save the life of his younger brother, who was in a drug-related dispute with Norris.

Kevin views his one week murder trial as a travesty of justice based on faulty theories by the prosecution and apathy on the part of his "public pretender." In the end, he was sentenced to life behind bars on February 7, 1992.

"I am here because of my overprotective nature. My will to survive won't allow me to give up and so I fight on."

Kevin finds great inequity in the fact that predatory serial killers, some with dozens of victims, have the same sentence as he does. He did not have a prior criminal history before the shooting beyond a DUII arrest.

His fight on technical grounds is a story for another time, says Kevin. He chose to focus on the constitutional issue for *Shame* out of the belief that declaring someone irredeemable for a lifetime is so serious that the legislature shouldn't have played god.

"This is our home and final resting place," he says of the situation facing those who are "on a slow walk to the death penalty."

At the heart of Kevin's constitutional argument is Article 1, section 40, of the Oregon Constitution: "The penalty for aggravated murder as defined by law shall be death upon unanimous affirmative jury findings as provided by law and otherwise shall be life imprisonment with minimum sentence as provided by law." That section was created through a citizen initiative petition filed as Ballot Measure 6 on July 6, 1983, and adopted by the people on November 6, 1984.

"If there was any question about what the people intended with 'minimum sentence as provided by law,' the voters should have been asked," says Kevin.

At the time voters approved Measure 6, the sentence of aggravated murder included the possibility of parole after twenty years, with a parole hearing after fifteen.

But then the Oregon Legislature decided to impose the sentence of life-without in 1989. On June 22 of that year, the Senate Committee on the Judiciary, which also involved House representatives, debated whether the legislature should unilaterally make that decision, or whether they should allow Oregonians to decide.

Kevin read through transcripts of the debates and discovered that the lawmakers' arguments revealed their prejudices and misconceptions. As an example, one senator could not fathom why the committee was even contemplating referring the matter to voters.

"Are we saying if the judge sentences someone to life, they will have to serve the life?" asked Senator Ronald Grensky. "We should ask ourselves how the parole board is able to take someone who has been sentenced to life and let them out prior to that. Now the law would be if somebody gets sentenced to life, they actually serve life. I don't think we need to ask the voters. I think they would love to see it. I oppose the referral idea."

Representative Phil Keisling expressed the belief that, because the bill was only tightening the language of Article 1, section 40, it could withstand a legal challenge and should not be referred.

Senator Jeanette Hamby took the opposing viewpoint, a belief that a public vote would protect the state against legal challenges for unconstitutionality.

She had this to say: "My initial thought in referring the bill was there was a great deal of confusion on the part of the public as to the criminal justice system. I think any opportunity we have to educate voters helps."

The Oregon District Attorneys Association strongly recommended involving voters and viewed the attempt to "tighten the language" as outright tampering. Dale Penn, speaking for the ODAA, said, "I don't believe people who supported the death penalty would say they really had the opportunity to come forward and deal with this bill. We believe the people should have a voice in it."

The DAs voiced their stance that they would only support the tougher sentence if the voting public had a chance to weigh in.

Ultimately, this chance was denied, and the Senate Committee on the Judiciary voted unanimously to impose the sentence of life-without, and to make it effective immediately, all without input from the voters.

The decision by the legislature was legally challenged and upheld by the Court of Appeals, which protected the state, explains Kevin.

Another issue troubles Kevin. Oregon established a moratorium on the death penalty in 2019 and reduced the list of aggravated murder conditions that could lead to a death sentence to only a handful of crimes. That means that people sentenced to the death penalty can now petition the court to serve life-without, but no move has been made to adjust the lesser sentence accordingly.

"Some guy who would have been on death row is now going to have the same sentence as I do—how is that fair?" asks Kevin, whose aggravating factor is no longer on the list.

There are very few people in this world, he says, who cannot be reformed to live a better life and he believes Americans intrinsically know that.

"I cannot understand how the death penalty can be deemed inhumane, while life-without sentences are allowed to continue," he says.

He served in the US. Navy out of his desire to protect and defend his fellow countrymen, just as he protected his brother. He took an oath to uphold the Constitution, although he feels strongly that the methodology used to come up with his sentence violates the principles he fought to protect.

"It is a shame that we live in the best country in the world. We preach forgiveness and second chances, yet we refuse to grant mercy and are so willing to waste lives. The key has been thrown away, yet I have learned there is more to life than where you lay your head down at night, and that allows me to keep the hope that justice will prevail."

"Stormy Days" by Toshio Takanobu from Oregon State Penitentiary

# We Need Mercy

*I was raised by my late aunt and uncle from the age of five, and neither of them were loving at all. There was no "I love you" or hugs and kisses in our household. My aunt and uncle were physically abusive to my brother and me and to each other.*

*My real mother gave my brother and me up to my dad at the age of four, and my dad gave us up to his brother because he had to go on the run. I didn't feel loved, nor did I know how to love.*

*As I got older, two things became very important to me: love and loyalty. I became an extremely loyal friend, even to the point of killing to protect my friends from the anguish of outsiders. In my eyes, I was looking for a real family, and since I was emotionally cold, the only thing I had to offer was a hostile nature to those who I thought were trying to hurt my so-called friends.*

*In short, I'm in prison for stabbing a woman who was sleeping with my friend's boyfriend because I believed in my heart that's what real friends did for each other. What led to my incarceration is that I didn't feel like I had any value, so I didn't know how to value anyone else.*

*In the very beginning, I was afraid that I wouldn't make it out of prison alive. Nowadays, I'm just afraid of falling over in a room full of strangers and no one giving a damn that my life has just been extinguished.*

*I realize every day that I put the keys to my life in someone else's hands.*

*I've done about a year and a half of my time in the hole. When you're in there with your radio, your TV, and all the rest of your property, it's not that bad at all. However, when you find yourself in the hole with nothing but your thoughts, it can be a whole different kind of animal altogether. I would often find myself meditating on all the evil that life had to offer because I didn't really have that many good thoughts to reflect on.*

*Most times, the hole doesn't have a window, so you begin to miss the simple things (like looking at the sky or seeing the sun rise). On a good day, you'll get outta bed early, work out, write a letter and, if you're very lucky, use the phone. However, on a bad day, the cell is your enemy and you hide from it under your covers. The walls are cold, the food has no taste, and no matter how much you try to plug your ears with toilet paper, you can't drown out the war stories being yelled through the doors of the cells around you.*

*The hole is a lonely place, and no matter how much you like spending time in your own space, the solitude eventually reminds you of that one person that you cannot help but long for.*

*In my daily routine, I wake up, yet I don't open my eyes because I'm still trying to hang onto the peace I had while asleep. It's only 4:20 a.m., but it's my most cherished part of the day because the prison is still quiet, and the foul nature of the joint hasn't invaded my space yet. I sit up and turn my TV on, knowing that world news is only moments away.*

*I take a few minutes to pray before getting down from my bunk to wash up and get dressed. Blue is the color we wear here, and although it comes in many different shades, it's now a color that holds no appeal to me. My family takes good care of me, so I wear Levi's and a Levi's denim button-up shirt with some white Nike tennis shoes, while others are forced to wear thin twill-type pants and shirt that the state provides because they don't have the same outside support.*

*After washing up, reading my Bible, and watching the news, I step out of my house (a six-foot-by-ten-foot cell) to face the day. Breakfast and lunch are served between 6:15 and 7:45 a.m., depending on which unit eats first. We get a hot breakfast on a tray and a cold lunch consisting of two bologna sandwiches to place in our little plastic tub to eat later if we want. We only eat two meals at the chow hall: breakfast and dinner.*

*After breakfast, I call my wife for a daily prayer and an "I love you" and to wish her a good day. I work maintenance here at the prison, so when the yard opens at 8:00 a.m., I wait for my boss to walk by and pick me up. Throughout the day, we will fix little things (the main thing being clogged toilets, blown lights, and some form of problem in the culi-*

nary). Our workday ends at 3:00 p.m., and after I lock in my cell for the prison's 3:30 p.m. count, I usually take a little thirty-minute nap.

Dinner is served between 4:00 and 5:15 p.m. and is often one of three meals: burgers, hot dogs, or corn dogs. We also get spaghetti, pizza, lasagna, and tacos, but only once every four weeks. After dinner, I usually shower and spend a couple of hours walking the dogs we have in the unit. I am part of the Pups on Parole program, which only thirty-six out of the fourteen thousand prisoners in this state can participate in. The program run through the Nevada Humane Society consists of eighteen dogs being placed in eighteen cells (two prisoners and one dog per cell) in a last-ditch effort to help them learn the skills needed to be a good family pet.

Each cell has a dog handler and a dog handler's assistant. The dog handler is responsible for teaching the dog seven basic commands: sit, stay, heel, come, leave it, no, and down. The handler is only responsible for the dog in his cell. The assistant is responsible for reinforcing everything that the dog handler has taught the dog. Assistants also take different dogs out throughout the day to make sure they can obey commands from individuals other than their handlers. I'm an assistant, and although I've only been in the program for six months, I already want to be a dog handler.

After I've spent about an hour and a half walking a few different dogs, I'll call my wife for a full half-hour good-night call and another "I love you." The rest of my night is usually spent watching a little TV and reflecting on the day. However, not a day goes by that I close my eyes for bed without thinking of Judy (my victim) and how I could've committed such a horrible and senseless crime.

Life is hard for prisoners with no outside support. If you just think about the necessities (e.g., food, water, clothing), you would think that the prison would adequately supply those things, right? Well, they don't. The only thing that the state supplies adequately is water. The food offered to us here is often of such a small portion that it's not even enough to sustain a healthy weight. The prison does its best to give us as much bread as possible, just to fill us up, and it's still not enough. The prison also feeds us items that aren't fit for human consumption at times. This isn't just my opinion, it's what I've witnessed with my own two eyes while working in three different kitchens in three different institutions throughout my incarceration. I'm talking about spoiled food that was seasoned and cooked to cover up the odor of its rankness and bread that's been nibbled and trampled on by mice—and yet knowingly placed on someone's tray and handed out the window at chow time.

Then there's the clothing here. The clothing is often used, which isn't that bad, but when it's already damaged, it becomes a problem. When you first get to prison, you are given two blue twill button-up shirts, two blue twill pairs of pants, two pairs of new socks, two new T-shirts, two new pairs of boxers, one pair of cheap slip-on canvas shoes, one wool blanket, two sheets, and one towel. All of which can be exchanged for new ones (or like new) every six months upon request. If it's wintertime, you may also be given a thin jacket/coat, which has no chance of keeping you warm (especially in the northern institutions).

Okay, now that we've covered what the state gives us, I'll explain why outside support is almost a must-have. Most of us in here like to be active with some sort of sport or exercise to stay in shape or just to keep from getting depressed. If you don't have the energy, however, to do these activities, your morale will plummet.

So those of us with outside help will buy—from the state commissary—extra food, snacks, and vitamins to keep up our strength and to give us those little treats from time to time. We'll also buy extra clothing suited for these activities, such as sweats, tank tops, and tennis shoes that don't fall apart on the first day. You also want to stay warm, so most of us want thick Levi's jeans and a good coat with a liner inside.

These are just a couple of reasons why outside help is good, but the number one reason why life is hard for those with no outside help is because you don't feel loved. Most people who don't feel loved have no incentive to do better, to be better. They are usually harder than most and will take what they can't buy or con you out of what they want.

There are not enough programs to help people get the job and life skills they need to succeed. The number one reason is that the programs aren't really designed to help. A lot of programs just look pretty on the outside, but they don't really provide you with any skills.

In this whole state, there are only about five vocational programs that teach you a trade—and only about five hundred prisoners are admitted to those programs a year. Out of those five hundred, only sixty-five or so will go on to get meaningful employment using the skills they learned *in that vocational program. A lot of these programs are outdated, while the world outside is on the cutting edge of technology. We need a lot more programs that teach us viable skills. Otherwise, you could be putting a guy back out into society worse than he left.*

*Prison teaches you a lot of patience (smile). Before I came to prison, I had a real messed-up way of thinking, and yet I didn't realize it. I now see that my thinking was twisted and so was my lifestyle. Since my incarceration, I've learned how to have real empathy for others, something that I had long since pushed out of my heart. I've also learned not to hate authority figures (cops, correctional officers, government officials).*

*The greatest thing that has happened to me since my incarceration, though, is that the Lord slowed me down long enough to show me that he really does exist. It wasn't one of those overnight deals either—it took six years to open my eyes (praise Yah).*

*Prison has changed almost everything about who I was. Before my incarceration, I was criminal-minded. I loved living a life of crime and making money quickly was the appealing part of my criminal past. I wanted to be a big-time robber/burglar ever since I was a little kid. I knew that I was ruthless and that the streets would always respect the gangsta that I was trying to be.*

*Nowadays I am no longer that little kid trying to be hard. I'm just a man trying to exhibit the love and mercy that God Almighty imparts to me every day.*

*People make mistakes and sometimes those mistakes are horrible, and yet I would like to see a justice system that practices mercy. Not just mercy for the rich and famous either. I would like to see the death penalty abolished and sentencing that reflects the crime.*

My name is John Bazile and I am forty-six years of age. I was sentenced to two consecutive twenty-year to life sentences with the possibility of parole for first-degree murder with the use of a deadly weapon. I have been incarcerated at Warm Springs Correctional Center in Nevada since December 31, 1997.

# A Call For Common Sense Change

Even if people can't get behind prison reform on ideological grounds, Paul Crowley, a retired judge with twenty-five years of experience on the bench, says they should get behind the movement out of public safety concerns.

With 90–95 percent of all inmates being released at some point, Crowley says it only makes sense to have them reenter society as changed human beings.

"If you don't do anything to make the person better when you have control of them, then you are going to let a more hardened person out into society," he says.

In Oregon where he presided over cases in the Seventh Judicial District for more than two decades, Crowley says the state constitution mandates that punishment for crime be founded on "protection of society, personal responsibility, accountability for one's actions and reformation."

In Oregon, 55 percent of released inmates get rearrested within three years of leaving prison, which Crowley sees as evidence that reformation is clearly not being achieved, so the will of the people is not being truly respected.

"Article 1, section 15 requires reformation. It says we must do it and we don't," says Crowley.

In order to truly rehabilitate people, he says Americans need to shift the focus of prisons away from retribution to restorative justice.

Under restorative justice, mediation takes place between the victim and offender to hold the offender accountable, but also paves the way for that individual to be able to redeem himself or herself.

This approach uses the theory that wrongdoing is an offense against an individual or community rather than the state.

Crowley supports the concept from the stance of a judge who has sent people to prison. and as the victim of a crime that took the life of his sister.

In 1981, Margaret Crowley, twenty-three, was killed by a drunk driver who smashed into her car doing sixty miles per hour in a rural area of northern Illinois.

"When he got out of the car, his comment was 'Accidents will happen,'" says Crowley.

The cocky attitude of the young male, who was not quite eighteen, continued through the court proceedings. The defendant admitted to having been drinking and smoking dope before getting behind the wheel. He was convicted of negligent homicide and several other charges.

"At one point, he said, 'What do you want me to do—cry?'" says Crowley. "What probably bothered me the most was his complete lack of empathy."

His sister's killer received only thirty days in the Crook County Jail and weekends behind bars for a year, in addition to a prohibition on driving and other conditions.

"At the time, that was considered an extraordinary sentence," says Crowley.

He was fourteen months younger than Margaret and in college finishing up an accounting degree at the time of her death. Ironically, Crowley had also been hit by a drunk driver who was so inebriated that she did not even know that she had plowed into the back of his car.

Crowley did not pursue a career in criminal justice because of his family's tragedy, but he felt the experience better equipped him to oversee jury and bench trials.

"When victims would go over the top in my courtroom, I was able to say, 'I understand, I've been there,'" he says.

The backlash from laws that did not truly hold offenders accountable led to the passage of tougher sentencing guidelines and, eventually, to mandatory minimums.

As the years passed, Crowley thought back to his sister's case and came to several conclusions. He had visited the Crook County Jail as a high school student and understood that the driver convicted in her case—a white male from a middle-class family—would not have had an easy time of it in an institution filled with hardcore criminals from disadvantaged backgrounds.

"I actually had some sympathy for his situation," he says. "That was one of two of the scariest places I've been to—the other one was the high-security ward at Oregon State Hospital where they house the criminally insane."

He worked with the mentally ill during years as a defense attorney, where he routinely handled legal issues for offenders in Oregon prisons and jails.

It was a frequent occurrence, says Crowley, for inmates to legally challenge the conditions of their confinement, sometimes for even the simple right to wear tennis shoes because concrete made their feet hurt. Indigent inmates were issued boots and no other footwear.

"You are in an environment that is covered in acres of concrete, have little access to sunlight, and have a poor diet," says Crowley.

Americans are always affirming their pets and willingly taking time to teach them good habits, but society seems to be all right with not giving humans the same degree of consideration, which he finds troubling.

However, he said the winds of change seem to be sweeping quietly across America as more and more citizens, legislators, and Department of Corrections officials come to the realization that mass incarceration is not working.

There is a growing interest in learning from Norway's model of reforming offenders due to that country's 20 percent recidivism rate, one of the lowest in the world.

Fewer than four thousand of Norway's five million people are behind bars, compared to seven hundred seven for every one hundred thousand people in the US.

Crowley says Norway's focus on repairing the harm done by prisoners, instead of just punishing them, brings about true rehabilitation.

For Norway, removing a person's freedom is considered enough of a punishment. Once inside, inmates are prepared to reintegrate back into society with vocational programs, such as woodworking and personal development programs to build self-esteem.

While it might be more expensive per inmate to run an operation like Norway's in the US, which has a population of more than 328 million, Crowley suggests the costs might even out with fewer criminals returning to prison.

That belief is borne out by a 2014 US Department of Justice report that strict incarceration increases recidivism rates, while facilities that incorporate "cognitive-behavioral programs rooted in social learning theory" are the most effective at keeping ex-cons out of jail.

Crowley has long spoken from the bench about the need to allow more flexibility in sentencing laws.

He says the refusal of an Oregon judge to enact the full penalty in a 2008 sex abuse case led to a state Supreme Court ruling that there could be some rare departures from M11 mandatory minimums.

That case highlighted the problems with tough penalties that are broadly applied, said Crowley.

Two criminal cases were consolidated in that case for consideration by the high court and required an interpretation of Article I, section 15 of the state constitution that "all penalties shall be proportioned to the offense."

In one of the cases, Veronica Rodriguez, an adult, touched a thirteen-year old boy when standing behind him in a room at the Hillsboro Boys & Girls Club, where she worked with at-risk youth. A staff member reported seeing Rodriguez bring the back of the teen's head in contact with her clothed breasts for about one minute. She was also observed running her hands along the boy's face and through his hair.

There were thirty to forty other youth and at least one other staff member in the room at the time.

The second case involved Darryl Buck, an adult male who touched a thirteen-year-old girl when she was sitting next to him while fishing. She leaned back to cast her line, which brought her clothed buttocks into contact with the back of his hand, which he failed to move, an occurrence that happened one or two more times.

When they stood up, Buck brushed the dirt off the back of the girl's shorts with two swipes of his hand. He took that action after she had warned him about violating her boundaries.

In both cases, Buck and Rodriguez had befriended the teens and spent a considerable amount of time with them, often alone. Rodriguez had sent the boy numerous messages that she claimed were meant only to be affectionate but which jurors felt were romantic.

A jury in Rodriguez's case and a judge in Buck's found that the physical contact made respectively by the defendants had been for a sexual purpose, which made them guilty of first-degree sexual abuse.

That crime carried a mandatory sentence of six years and three months under M11.

In each of these cases, however, the trial judge determined that the mandatory minimum was "not proportioned to the offense" and imposed shorter sentences—sixteen months in the case of Rodriguez and seventeen months in the case of Buck.

The state appealed the rulings, and Rodriguez and Buck cross-appealed their convictions.

The Court of Appeals upheld the convictions and agreed with the state that the trial courts should have imposed the mandatory minimum of seventy-five months.

The consolidated cases then went before the Oregon Supreme Court, which affirmed the convictions but reversed the length of the sentences. Justices determined the time Rodriguez and Buck would spend behind bars violated the constitution's requirement for a reasonable penalty.

The high court applied the "shock the moral sense" test to the cases, based on a 1921 law. In order to protect defendants from cruel and unusual punishment, as required by the US Constitution, that law required punishment to be seen by reasonable men as right and proper under the circumstances.

Crowley says the supreme court ruling on these cases paved the way for some flexibility when imposing penalties under M11, but the circumstances under which discretion can be applied is extremely limited, so sentences have seldom been changed.

"Our system was absolutely broken before M11, when we had three thousand beds for prisoners in our entire state and inmates were serving six weeks for lesser crimes and eight years for murder," says Crowley. "That wasn't working, but this isn't either."

# Part I
# The Row: Either Life Is Hallowed Or It Isn't

Executing condemned prisoners is a more premeditated and calculated killing than any inmate on death row could devise, says Frank Thompson, retired superintendent of the Oregon State Penitentiary.

"The only difference is that these killings are sanctioned by the state and the identity of the executioner is cloaked by law," he says.

Although the average citizen will never look into the eyes of a death row prisoner while lethal drugs are being administered, Thompson says citizens should share the burden of a flawed and inhumane policy that does not make communities safer and victimizes prison staff.

"Vengeance is not the stuff good legislation should be based on," he says. "I do not believe that emotions should be the driving force behind establishing sound policy."

He became a strong voice for abolishing the death penalty after presiding over Oregon's last two executions in fifty-seven years.

The state's last two governors have enacted a moratorium on executions, but Thompson and others want to see the death penalty repealed altogether.

Don't think that he's against executions because he's soft on crime, says Thompson, who firmly believes there are some people who need to be locked away for a lifetime.

"I am convinced that life, on a moral level, is either hallowed or it isn't. And I want it to be," he says.

Asking Thompson about his emotional state on execution days in 1996 and 1997 earns an indecipherable look and a deep frown.

"You have to understand how I got to the point of having to kill someone," he finally says.

Thompson came from Arkansas in 1994 with powerful childhood memories of the lynching of Emmett Till, a black man who was killed by white men in 1955 because he allegedly "flirted" with a white woman. Thompson's childhood was a time of segregation and racism that resulted in the death of many civil rights workers. In addition, his sister was killed in a violent act.

"Those things were very vivid in my mind and my psyche," says Thompson. "I felt there was a place for capital punishment for people that did certain things, that it was a just sanction."

That belief was reinforced when his best friend and then his cousin, both police officers, were killed in the line of duty. The man who murdered his cousin was eventually executed for another crime, which left Thompson feeling that justice had been served.

He enlisted in the military and spent his entire career in law enforcement and corrections before accepting the responsibility of running the penitentiary in Oregon. He carried the mindset of a soldier who trains to go into harm's way for the greater good.

"When asked if I could conduct an execution, I said that I would have no problem," Thompson recalls. "The death penalty was part of the criminal justice system and I had to be prepared for all of the duties that a superintendent could be called upon to perform."

Flashing through his mind, even as he answered that interview question, was the botched execution of Ricky Ray Rector, forty-two, that had occurred a couple of years before he left Arkansas. That night inflicted such deep trauma on the execution staff in his home state that the chaplain resigned in moral outrage.

"There's no way to come up with a protocol that is completely fail-safe," says Thompson.

The execution of Rector, a mentally disabled black man, was carried out at the Cummins Unit on January 24, 1992. He had been given the death penalty for the 1981 murder of police officer Robert

Martin in Conway, Arkansas. He was sentenced to life for the murder of Arthur Criswell.

After killing Criswell in a restaurant, Rector agreed to turn himself in to authorities but instead shot Martin, the officer who had negotiated his surrender, in the back. He then shot himself in the head in a suicide attempt. Although he lived, Rector's frontal lobe was destroyed.

His defense team argued that he was not competent to stand trial because he could not comprehend what was happening to him. However, after hearing conflicting testimonies from experts, a judge determined that prosecution should proceed.

Because he had shot himself following the criminal acts, Rector could not use insanity for a defense. The Supreme Court has held that the Eighth Amendment prohibits the execution of someone who is "unaware of the punishment they are about to suffer and why they are to suffer it."

It would be reported that Rector was so mentally impaired during his last hour on earth that he told corrections officials he was saving the pecan pie from his last meal "for later."

When Rector was strapped to the gurney for his execution, a medical team of five people ended up working for more than fifty minutes to find a suitable vein for the intravenous line that would carry lethal chemicals into his body.

According to reports, Rector attempted to help medical personnel locate a good vein. Witnesses said he seemed to think the execution was an ordinary medical procedure.

People outside the curtain drawn around the death chamber reported hearing Rector give eight loud groans of pain during the search for a vein. At some point, a scalpel was used to cut his arm in an attempt to aid the process.

When the curtain was finally pulled back, witnesses saw blood on the sheets of the gurney where Rector lay. He was heard gasping for air before the drugs stopped his heart.

"I carried all of that with me," says Thompson. "I came to Oregon with the realization of how an execution can affect staff. With this being the first execution in thirty-two years and the very first use of lethal chemicals, I knew that the media would be watching my team, and if something went wrong, it would be the biggest news in corrections history."

Although he was prepared to carry out a death sentence, Thompson hoped that would not happen under his watch. However, he had been on the job eighteen months when he was instructed to prepare for the execution of Douglas Franklin Wright, fifty-six, who had waived his appeals.

The Oregon Supreme Court had cleared the way for Wright's execution when it denied motions to block the procedure.

Wright had been sentenced to death on October 11, 1993, for luring five homeless men to a remote area of Wasco County on the Warm Springs Indian Reservation with the false promise of work and then shooting four of them. One escaped to call the authorities.

Wright was prosecuted for three murders because the fourth victim was a Native American and that case would have been tried in federal court. Later, Wright admitted to killing a ten-year-old boy in 1984.

"At that time the protocols were still for death by the gas chamber, although Oregon had adopted lethal injection as the method of execution," explains Thompson. "I had to rewrite the protocols and then educate staff about how to do it right. I ended up knowing more about taking a life than anyone else in that prison."

Corrections officials are not trained to take lives, so Thompson utilized his military background to set up a series of training sessions that would teach them practical skills, as well as how to morally disengage themselves from the process.

"I trained, I trained, I trained," he said of the weeks leading up to Wright's execution. "The assistant superintendent came to me and said, 'Boss, they are tired, they get it,' and I said, 'That's what I want to hear—tell them to go back and do it one more time.'"

The overtime bill for training came to $85,000, but Thompson felt every penny was worth it because he could not get the chaplain's resignation in Arkansas out of his mind.

"I cannot put into words the anxiety I felt about the possibility of a botched procedure," he says.

His next challenge was to pick the executioner, his responsibility by law. The identity of that individual had to be kept secret by state statute.

"I didn't know how to go about searching for somebody without other people knowing," says Thompson. "But I disregarded anyone who volunteered to take that life because I suspected their motivation."

His dilemma was resolved when a young corrections officer stopped by his office and offered to take on extra duties to relieve Thompson's burden during a time of high stress.

"I thought about it a minute and I felt that he was the right one, he had the right attitude," says Thompson.

When he later called that officer in to request that he take on the grim job of the executioner, Thompson says the gravity of the request made the man bow his head.

He recalls the officer saying, "When I came in here asking what I could do to help, I didn't think it would come to *that*."

Like Thompson, the officer felt prison staff had a sworn duty to uphold the law, so he reluctantly agreed to learn the right techniques for handling the syringe that would end Wright's life.

"His moral hesitation was superseded by his sense of duty," says Thompson.

The executioner was secretly trained behind closed doors in the art of lethal injection. Thompson had him practice drawing water into a syringe and depressing the plunger just hard enough to make the liquid flow out at a rate equal to gravity, which would result in a "gentle" infusion of the lethal chemicals into the veins of the condemned man.

Like most states, Oregon has authorized a three-drug combination for lethal injections: sodium thiopental to induce unconsciousness; pancuronium bromide, a paralytic, to stop breathing; and finally, potassium chloride to stop the heart.

If everything goes as planned in a lethal injection execution, the condemned prisoner dies within ten minutes.

"I told my executioner to practice on that syringe until his thumb got tired," says Thompson.

He said Wright was placed under surveillance twenty-four hours a day for the last several days of his life so that he could not commit suicide, which Thompson viewed as a grim irony.

"If he harms or kills himself, we would be depriving the people of Oregon of the right to do the same," he says.

Thompson felt the "chaplain riding on his shoulder" as he assembled the team to end Wright's life on the night of September 6, 1996.

He had already explained to the condemned man exactly what would happen to him.

"There's this haze —a moral detachment—that a person who's been trained to do something they don't want to do goes into," Thompson says. "I didn't have time to really think about what I was doing. I don't even know if I was hungry that day."

The executioner was brought into a special room where he could not be seen by medical and prison staff or witnesses assembled in seats on the other side of a glass wall.

"We wanted to conduct the execution professionally and with as much dignity as humanly possible," says Thompson.

Behind a curtain drawn so witnesses could not see, Wright was strapped to a gurney and intravenous lines inserted into each arm so there would be a backup if the first attempt failed. Long tubes connected the needle through a hole in a cement block wall to several intravenous drips. The first was a harmless saline solution that started immediately.

Once the drug delivery system was in place and the saline flowing smoothly, the execution was set to go.

Thompson gave the nod to have the curtain opened. Witnesses, including members of the victim's family and media representatives, had a clear view of the gurney where Wright lay.

Thompson asked the condemned man if he had any final words, but Wright only mouthed "I'm sorry" to the mother of one of his victims. She nodded in response.

It was then time for Thompson to direct the executioner to begin administering the drugs.

"At that moment, I knew I wanted to get it over with, that was my all-consuming emotion," says Thompson.

He pronounced Wright dead shortly after midnight on September 6. The execution had been successfully performed at a cost of nearly $300,000 to the taxpayers.

But the true price was much higher, as Thompson quickly came to realize. He was haunted by the immorality of a society that set up such extravagant protocols to take a human life.

After the death of Wright, involved prison staff reported varying levels of distress and a couple of employees left their job. Thompson worried that officers would turn to drugs and alcohol to cope with the trauma and depression.

"It's hard to avoid giving up some of your empathy and humanity to aid in the killing of another human being," he says.

Eight months after Wright's death, Thompson and his team were called on to execute Harry Charles Moore, fifty-six, who had also waived appeals.

Moore had been given the death sentence for the 1992 murders of relatives that he thought would be moving to Las Vegas with his estranged wife and infant daughter, which he believed would expose them to a life of prostitution and drugs.

"I was a good corrections officer and a good soldier, so I began planning again," says Thompson. "I also began saying that when I was able, I was going to do something about state-sanctioned killings."

He never told staff outright how deeply convicted he was to end the death penalty, but word of his opposition got around and some of the officers asked how he felt. Thompson told them that, while he had personal objections, they all had a job to do and he would not bail out.

Anyone who felt similarly opposed was allowed by state policy to back out of the assignment, but Thompson said no one did because of their desire to ensure the job was done professionally.

"Despite the qualms and the cost, the job gets done. That's the way it's supposed to work," says Thompson. "Capital punishment keeps grinding on, out of sight of society."

Moore died at 12:23 a.m. on May 16, 1997. The second time around, Thompson chose not to stand at the foot of the condemned man's gurney; instead, he directed the execution from the other side of the glass wall.

His opportunity to work for repeal of the death penalty came with his retirement in 2010. Thompson now travels the country sharing his message and his opposition voice has been aired in broadcasts and printed in major publications.

For the last ten years, Thompson has undertaken the job of educating legislators as a board member of Oregonians for Alternatives to the Death Penalty.

"The process of an execution creates a totally new and unnecessary set of victims—the men and women who carry out the taking of a human life," he says. "They are needless casualties because we have life without parole—the state dishonors us by putting us in that position."

The mindset of Americans needs to change, says Thompson, who is hopeful that the pendulum of capital punishment is swinging in a new direction. He said the sheer cost of maintaining the existing prison system and inmates on death row is driving the discussion for change.

"Our society really doesn't think about this 'out of sight, out of mind' travesty of societal indulgence, and it is killing us morally," he says. "The issue goes to the very core of who we are as a society, especially when we have civilized societies that have abandoned this notion in its entirety."

He said the chance that an innocent person could be executed should also be morally unacceptable to Americans.

If capital punishment is not abolished outright, Thompson believes it should be the civic obligation of every lawmaker in states where it is enacted to participate in a lottery system to carry out an execution, a sort of jury service.

"Why should the people who are responsible for making capital punishment into law in the first place be exempt from assuming some of the responsibilities and psychological burden of killing?" he asks.

The words of Martin Luther King Jr. keep Thompson going when he is attacked by death penalty proponents for wanting to 'let murderers escape their 'just dues.''

"We're got some difficult days ahead," said King to an overflowing crowd in Memphis, Tennessee, on April 3, 1968. "But it really doesn't matter with me now, because I've been to the mountaintop... I've seen the promised land. I may not get there with you. But I want you to know tonight that we, as a people, will get to the promised land."

Thompson, who served in the Army and was stationed in Korea, compares the growing public sentiment against the death penalty to the antiwar movement of the Vietnam War. As the calculated outcomes failed to materialize, he said the American people became more and more reluctant to put boots on the ground.

"We need to come to that same mindset about the death penalty," he says. "America should no longer accept the myth that capital punishment plays any constructive role in our criminal justice system."

Untitled by Imani Williams from the hole at Oregon State Penitentiary

||||||||||||||||||||||||||||||||||||||||||||||||||||||||||||||||||||

# Fighting The War Within

*My mom went to San Jose State in California and graduated. She decided to have only me as a child. But my mom chose to work at the post office, so she could go to the bar and shoot pool.*

*She would take me to school about 8:00 a.m. and pick me up, or my dad would, and she would be out the door by 8:00 p.m. to go out to the club five or six days a week.*

*My mom kicked my dad out because she was tired of being hit domestically, and I hated my dad for hurting my mom. That's why I can't understand why I hurt women. But my victims were in a domestic relationship with me, and I have abandonment issues. When issues arise, I am like Dr. Jekyll and Mr. Hyde—I just transform.*

*Most of my life, I was raised by kids who were poor and homeless. My dad paid child support, but I did not want to live with him because he hit me too much. My dad broke my jaw at nine years old, and I told people I had braces. My mom used to tell me to lie about what happened.*

*I was the only kid in my neighborhood who had no food in the fridge, and the ghetto kids raised me on morals and principles that I did not agree with.*

*My mom brought stray men home who sold drugs, and I looked up to the people around me; yet my mom used to say, "I don't want you to grow up like my boyfriend." So I'd ask, "Then why did you bring his ass here?"*

*My mom loved being with men she could control with her money, my money, and my grandmother's money. Yeah, she stole and kept most of the money, even though I had a lot as a teenager.*

*I regularly had fifteen friends at my house, and my mom was gone all night. So we would plot and do stuff that normal kids wouldn't do.*

Guns and drugs and violence. But we could never seem to make money because we tried to kill everything, or at least bet on it.

A lot of us died at a young age. In Oakland, California, you go to jail, die, or become a dope fiend between the age of thirteen and eighteen.

My dad got married to a lady whose brother was a cop and he would talk to me. I would say, "I'd rather go to prison than to Princeton." I was like thirteen years old. Sinister thoughts.

My grandma used to talk bad about my mother, and it made me mad, but I should've listened to her and stayed in the house with her and gone to school and hid from the hoodlums. So I chose my life story.

I hated not having a brother, a sister. I hated my mom. I hated my dad. I hated them so much, death was the only thing that could keep us apart, so I chose to part ways and that's how I ended up in Oregon.

I came to Portland in 2004 or 2005, and I wanted to change. I had no record of any kind.

I relapsed in my drug use, and there's one thing I will say about downtown Portland: anybody can go up to the rescue mission and not only get a bed to sleep up but become a member of the eighteen-month recovery program.

I used to say, "Hell nah! I just need eighteen hours of sleep and I'll be all right." I never wanted to submit fully. By the time I did, it was too late.

Opportunities presented themselves many times. White people came up to me and tried to rescue me, but I ran away from their homes and their food to be back in the streets. To be homeless is a choice thang and not a forced thang.

I can't speak for nobody else but me. I lied in the streets, stealing every day. Getting high every day. Wanting to change for the best but staying the same for the worst. I hurt, yet I thirsted for corruption and I hungered for self-destruction. Food for thought: I felt like the bad apple on my family tree.

A strong foundation with education is all a child of God needs to believe. But I had to wanna change before I could do anything out of the ordinary.

Life's a trip, but it doesn't come with a map. Many men are dying here from stress, and many are leaving and coming right back because *they can't stay away from the altercations, women, and drugs. It's a dangerous combination.*

*Many here have skills but aren't ready to use them. Some like it here because we get three hots and a cot. Free water that's hot. Television with cable. It's safe here. You won't die from a weapon here; there's two to ten odds of old age. Likely, cancer or an overdose. Suicide maybe, but violence no.*

*I've beat people with objects because they stole from me, but that's not the way to conduct business, so now I say, "If I loan it to you, I've already convinced myself that if you don't give it back, then you can just have it." But people still wanna take the debt and owe me. I be like, "You don't really wanna owe me, just look out for me and return the favor."*

*I'm in the process of changing my way of thinking. As a kid, I used to disagree with all my friends, and I got beat up for it. But I was right, and they were wrong. Should've chosen better friends.*

*Sometimes, I think I just got caught. Many people have gotten away with murder, robbery, etc.*

*I let peace be my salvation now because I've been at war with me, myself, and I since I've been born.*

*Anyone can start from now and make a brand-new ending/finish. If you always do what you've always done, you'll always get what you've always gotten.*

*So I try to teach myself that anger is a wind that blows out the lamp of the mind.*

*I'm learning how to deal with pressure—as you know, pressure bursts pipes but it can also make a diamond.*

*I am learning how to love me because I've hated life for so long, it's just sad to say that life had an evil meaning once upon a time. But today I stay in the light and out of the darkness, which led me here.*

My name is Imani Williams, and I am forty-two and serving time at Oregon State Penitentiary. I was convicted of felony murder and second-degree assault and sentenced to thirty years, of which I have served fifteen.

# Better Treatment For Sons And Daughters

The reason most inmates don't overcome drug addiction is because illegal substances are easy to get in prison and the vast majority of treatment programs are being run without the expectation of success, says Michelle Brandsma, a certified addictions counselor.

"If chocolate cake is sitting on your counter all the time, eventually you are going to taste that chocolate cake—it's inevitable," she says of the situation.

Only a dissertation away from her doctorate, Brandsma has a long pedigree in the field of treatment and has come to the belief, based upon her firsthand experiences, that prisons aren't really committed to rehabilitation. She has worked in the field for fifteen years, ten of which were in the penal system.

"I got tired of seeing nothing good come of what I was doing," she says of stepping down from overseeing programs in Oregon and California. "I left the prison system because I just ended up feeling like I really couldn't make a difference."

The biggest obstacle to change is a monolithic bureaucracy that is more concerned about appearances than results. There is a lot of talk about treatment, but the recidivism rate of addicts tells the true story, she says.

A review of recidivism in fifteen states undertaken by the US Department of Justice found that one-quarter of inmates who are released end up back in prison within three years for technical violations, the majority because they tested positive for drug use.

That is a significant public safety issue, noted federal officials, because 50 percent of inmates were high during commission of a crime, often to obtain money for more drugs.

The National Institutes of Health reports that 80 to 85 percent of prisoners who could benefit from drug abuse treatment do not receive it. The dire need for treatment of this population group is exacerbated by their being at high risk for infectious diseases that can be passed on to others, such as human immunodeficiency virus (HIV) and hepatitis C.

Not treating a prisoner is a missed opportunity to not only protect the general public but to help a valuable human being turn his or her life around, says Brandsma.

Her methodology for treatment was "Uncover, Discover, and Recover" and she helped inmates realize faulty thinking patterns and learn new ways to deal with life challenges. That is the way parents teach children how to become contributing members of society and it is the type of approach prison needs also, says Brandsma.

"What we are doing now is like punishing a kid for two or three years because they made a mistake, which just doesn't happen in the real world. This just isn't working. We expect people with substance abuse issues to live in the general population and change their lives when we could not be exposed to that level of temptation and make it outside. Those who do want change are given the feeling that no one cares."

She said two minimum-security institutions in Oregon—Powder River and Deer Ridge—are the exception to an otherwise apathetic system. In those facilities, she said inmates getting ready to be released are immersed in highly effective restorative programs.

"They are eating and sleeping treatment—there is a high degree of accountability," she says. "They are working on themselves the whole time they are there. The goal is to get them dealing with as many issues as they can before they get out into society."

She praised corrections officers in Powder River and Deer Ridge for genuinely listening and working with inmates to help change their behaviors.

"Inmates with substance abuse problems are lucky to get a few hours of treatment a week at most prisons, which isn't going to do them any good," she says.

Her professional assessment of the situation was that the end result of warehousing people without true rehabilitation programs is that both staff and inmates experience a high degree of despair.

"We use inmates for labor that makes a profit for the system instead of teaching them new skills or self-knowledge," she says. "No one inside really believes in the system and yet they all have to continue functioning within their designated roles."

In order to succeed on the outside, Brandsma contends that prisoners need to reflect on their mistakes and how their actions negatively affected other people, not only the victim but their own families.

"Our treatment of inmates needs to be therapeutic. They need to look at what got them there and decide if they are 'on vacation' or really want to stay out because that is going to take a different kind of work."

People can't expect someone off the streets to turn things around without an understanding of their life circumstances before incarceration, she says.

"Most of us have no idea what it's like to have grown up in gangs. When we ask them to turn their back on that lifestyle, we are asking them to give up a 'family,' and that is going to be difficult."

The key to working with prisoners, she says, is to be aware of their games to manipulate you but remain compassionate.

"I think what has to happen is that corrections officials need to quit seeing prisoners as a paycheck or an amusement. If they get to know them as people, then they will have to look at them differently and treat them differently."

During her time behind the wall, Brandsma observed guards who exhibited the same criminal thinking as inmates.

"Some of the staff follow the rules only when it benefits them," she says.

It was the ultimate irony, she says, that corrupt guards smuggled in drugs and then raided the cells of prisoners they had sold contraband to, seizing it to sell another day.

Brandsma saw police officers in Los Angeles with gang tattoos interacting with inmates and wondered what deals were being made. Even more troubling, she witnessed guards in several institutions abusing power because they knew that no one would listen if the inmates complained.

Sometimes, just for fun, guards acted like they were best buddies with an inmate to give the appearance that they were working together, which set the prisoner up to be labeled a snitch and attacked, recalls Brandsma.

"There is a lot of manipulation. An attitude among corrections officials that 'I can treat you any way I want to because I am the boss.'"

Not all guards are corrupt, she says, and many truly care about inmates, but the prison system accommodates authority figures who don't want to play by the rules.

She said life behind the wall is especially difficult for a mentally ill inmate because they cannot navigate the brutal code and often end up in the hole or protective custody due to dangerous run-ins with predators.

Brandsma remembers a man with schizophrenia having other inmates whisper in his ear that the food was poisoned, so he quit eating. He started losing weight, but no one seemed to notice until it became enough of a health crisis that he required medical attention.

Another incident that sticks in Brandsma's mind is what happened to a prisoner from the streets who was working to turn his life around. Inmates who wanted to prove a point about who was in charge jumped him and stabbed him while he watched TV. He was placed in solitary confinement for his own protection.

"If you do see a problem and try to point it out, you are the problem—whether you are an inmate or a staffer," she says.

If the focus of prisons changed to restorative justice, Brandsma believes success stories would become commonplace.

She said many inmates come from highly unstable backgrounds where they learned survival skills but never had the opportunity to explore higher levels of thinking, such as finding a purpose to benefit others.

"Locking people in a cage when they screw up isn't going to change anyone for the better," she says. "Some inmates deserve to be in there for a longer time or maybe forever, but we should still treat them as human beings, like we would in the real world."

It takes money to help inmates earn a GED, become better parents, complete college classes or vocational training to acquire job skills, and as a result, improve their self-esteem, says Brandsma.

She contends that the return on investment would be prisoners walking out the gate with confidence in their futures, the ability to become contributing citizens.

In today's world, she says an inmate leaves prison with the deck stacked against success.

For starters, the parole officer often views the felon in the same suspicious way the guards did and treats them negatively instead of trying to be supportive.

"In this field, people are all looking through the same lens and that needs to change," she says.

She believes most people don't really know what a dismal failure prisons are. Once educated, her hope is that they will demand real change and elect leaders who will make it happen.

"Prisoners are human beings, they are our sons and daughters, and everyone deserves to have an opportunity to prove that their mistakes are just that—mistakes."

||||||||||||||||||||||||||||||||||||||||||||||||||||||||||||||||||||

# Part II
# Kat: The Fire To Survive

*Nobody looks good in their darkest hour, but that hour shapes who we become because of our experiences. We stand strong or we cower. A choice is made in a split second. State of mind and the natural-born instinct to survive is real and absolute. You never know how you will respond until you face the trauma.*
—Kathleen Blankenship

Her shoulders were back and her chin up the day Kathleen "Kat" Blankenship was transported from the county jail to the only women's prison in Oregon.

She walked through the door determined to avoid trouble if possible but willing to stand up for herself if challenged.

"I hadn't lived the street life and I had never had a problem with drugs or any other type of criminal behavior, so I wasn't as tough as some, but I knew it was important to let people know that I wasn't going to be messed with," says Kat.

It was 2003, and she had been sentenced to twenty-five years at Coffee Creek Correctional Facility for murdering her abusive cop husband. She had vowed to never quit fighting for her freedom from what she saw as a blatant injustice.

"I walked in telling other women that I was going to win my case and go home," says Kat, who was forty at that time.

Her mother and ex-husband were raising her two traumatized sons, then nine and ten, who had been sexually molested by Walter Blankenship, the man who had held a gun against her head and threatened to kill her entire family before she gained control of the weapon and used it to defend herself.

"At what moment does a man, who otherwise seems sane and good, choose to indulge in his own darkest desires? What turns an ordinary man into a monster?" she later wrote. "I have no answer to that, but I can tell you what it was like to live with such a person and survive not only his abuse but that of the legal system."

Kat had not been allowed to plead self-defense at her trial, and she planned to legally challenge the right of her lawyer to deny her the right to speak out in court.

"There is a saying that the truth will set you free, and I knew it would. I just didn't expect it to take ten years!" she says. "I put it out to the universe, and I spoke it into existence."

When she arrived at the prison in Wilsonville, Oregon, which houses about 1,600 women, a small percentage of the overall prison population, Kat was prepared to be abused by guards because Walter had been in law enforcement.

Instead, she said some guards who knew Walter to be an "asshole" expressed compassion for her situation.

Other corrections officers were less kind, but many of these authority figures were in the job for the power so they mistreated most inmates. In fact, sexual abuse of female inmates by guards of both genders was common. Corrections officers often performed "bare" skin searches at will, either for some perverse pleasure or to humiliate the inmate, says Kat.

Although a women's prison doesn't have the high level of violence among inmates reported at institutions for males, she said there is still a "predator and prey" mentality. The weak are dominated by the strong.

Kat earned respect by giving respect and learned that there were a lot of good people around her. Many were women who, like her, had been imprisoned for injuring or killing an abusive partner.

She saw for herself the havoc wreaked on their lives by mandatory minimum sentences that did not factor in who they were as a person.

"That's the most inequitable law they ever passed," Kat says. "Every DA interprets it the way they want to get the results they want. It's all about claiming a win."

Ironically, she said being in prison was the beginning of her quest to heal the brokenness inside that had led her into abusive relationships.

"Sometimes in life, you have to look at your own reflection, and it isn't pretty. I learned a lot from my prison counselor because she allowed me to find me."

Kat had been adopted when she was three days old in 1963 by older parents who had long wanted a child.

"They had been married for twenty years before I came along, and they spoiled me with love and devotion," she says. "I was surrounded with a mature family fabric, a grandad, aunts and uncles who doted on me, showing me unconditional love and acceptance."

Like most little girls, Kat had the fairy-tale dream of marrying Prince Charming and living happily ever after.

"I never thought about things like self-defense and being abused or the need to protect myself and family from a predator or trials and fault lines," she says.

Somehow, even though she excelled at school and had plenty of affirmation in her life, Kat lacked self-esteem. She craved the approval of others for fulfillment and that set the stage for her to make poor choices in men.

"I held on so tightly to relationships that I couldn't allow them to mature in a healthy process," she says. "I created more trouble from my need to control my environment. I tried to earn love to fulfill the need inside of me to be accepted. I didn't trust. I couldn't truly allow anyone in because it would expose my vulnerable spots, my need to be needed."

She picked partners who had suffered trauma in childhood and failed in other relationships. By loving them enough, Kat was sure that their lives would turn around and they would love her the more for it. Instead, she ended up being the target of their rage and deviant behavior.

"I would get lost in trying to make them happy, give them whatever I thought they needed to fulfill that voice I perceived lacking. I just couldn't do enough," she says. "I stuffed all my needs and values down so deeply, my own happiness was no longer easily known. My foundation became severely bruised, damaged to the point I no longer had any energy to put into my own well-being. I was too busy being a mother, daughter, wife, and friend. I did not have time for me. I did not love myself. I had no value within me, and I began to believe that I truly was the cause of the cruelty and abuse."

Her pride and ego became a driving force for hiding the nightmare of her life with Walter.

"I was successful personally and professionally in the eyes of society. I was too ashamed to admit what was going on behind closed doors," she says.

Under the shame and guilt was fear—fear of rejection, fear of being alone, fear of abandonment, fear of retaliation if she tried to leave.

"I was on autopilot. I appeared to be functioning, but I wasn't really living. I was just existing. My validation for existence was totally tied to another's opinion and acceptance."

In prison, Kat worked hard at strengthening her soul—and getting her conviction overturned.

She did not lose hope when the Oregon Court of Appeals upheld her conviction without opinion. She refused to give up when the state Supreme Court denied review, as did the United States Supreme Court.

Instead, Kat educated herself on the appeals process and challenged the system for denying her the right to a fair trial.

"My trial was a joke," she says. "I was told by my attorney that I would put a nail in the coffin if I testified about Walter's abuse or what really happened that day."

Her challenge of the trial process was heard in a Washington County Circuit Court, a post-conviction appeal. Judge Stephen Price ordered that her case be returned to Umatilla County for a new trial.

With that ruling, Kat became the first woman in Oregon to have her case overturned at the post-conviction level of appeals. It was May 2008, and she had spent seven years behind bars.

"When I won my case, my friends inside wrote thoughts in a journal about me and the most common theme was that I was an inspiration to them because I never gave up. I walked my walk every day the same," says Kat.

Despite her victory, it would be another three years before she returned home to get reacquainted with her sons, one of whom struggled with abandonment issues and the other who was angry with her for not protecting them from Walter.

In May 2009, Kat returned to the Umatilla County Jail as the state prepared to try her again. This time the Hood River-based law firm of Morris, Olson, Smith, Starnes, and Raschio took on her defense.

Jack Morris was the lead attorney and was cynical enough after a long career in criminal defense that he did not initially believe the story Kat told him. However, he set about proving her case and eventually arrived at the conclusion that she was telling the truth.

His investigator found witnesses who verified that Walter had an explosive temper. The team hunted down other victims of his perversion and learned about complaints filed against him for inappropriate contact with juveniles that had been hidden by the police department.

While in prison, Kat received an anonymous letter with an article inside about a cold case involving the unsolved murder of a woman at a local reservoir.

"Your husband is responsible for this one," the letter stated.

Kat turned the letter over to the DA, who refused to investigate the allegations.

"It just rang true in my heart," she says.

She was optimistic that a new trial would reveal the truth about Walter's character and how the system had aided and abetted his abuse.

Dr. Reid Meloy, a renowned forensic psychologist, was brought back to evaluate Kat. He determined that she had been extremely emotionally disturbed at the time of the shooting and that she had acted in self-defense.

Dr. Anne Marie Smith, who conducted evaluations for the Oregon State Hospital, agreed with Meloy's assessment.

Then Dr. Scott Reichlin surprisingly reversed his opinion from her first trial and said Kat could have acted under extreme emotional distress. He also stated that he believed it inappropriate for a mental health professional to issue an opinion on the capacity of a defendant and that a jury should decide the matter.

As a result of Reichlin's conclusion, the state filed a motion to delay the trial in order to secure an additional evaluation.

A short time later, state prosecutor Dean Gushwa left office after being charged with several counts of misconduct. His original cocounsel at trial, Christopher Brauer, had become a judge and was therefore unavailable to assist in the case.

The cost of Kat's original trial had been estimated by Gushwa at over $1 million, and a retrial was expected to cost even more. Nevertheless, the state refused to consider a settlement.

Instead, Rachel Bridges, an assistant attorney general, made repeated efforts to postpone the trial to line up another expert to evaluate Kat.

The defense vigorously opposed each request for a delay and the prosecution finally reconsidered a settlement to the case.

If Kat pleaded guilty to the charge of manslaughter, she would receive credit for the years she had already spent in custody, so the ten-year sentence would be fulfilled. She agreed to the deal to get home to her family.

At her final hearing in January 2011, Morris pointed out that the state had provided nearly six thousand pages of material that had not initially been offered during her first trial.

Judge Garry Reynolds took the prosecution to task, declaring that he was completely "dismayed" by the way the case had been handled.

"It was definitely the good ole boy system at work," says Kat.

At the age of forty-eight, she was finally free to start a new life, with the added layer that she had vowed to help others wrongfully convicted.

"You have to have the fire inside you to survive and that's one thing I've learned about myself," she says.

Untitled by Jorge Cabrera

# The Underdog

*I was born poor, black and ugly, neglected, abused and rejected.*
*I grew up sad, depressed, angry, and alone,*
*At age 13, I ran away from home.*
*I squatted in abandoned buildings and homes,*
*in the Mission and Haight District in San Francisco, California.*
*I was so lost, so sick, so inflicted,*
*So inflicted with so many addictions.*
*I was addicted—alcohol addiction, drug addiction, sex addiction*
*Addicted, addictions, a dick!*
*I've always been the Underdog,*
*Sometimes, God, I even think I'm your favorite one.*
*You have always taken me to the brink as the razor cuts deep,*
*So deep I fell asleep, my heart skipped, then lost its beat.*
*Two times I died, yet I'm still—*
*Still a mess, a hot mess, a train wreck,*
*Still the Underdog.*
*I'm something like a Wonder Dog; I overcame,*
*I've overcome, I'm overdone!*
*Yet I'm still, I'm still the Underdog.*
*Such is the life of one that lives against all odds*
*Such is the life of the Underdog, I'm something of a Wonder Dog,*
*Baby, I'm still the Underdog.*

Travell "Paycheck" Holmes
A man in a cage

# Whatever You Do To The Least

"If you treat people cruelly, they will respond cruelly," says Roger Martin, a former Oregon state legislator who now lobbies for prison reform.

"I knew the system and how it worked, so I felt that I could make a difference working within it," he says of his role.

Even if public safety and spiraling costs don't concern citizens, Martin contends that a nation that identifies as Christian should look at the issues from the biblical perspective of mercy and grace.

Matthew 25:36–40 says, "I was naked, and you gave me clothing. I was sick, and you cared for me. I was in prison, and you visited me. Then these righteous ones will reply, 'Lord, when did we ever see you hungry and feed you? Or thirsty and give you something to drink? Or a stranger and show you hospitality? Or naked and give you clothing? When did we ever see you sick or in prison and visit you?' And the King will say, 'I tell you the truth, when you did it to one of the least of these my brothers and sisters, you were doing it to me!'"

Another verse, in Hebrews 13:3, says, "Continue to remember those in prison as if you were together with them, and those who are mistreated as if you yourselves were suffering."

Martin says, "It's all well and good to pray for people, but we need to change the system. This is not a partisan issue, it's a humanitarian issue."

Reformers have been successful at getting some changes made that benefit prisoners, such as a bill that allows them to sell the art they make online, but Martin says the deep systemic changes that need to be made remain largely elusive.

The problem is reaching critical mass with the cost of running US prisons continually rising and now threatening other state services.

According to the Oregon Department of Corrections, the cost of maintaining an inmate per day is about $108.26, or $39,400 per year. That cost is up from $84.81, or about $31,000 per year, just four years ago.

Those costs are related directly to prisoner care and housing. Additional millions are being spent for operations and employee salaries, says Martin.

The cost per prisoner goes up exponentially for inmates with serious health problems, the elderly, and inmates with mental disorders.

Larger populations and longer sentences have turned many prisons into nursing homes and hospice services must be provided, says Martin.

Several years ago, *The Oregonian/Oregon Live* reported that a forty-year-old inmate might have an annual health expense of $776, while an inmate over age seventy might require $6,527 in health care a year.

The US Department of Justice reports that 64 percent of local jail inmates, 56 percent of state prisoners, and 45 percent of federal inmates have symptoms of serious mental illness. It can cost twice as much to incarcerate these individuals.

Most mentally disordered inmates are not violent criminals, but if convicted and sent to prison, they don't receive the treatment they need and end up leaving prison more traumatized. They often stay longer than their counterparts without mental illness and are at greater risk of victimization. Often their mental health condition deteriorates while they are being "warehoused" without adequate treatment, says Martin.

US DOJ reports that state and federal prisons have anywhere from 1.2 to 1.9 percent of inmates infected with HIV, another expensive condition. Many of those cases are not discovered until the offender is tested at the county jail level.

The illness can be treated with a very expensive and potent drug referred to as a cocktail, which is a highly active antiretroviral therapy. The Centers for Disease Control and Prevention estimates that the cost per month to treat these patients is about $1,863, or an annual average of $22,356.

Lawmakers need to overhaul the criminal justice system or continue to watch corrections eat up more and more revenue, says Martin.

Spiking costs have initiated a philosophical discussion that leaves hope for positive change. Officials must decide whether large number of inmates should be released early or if states should retool the way they manage corrections.

It is time, says Martin, for people to push legislators to allow a range of sanctions for lawbreakers so fewer people end up in prison. And those who do are treated with the respect and dignity owed a human being.

Martin was elected to the Oregon State Legislature in 1966 and served until 1979, when there was a push to reduce crime by imposing stricter sentences. He became a lobbyist almost forty years ago, at first for commercial interests and then later for the Oregon Catholic Conference, which wants to see the death penalty abolished.

When former Oregon governor John Kitzhaber put a moratorium on the death penalty in 2011 out of the belief that "it fails to meet the basic standards of justice," Martin was asked by the Catholic Conference to focus on overall reform of the criminal justice system, including getting life without parole sentencing rolled back.

"We need to give a second look at the sentences of older inmates when they clearly pose no threat to society," he says.

He describes parole boards as "dysfunctional" because their focus is on the original crime and not where the inmate is in terms of mental and emotional development and rehabilitation after years of incarceration.

"They seem to be trying to keep the person behind bars and I don't think the inmates get a fair hearing most of the time," he says. "They can have a job lined up, a good support system in place, and evidence that they have completed programming and rehabilitated their thinking, and they still get denied."

He says district attorneys are also opposed to changes in the system and fight hard at the state capital to keep the mandatory minimum and other punitive measures in place.

If the people demand that the failing system be overhauled, Martin is confident that it will happen. "Nothing will change the mind of a legislator quicker than a few phone calls from constituents."

# Part II
# Keith: Prison Dangers Are Real

*The penitentiary breaks people. If you are not care-*
*ful, you are not doing the time, the time is doing*
*you.*

—Keith Ward

At the age of twenty-eight, Keith Ward was sentenced to thirteen years in a Nevada prison for armed robbery, and no one who knew him was surprised by the verdict.

He had been in and out of jail since his teenage years for crimes related to a serious drug addiction.

Keith had learned enough in his travels through the criminal justice system to know that prison was a "gladiator school." There were predators and prey and he had no intention of being a victim.

"In this environment, you have all types of people—you've got weak and strong," he says. "I am not a weak person. I grew up on the streets and know how to survive."

Determined to avoid joining a gang, Keith knew that standing up for himself would be important.

"When you first come to prison, you are a little scared because you don't know what to expect," he says. "The first thing you learn is that it's all about respect because if you don't have respect, you're gonna run into the wall."

Many inmates, particularly those who are young, join the gang of their ethnicity to have "two hundred to three hundred other guys backing you." Being in a gang means you have support if you go to the hole for an infraction and there is always money on your books for commissary.

"If you don't have outside support, that gang starts to look like a family," says Keith, sixty-four.

The flip side of being in that "family" is that you must do whatever the gang leader says, even if that means running drugs and other contraband—or murdering someone. Gangs are always fighting each other for control so joining one almost always guarantees violence.

"You will always have to do something for them," says Keith.

Being a lone wolf required that he stay vigilant. A brawl at Southern Desert Correctional Center could start just by someone getting bumped while walking down the hall or an inmate being in a bad mood.

"Things can go from zero to sixty in here at any time and you have to be ready."

He recalls an encounter on his first day of prison that set the stage to establish respect.

Keith was going through the line in chow hall, and one of the servers complimented the watch he was wearing.

"You ever thought of selling it?" the man asked.

"No," replied Keith.

"Then someone's gonna end up taking it from you," the man said.

Irritated and feeling threatened, Keith sat at a table and was discussing the incident with other inmates when he observed movement out the corner of his eye.

The server came up behind him, and without thinking, Keith turned and stabbed him with his fork. He later learned the injured man, who recovered from his wound, had just wanted to make an offer for the watch.

"So I went to the hole for sixty days right off the bat," says Keith.

When he got out of isolation, he was unsure if his victim belonged to a gang or had other associates who would retaliate. He was ready for anything.

But in the prison hierarchy, the strong are admired—even if grudgingly—for their ability to dominate the weak.

"I got back to my cell and my cellie says, 'You pretty tough.' I only had a few more problems after that, and then I was left alone," says Keith.

He said the Convict Code that is portrayed in movies is real, and it is strictly enforced by the inmates. Failure to follow these protocols that bind the penal societal system together can get you injured or killed:

- Never snitch on another inmate. Don't have loose lips or put an inmate on the spot in front of guards.
- Mind your own business. What someone else is doing is not your concern, no matter what.
- Don't put yourself above others, such as cutting in line. There are long waits in lines for everything, so this is a sign of disrespect and you will be "checked" by another inmate.
- Don't exploit inmates. If you make a promise, keep it. Don't steal, don't sell favors, and don't renege on bets. If

you run up a gambling debt and don't pay up, you could be injured or killed.

- Do not call someone a punk, because inmates take that term seriously. A punk is someone who doesn't stand up for himself, so the term is considered an insult to manhood and a challenge to fight.
- Maintain yourself as a real man. Don't whine, cry, or demonstrate any kind of vulnerability. Always appear tough.
- Never steal. Your own friends in prison will beat you up for taking something from someone else.
- Don't mess with homosexuals or you risk a beating. These inmates are shunned by the general population.
- Don't trust guards. No matter how nice the official is, he or she is not on your side.

Keith says sex offenders and prisoners who have hurt women or children are despised by the inmate population. In some cases, they pay "rent" from their commissary, and in others, they risk an attack if they come out of their cell for more than a quick shower and a meal.

There is a distinctive language among prisoners. A knife is called a shank or shiv. Homemade jailhouse alcohol is pruno or hooch. Prescription tranquilizers used to calm antisocial inmates are called brake fluid. Elderly inmates are referred to as old heads, and middle-class inmates who identify with staff members are known as square johns. An inmate who constantly complains about being wrongly convicted is called a rapo. Mentally ill inmates are called dings or crazies. Prison money is referred to as scrip. Newcomers to the prison are fish. Prison informers are squeals, snitches, or rats. Telling secrets or offenses to a person in authority without directly naming the inmate is called dry snitching.

Keith quickly learned about the thriving black market after entering prison. You could get anything you wanted, from phones to heroin. Some drugs came through the visiting room, but the majority were smuggled in by guards or vendors.

"I was a heroin addict when I came in, and I was a heroin addict when I got out thirteen years later," he says.

Within three years of walking out the door the first time, Keith was back inside—this time with a life sentence for being a habitual offender. At the age of forty-four, he had been convicted again of armed robbery, this time with the added counts of kidnapping and coercion.

For months he had been a fugitive, catching rides with truckers and staying at cheap motels in several states before deciding that he couldn't keep living that way. He finally walked into a police station in Virginia and gave himself up.

"I thought they would go easy on me because I turned myself in and I was shocked, shocked, when the judge put me in for life," says Keith.

He has served twenty years of the second sentence in several different prisons and has the possibility of parole in 2023.

He was part of the Scared Straight program before it folded and felt the opportunity to tell troubled youth about the "world of hurt" that awaited them was worthwhile.

"I told those kids, 'If you don't know how to fight when you get in here, by the time you leave, you'll have learned.'"

In the early days, Keith found that running a hustle was a good way to make a buck if you didn't have outside support. He once spent eighteen months in the hole after getting caught moving contraband.

"I just stopped running drugs because I knew there was no future in it," he says.

He has also been in the hole for twelve months and a few lesser stints, mostly for fighting.

Being isolated requires a lot of mental discipline, he says, because so much unoccupied time allows your mind to play tricks on you. He has witnessed numerous men needing meds for psychotic conditions after a long time in the hole.

"I slept a lot," he says. "I stand strong, so I could survive it, but it breaks weaker people."

At one point in his incarceration, prison officials accused Keith of being the shot caller for a gang problem in another institution.

A shot caller is the leader of a gang who issues orders for members inside and even orchestrates drug and gun trafficking on the streets.

"Something happened, and the administration thought I had something to do with it," says Keith.

One reason the guards might have thought that is because, for the most part, he gets along well with gang leaders. "I just stay out of the way. I don't really socialize with anybody, but I'm pretty well liked."

Even if you don't join a gang, when there is a riot involving your race, you are expected to defend your own, says Keith.

If you do not, then no one will come to your aid if you are attacked, so everyone will know that you are unprotected.

As you age in prison, you refrain from getting involved in nefarious activities because your soul longs for peace and you don't want to mess up any opportunity you have of returning to the free world, says Keith. "You want to stay on your A game because you got your eye on the gate."

Unfortunately, Keith says most inmates don't have outside support because they have either burned bridges with bad life choices or been inside a long time and their parents have died.

"If you don't have anyone on the outside, you don't give a damn."

After more than thirty years behind bars, Keith has seen men leave only to be back inside a few months or years later. The problem, he says, is that there is not enough programming available to teach inmates the skills they need to succeed outside.

When they get out with a $25 gift card and a bus ticket and have nowhere to go, they end up hanging out with past associates and gradually revert to familiar patterns.

"That's what happened to me," he says.

Keith does not consider himself institutionalized despite being incarcerated for decades. Unlike some of the men, he does not think of prison as his home.

Prison is a brutal environment that offers a life of deprivation. And danger is always lurking, he says.

A couple of years ago, guards at his prison uncovered a plot where a white gang was stockpiling knives made in the machine shop for an attack on the blacks.

Although the blades were confiscated in a shakedown of cells, Keith taped the books he owned around his waist to serve as a shield in case the attack still took place.

"You never know what any day will bring," he says. "Before something big happens, you can feel the tension, and everyone is on edge. Then the riot breaks out in the yard, and you are laying on the ground with a gun in your face [guard] while they sort things out."

One of those violent encounters at his facility in 2017 made the news because three men died, and many others were injured. Tensions ran high for several weeks and the guards were quick to fire birdshot at any group of men inside who became rowdy, even if no one intended violence.

Inmates standing nearby also got peppered by pellets even though they were doing nothing wrong.

"Since I've been here, I've been Tased, pepper-sprayed, and hit with rubber bullets and bird shot," says Keith.

He said some guards are good and treat inmates like they are human beings; others abuse their power. Either way, you learn early on that no corrections official is your friend.

As an old head, he is much more tolerant than he once was of perceived disrespect, but he still has a personal code to live by: "If you say something to me, okay, well, you've got that. But if you touch me, now I've got that."

Untitled by Allen Howard

# Stinkin' Thinkin' Led To Crime

*My name is John A. Harris Jr., and I am fifty-one years old. I'm in prison (Nevada) for assault and battery. I've been locked up at Warm Springs Correctional Center for five years and they gave me ten years.*

*It was a combination of me being a drug dealer/addict/gangbanger that led so many people to hold me in contempt for this time I'm serving.*

*And I almost forgot to tell you that I was born and raised in Denver, Colorado. On the east side by the Five Points. Thinking back on my younger days, if I had died, my tombstone might have read "Good Riddance to Bad Rubbish."*

*My mother was stabbed (but not killed) right in front of me by my stepsister, whom I used to look up to since I didn't have an older brother. She was the one who got me hooked on weed at age nine.*

*But back to what happened after she stabbed my mother...*

*I had this chip on my shoulder that felt justified and I felt lost in dark waters, like I was one of those old sunken pirate ships lost in the deep. Because of what happened to me so young, I had this gigantic hole where my heart was supposed to be.*

*I was blinded by a sense of entitlement and I didn't realize that this hole was larger than anything that this world could even hope to fill.*

*So sin made me a true slave to my appetites, which left me pining for more sex, money, drugs, gangbanging, and control. As a result, I have been in and out of prisons and hospitals my entire life.*

*Then came a breaking point when I listened to one of Satan's deadly lies and took 250 pills from my parents' medications.*

*I was twenty-two years old at the time, and I felt I couldn't be killed by gangbanging or selling drugs, so why not take the pills? On top of that, I drank a half gallon of some white rum.*

*I remember making a phone call to my cousin's friend to ask that she tell my mom and dad that I loved them and not to feel sad that I was gone—and not to cry. She sensed that something was really wrong and told me to hold on and not to hang up the phone.*

*Then she got hold of my mother, who came home and brought the medical people with her. They called the ambulance to take me to the hospital, and I died on the way there. I was what they call DOA (dead on arrival).*

*They put me in the morgue, and I woke up with my black pants and white T-shirt covered with all kinds of black stuff. It was so, so cold in there, and I could see a black janitor sweeping the floor through a window.*

*I was in a room with no phone and I wanted to know how much my bond was because my stinkin' thinkin' was so off. I didn't even realize that I had died and came back to life.*

*The janitor ran and got two more big black guys in all-white suits, and they walked me to some white lady sitting at a desk with a folder that had my picture on it with some red letters that said DOA. I didn't know what that meant at the time, but by the look on the lady's face, it wasn't good.*

*She told me that I better call home at once. My mother answered and hung up after telling me to quit playing sick jokes on her because her son, Jonny Jr., had died.*

*I had the lady at the morgue call my mama to tell her that I wasn't dead. I was really mad, scared, and confused because I didn't understand what had happened to me.*

*I ended up walking down the street with no shoes on, and I felt so lost.*

*After that, I didn't stop gangbanging and selling drugs and using them.*

*One day I was hangin' around da hood and these dudes came around one corner. While I was looking at them, five more dudes wearing red and brown with 49ers baseball hats started to spray my way with a bunch of bullets. All I heard was a lot of women screaming at the top of their lungs. I didn't know why, because I was fine—at least that's what I thought.*

However, they weren't looking in my direction, and when I saw what they were looking at, I couldn't believe what I was seeing. My li'l brotha from a different motha was lying on the ground in a puddle of blood.

I got up to go to his side and fell face-first because I was also bleeding very badly. I passed out, and when I came to, my mom and dad were next to my bed in the hospital. I asked them where my li'l bro, known as Domino, was. At first, they didn't want to tell me that he had died. But finally they did, and I screamed hella loud with tears coming out of my eyes like there was no tomorrow.

I promised that I'd get the person who pulled that trigger and took the life of my bro—and I meant every word that I said. My mom and dad pleaded with me not to be like that, said that they didn't raise me to be no gangbanger and that God had spared my life, so I should be grateful.

But at that time, their words just went in one ear and out the other because I was full of hate and revenge, and the theme song going through my mind was "play at your own risk."

As soon as I could, me and some homies dressed in all black and loaded up all of our straps and got in the whips to start rolling down the streets. We went to the little park in the back of the rec center where the gang that shot my brother hangs out.

But as soon as we got there, the gang unit rolled in with red and blue lights flashing. They were everywhere with their straps out, yelling at us to come out of the car with our hands in the air.

Lo and behold, there was a cop that was an OG (original gangsta) on that task force named Doken. He was cool if you were cool and gave him his respect. But man, if you didn't and tried to play him like a mark or a buster, you had another thang coming.

Well, rollin' right along… As I came out of the whip, Doken met me. He and I have a lot of history, and he asked me what in the hell I was doing over on this side of town. He started to pat me down and that's when he found my Nina and two clips fully loaded and a .38 special snub-nose with hollow points.

He told me that he knew I would be out for some get back because I had lost Domino and that's why the gang unit was out so thick.

*Doken said he was very sorry for my loss, but there was no need for both of us to be gone. Because I had the guns and some crack sacked up in rocks to sell, he said that he would book me in the Denver City Jail for possession of a controlled substance.*

*I went to the holding tank where all the Crips were put together. But we didn't all get along, like Rollin' 30s and the CCR (Compton Crip Ridarz). There happened to be two of them in the tank and three of us.*

*I was the ringleader, so I kicked it off by socking one in his nose and breaking it. Blood flew everywhere and then my homies got the other one and broke his arm.*

*By that time, the deputy saw what was happening and ordered us to lay on our stomachs with our hands behind our backs and our feet crossed. They handcuffed us and took us to the hole, where they put us in single man cells to keep us from hurting anyone else.*

*After interrogating us, they took me back to the unit where everyone was a gangbanger. I told my homies that when I found out who killed Domino, I was gonna lay him down.*

*Lo and behold, about a week later, I was shackled and on the way to my arraignment. I was facing sixteen years in prison because I was in a gang, and I was hella mad at the world.*

*I blamed the white man for me doing a black-on-black crime. Wow! Huh? I know.*

*On the ride back, I was letting everyone on the bus know that I was gonna smash the mark that killed my brotha. RIP.*

*As soon as we got back to the jail, the dude that sat next to me coming and going from court took off real fast to the door of the holding tank. One of my homies said he was with the gang that killed Domino.*

*I looked toward the tank door and met the guy's eyes. I let him know that I knew who he was; I found out later he was known as "Handy."*

*I learned that he only got five years because they said we started the fight when the system failed me and Domino.*

*They gave him self-defense even though they came to our neighborhood—so he must have had a good lawyer and the judge wasn't fair.*

*I took a deal because sixteen years was too much for me, and I was hoping that I landed in the same penitentiary as Handy so that I could take real good care of him since the court system hadn't served up justice.*

*A week after I was sentenced, I was sent to Cannon City where you are given your prison number. After I got out of the testing unit, they send me to Ordway in Crowley County, which is a medium-security prison.*

*When I hit the yard holding my bedroll and was walking toward my unit, a little short black dude approached me and asked where I was from. I told him I was an Eastside Rollin 30's and then I asked him where he was from. He was a Palmer Blocc Crip out of Compton, California, who was called Shorty.*

*He took me to the unit, and I saw more than a few of my homies there. After we chopped it up, we were hanging out in the yard and then we walked by the barbershop, and I saw Handy, who was with his homies.*

*I opened the door, and everyone was laughing and just having a good ole time. But when Handy locked his eyes with my eyes, he knew in his heart that it wasn't any laughing matter. He could see all the hurt and pain there. I told him that I needed him outside "Now!" and his homies got mad.*

*They followed him, and now it was five on five. I told them that it was just between me and Handy, but I could see in their eyes that they were not gonna let one of their homies get smashed.*

*I threw a fast right cross to Handy's jaw, and then all hell broke loose in the yard. It was 8:30 p.m. on July 18, 1995. Woody got stabbed. Miami got cut with a razor, Bear got pushed through the barbershop window, Tybud got knocked out, and Ken-Dogg got shot by the CO from the gun tower, while the rest of us got pepper-sprayed.*

*I got booked for another assault because I broke Handy's jaw in three places. They kept me in the hole for a year, and toward the end, I was acting crazy, so they took my sheets, blankets, towels, and mattress away. Then they brought in a fire hose and sprayed me with ice-cold water. For the rest of the night, I was shivering but I wasn't kicking on the door calling them a bunch of bitches.*

*It was damn strange that I started to feel so warm with my T-shirt and boxers dripping wet while I was sitting in a corner of the cell. Then I heard a voice telling me it was gonna be all right.*

*The next day, the CO brought me a brand-new mattress with new sheets, blankets, towel, and even a pillow. I was scared because I thought* it was a trick, but then they told me to get dressed because I was going back to GP (general population). I asked why, and they said they didn't know why.

When they took me to my new cell in another unit, I saw all the spiritual stuff, and I told the CO I wasn't going in there. He said, "Oh yes, you are," and I said, "No, I can't, this guy is a Christian and I'm not."

The CO told me that he would block any move that I might try to make to another cell. I went out to the yard with the homies, but things were different after what I had done, so I went back to the cell.

My cellie was there and introduced himself as Clarence. I told him who my gang was and then I lit up a cig and started to smoke. He just sat there smiling, but he asked me to please not smoke in the cell while he was in it.

Usually, I would have flashed on him and kept on smokin', but I didn't; I just went to the bathroom down the tier to smoke.

He was so humble, and I didn't understand it, but God used this man to help me realize I needed a relationship with our Heavenly Father.

My cellie called me Knucklehead because I would turn around and do the opposite of what he had just told me not to do, like smokin' weed or drinking pruno or gaming or set trippin'. He kept on being the true big brother that I needed and helped get me paroled in May 1996.

That's when I came out to Las Vegas and met my wife, Rosemary, and she took me to church.

I finally let go and let God into my heart.

But the struggle is real.

III

# Never Give Up, Not Even For One Minute

Nothing can take away the pain of having a child in prison; there is not a day when worries about his safety and well-being do not pervade your thoughts and dampen your spirits.

And yet life has to go on—there are hundreds of daily tasks to take care of, other family members that need your time and attention. So you find a way to compartmentalize the heartache, the worry, and the fear because it is the only way you can carry on.

And no matter what you are going through, you must absolutely keep hope alive for your child because that is his lifeline in a dangerous world. He needs to remember at his darkest moments that one day he will be free to laugh again, to find his purpose, and to start his own family.

Those thoughts were recently expressed by Dr. Barry Bacon and his wife, Shelley, of Colville, Washington, about having a son incarcerated for more than a decade in federal prison.

Faced with one of the worst nightmares a parent can envision, they have learned to draw upon their strong Christian faith for strength, especially when feelings of helplessness swamp them.

"The system doesn't care about Patrick, and there is nothing you can do when things go wrong in there," says Shelley.

When things go bad in prison, they really go bad. Patrick's struggles to stay clear of gang politics have caused him injury and forced him to inflict bodily harm on others.

"He has continually tried to protect us. He doesn't whine and he doesn't complain," says Shelley.

Barry says having a loved one in prison presents an opportunity to learn what unconditional love really looks like.

"I keep telling my son 'I'll never go away' and 'I'm here, I'll always be here.'"

Barry says Shelley's passion to take care of Patrick and their other three children has been unwavering no matter what the last years have thrown their way, but there is a fragility to her now that wasn't there before tragedy struck.

Shelley says sharing the emotional burden of having a child in harm's way with Barry has made tough times bearable. "I'm really thankful to have someone to walk this road with me."

Their education about the failure of America's criminal justice system began when Patrick robbed two banks at the age of nineteen, she remembers.

"He had hitchhiked to Montana to visit a friend. He has this crazy idea he was going to get money and fly to Hawaii to see a girl he was interested in."

On December 15, 2003, Patrick hot-wired a van in Billings, Montana, and then rammed it into a pawnshop, where he stole a couple of guns and some ammunition. Somewhere along the way, he also stole a bicycle.

He then went to a bank in town and passed the teller a note demanding money. She became so upset that Patrick panicked and left without the cash.

Shelley says Patrick used the stolen bicycle as the getaway vehicle because he had heard that would make it much easier for him to evade police. That did not turn out to be the case as he was found hiding behind a dumpster near the scene of a second robbery.

"It was right before Christmas, and I get this late evening phone call from a detective asking if I had a son named Patrick," says Shelley. "We were just in shock after being told that he was in jail."

The Bacons were not a family that had problems with the law, so Barry and Shelley weren't sure what to do next. They knew Patrick needed a lawyer, but they didn't fully understand the gravity of the charges against him.

While he had not been seen with a weapon, the tellers reported that Patrick had alluded to having one. No guns were found in his possession at the time of the arrest.

"Our son had not been a delinquent, so we just didn't expect this," says Shelley. "The only problems we had with him were just stupid teenage stuff."

Like the time Patrick wanted to be a model at age fourteen and ran away after his parents told him that he had to stay in school and couldn't seek his fortune in Seattle, a big city more than three hundred miles away.

Barry remembers Patrick using his car without permission one time, but those were the biggest problems with their teenage son. And those acts of defiance were more than balanced out by Patrick's willingness to help others, such as accompanying his father on a mission to Guatemala and going on another one to Africa with his parents and older sister. In all these trips, the Bacons worked to alleviate the suffering of the homeless and poverty-stricken families.

"Patrick is very caring. He is real and genuine and looks out for the underdog. He refuses to let them be bullied," says Barry.

The Bacons believe a deeply embedded sense of social justice is behind Patrick's problems with gangs in prison.

Patrick had been going to college and was close to getting his associate degree prior to the ill-fated trip to Montana, recalls Barry.

However, Patrick had been struggling internally with depression and his thoughts had begun unraveling to the point that he felt a fresh start was needed.

When Shelley got the call from a detective about the robberies, her first instinct was to say, "I'm glad you caught him, he shouldn't be out there doing things like this."

Their oldest daughter, Allison, had just been accepted to medical school, but there was no celebration in the Bacon household as Barry and Shelley struggled to deal with Patrick's situation.

"I would be in the grocery store and people would come up to talk, and I would be trying to carry on a conversation, but I was just barely holding it together," Shelley recounts.

She and Barry were filled with shame tied to a guilty feeling that somehow they were to blame. They would have preferred no one know about Patrick's arrest, but they were aware that, with Barry being a prominent physician in a small town, it would be impossible to keep it quiet.

"I grew up in Minnesota, where we stuffed things in," says Barry. "After we decided that we should tell the congregation at our church, I asked Shelley, 'Can we pretend everything's normal for just one more week?'"

Shelley told her husband that was not a good plan. She felt it was important for their church family to hear the news as soon as possible and to hear it from them before it became public.

So the Bacons wrote up a statement about their situation and read it to their fellow parishioners.

"Everyone was just so supportive," says Shelley. "There was such disbelief. Patrick had had every advantage, he was loved, he was gifted. He'd never even been sworn at, never heard any swearing in our house—ever. No one smoked, drank, or did drugs. He had the American dream."

She and Barry naively thought everything would be sorted out fairly in the criminal justice system, so they answered every question posed by police. Shelley even volunteered stories about Patrick's childhood exploits, never dreaming they would later be used by a prosecutor and judge to paint him as a delinquent.

Due to their family's good reputation and standing in the community, Patrick was released in April 2004 to return home after he pleaded guilty to two counts of bank robbery.

The ten-year concurrent sentences were suspended if he obtained mental health treatment, got a job to pay restitution, and stayed out of trouble.

A counselor working with Patrick concluded after a few visits that he was at high risk to commit another robbery, which made him a threat to others. For that reason, he was involuntarily committed to a psychiatric hospital and spent his twentieth birthday there.

When he was released several days later, he was angry with his parents for allowing the commitment.

Understanding what is going on with their son's mental state has been difficult, says Shelley. His psychological evaluations have been "all over the map," and he has been diagnosed with everything from schizophrenia and bipolar disorder to personality disorders.

The Bacons dispute these diagnoses but do agree with experts that Patrick suffers from ongoing depression, which they believe has contributed to his erratic behavior.

There was a bright spot during that year of turmoil that still draws a big smile from Barry. Their daughter Allison married in June 2004 in a beautiful outdoor ceremony on their scenic property, and the entire family was together for a few joyous hours.

"It was one of the most glorious days of our lives," he remembers.

The following month, he and Shelley went on a cruise for their twenty-fifth anniversary. They had misgivings about leaving Patrick at home, but he promised to stay out of trouble and to take care of the place.

"We came back to chaos," says Barry.

Not only was the house a mess and the animals uncared for, but Patrick was gone.

Shelley tracked him down in Spokane, about seventy miles south of Colville, but could not get him to return home with her.

"One of the hardest things I've had to do was to leave him there," she remembers.

In September, she got a call from Patrick, but her joy quickly turned to dread. He was in jail after being arrested for robbing a bank in Spokane, which he denied. He asked Shelley to pick up his backpack from an abandoned building where he had been staying.

She and Barry retrieved the backpack and looked through it. Inside, they found latex gloves, which the bank robber had been described as using.

"Why do you think these are here if our son is innocent?" Barry asked Shelley.

The Bacons debated about what to do with the potential evidence. In the end, to spare the family greater humiliation, they called the FBI to report what they had found.

"It's not easy calling in the authorities on your own son," says Barry. "However, we realized that Patrick was in no condition to be out in society. He would harm himself or others."

They were told by authorities that a search warrant would have been executed if they had not cooperated because there was already substantial evidence against their son.

"I made sure the younger two kids were somewhere else when they came in and took the backpack," says Shelley.

In January 2005, Patrick pleaded guilty to the third robbery, and the information Shelley had provided about his childhood misdeeds was used to make him appear a public menace who qualified for the maximum allowable sentence.

"The judge picked up on what I had said and told Patrick, 'You've been a bad kid for years,'" says Shelley. "You know he's wrong, but what are you going to do? I've learned not to give the system more than you need to."

Patrick was sentenced to four years in a federal prison and sent to Louisiana, where he ended up assaulting another prisoner, who was tied to a gang. Six more years were added to his sentence and Patrick was transferred to a super-max prison in Colorado where Somali pirates and other hardcore criminals were housed.

For seven years, Patrick was in isolation and it was five years before the Bacons were allowed a "no contact" visit, which meant they were separated by a glass partition from their son.

"You don't realize how much emotion you are holding back just to keep walking, talking, and doing your job," Shelley says of those years.

Patrick assured his parents that isolation was the best place he could be because he didn't have to deal with prison politics.

"On more than one occasion, we've been told by guards that we've got a really nice son, that he's very respectful," says Shelley. "He's a citizen in his head. He's made a conscious decision to be that, even in there."

In June 2015, Patrick was released to a residential reentry center in Spokane, although he disagreed with the need for a step-down program instead of being allowed to go home.

About two months into his stay, Patrick got into an altercation with another resident and was sent to jail for a few days. He then ended up behind bars again for a short stint after being thirty minutes late for curfew.

However, it was his wish to come home for Thanksgiving that landed him in big trouble, remembers Shelley.

Patrick had requested a pass from his caseworker to go home for the holiday. After years of looking at the photos Shelley sent him behind bars of the family gathered around the table, Patrick had a deep longing to share that moment with them.

"He was asking, asking for a pass, but his caseworker didn't get around to it," says Shelley.

Patrick thought he might have to spend a few days in jail if he went home, but he felt it would be worth the cost. So he made the trip without permission.

"At that point, we were saying, 'We don't blame you, this is ridiculous,'" remembers Shelley.

Patrick then decided that he would do everything he could to rebuild his life without going back to the reentry center. He decided to live in the fixer-upper house his parents had purchased for him in Spokane and went to work every day. However, on December 15, four US marshals showed up at the residence to arrest him, four days before he would have been done with the reentry program and his prison sentence.

In early 2016, Patrick was sentenced to another year in prison for going home for Thanksgiving and shipped off to a federal prison near Victorville, California.

During his incarceration, Patrick was involved in an altercation with a fellow inmate—a friend—and inflicted superficial injuries to the man's head and chest. He would later tell his parents that he had been threatened by other inmates with serious harm if he did not take that action.

Patrick was supplied with the shank and instructed to use it for the attack.

He was disciplined by prison officials for the incident but was not charged, and he completed his sentence in May 2017.

For seventy days, Patrick was a free man. He worked two jobs and reintegrated back into society without incident. His parents were helping with renovations, and Shelley said her son seemed relaxed and happy.

Patrick came to Colville the first weekend in August 2017 to celebrate his parents' anniversary. A few days later, he was to join the other three siblings at the Doctors' Concert that Barry and Shelley organize every year to raise money for their nonprofit to help the homeless.

Two days before the concert, Patrick was arrested by US marshals when he went to a regularly scheduled meeting with his parole officer. He was charged with assault for the incident in 2016.

His case went to trial, but the judge did not allow the defense to mention anything about his mental health history or the threats he had received that caused him to feel he had no choice but to carry out the attack against his friend.

He was found guilty by a jury trial.

In a recorded statement made for the sentencing, the victim told the judge that Patrick was likely pressured into the act by gang members, whom he mentioned by name, and that he bore him no "ill will." He appealed to the court not to give Patrick any more time behind bars.

Nevertheless, Patrick was sentenced in April 2018 to ten more years in prison.

He was sent to a federal facility in Kentucky but then moved to Florida after he was jumped by three inmates on one occasion and stabbed in another.

The Bacons are appealing the latest sentence on the grounds of viable duress, that Patrick could not reveal what had really happened because one of the gang members, a codefendant, was present in the courtroom and had been placed in the same cell during the trial. Implicating that man would have put her son's life at risk, says Shelley.

If the appeal fails and Patrick serves out his entire sentence, his release date will be April 2026.

"Patrick is not a throwaway person," insists Shelley. "And that's how society sees him."

The years of solitary confinement in Colorado took a toll on Patrick's mental health, says Shelley, and he tried to commit suicide by cutting an artery in his arm in 2012. His wound was bandaged, and he was left in his cell with dangerously low blood pressure by apathetic guards, who didn't even make water readily available to help his body cope with severe trauma.

Instead, Patrick, who had been vomiting and defecating from shock, had to belly crawl to the door in his weakened state to get the guard's attention so that he could get a cup of water. He was so dehydrated that he couldn't speak.

"When we visited shortly after that, he looked really pasty but said he was fine—he didn't tell us until later," says Barry.

As a doctor, he is appalled about how the situation was handled and how close his son came to death.

"These people are incompetent, they don't have any idea what they are doing, and worse, they don't care," he says.

Shelley now feels heartbroken not only about the victims of a crime but the families of defendants. She is skeptical about news reports that paint a suspect as a villain because she knows from personal experience that there is another side to the story.

"I have so much empathy for the families of prisoners," she says. "They say having a supportive family is the best chance an inmate has of rehabilitation, but then they make it so hard for us to visit and stay in contact."

The Bacons fly to Florida twice a year to see Patrick and try to stay in touch by phone, although he is limited to three hundred minutes a month. The costs to communicate are high enough, says Shelley, that poorer families would be unable to stay connected.

"This was never really part of our plan for our family. But going through all this has given me a little peek into God's heart and the incredible pain we cause him. I put myself in God's mind now and I feel his pain."

*On Dec. 19, 2020, Patrick Bacon was found dead in his cell at United States Penitentiary Thomson in Illinois, where he had been moved a couple of months earlier. At the age of 36, Patrick lost his battle to keep hope alive in a system that turned his mistakes into tragedy.*

||||||||||||||||||||||||||||||||||||||||||||||||||||||||||||||||||||

# Part II
# Trevor: Guess Who's Coming To Dinner?

*I completely understand if there are hesitancies and concerns about who I am. I value being an example to be pointed to that suggests we are not our worst decision in life; people can grow and change.*
—Trevor Walraven

Try bringing your boyfriend home to meet your parents when he is a convicted murderer who may or may not stay out of prison, and see what reaction you get, says Loraine McLeod, who did just that.

"Dad was not fun to deal with—he was a little worked up," she says. "Mom was good about it comparatively, although she had told me that I 'better not marry a lifer,' and the first thing that went through my head was that I was so proud of her terminology."

Loraine, who was then twenty-three, knew that once her family got to know Trevor Walraven, they would see him as the intelligent and insightful man she had gotten to know through letters and visits to prison.

Five years later, she has been proven right.

"Now they both love him. My dad texts Trevor more than he texts me. It took some time for him to get there, but they like him now because they see that I'm doing well," she says.

When her father heard Trevor speak, it clinched the deal because the ex-con took responsibility for the killing of an innocent man during a carjacking in 1998. He spoke of the need to live with purpose to make up for the harm he had caused.

"There is a humility that comes with the recognition of the harm I've done. I see my freedom as a privilege," says Trevor.

There was a fleeting moment, admits Loraine, when Trevor was released from prison after serving more than seventeen years that she worried about what he would be like on the outside. Never once did she fear he would harm her; instead, she wondered if he would be as attentive and responsive to her needs as he had been while incarcerated.

However, Trevor's calm way of dealing with challenges, something she learned to rely on during the early days of their courtship, helped soothe her worries.

Prison gave Trevor plenty of time to reflect on who he wanted to be, in or out, and what he wanted to accomplish—so he hit the ground running as soon as he was free to make choices.

"I live now as I lived inside," he says. "I was always businesslike, very professional. I didn't bullshit, I didn't mess around—I wasn't a tough guy, but people knew that I was going to be taken seriously."

When his conviction was vacated on technical grounds last year, Trevor joined Loraine in the free world before the state rearrested him, and he was back in custody for nearly four months before his attorneys got him released.

"Having him ripped away is probably one of the hardest things I've gone through," she says. "I was bawling my face off, and it took a toll on my mental health—I did not feel complete."

The legal battle for Trevor's freedom is still going on, and Loraine admits the uncertainty is difficult to live with.

"I have anxiety about it," she says. "But I'm surrounded by people who understand what is happening, and they provide support. We don't dwell on it very much. We just take one day at a time."

She plans to stand by Trevor no matter what the future holds, even if that means he serves life behind bars.

They are engaged and excited about making wedding plans amid her schooling and his advocacy for prison reform.

It has become a regular part of their weekly routine to have Trevor speaking to a college class or a group interested in changing the penal system.

As a shy personality, Loraine said it is amazing to see how comfortable Trevor is at the podium.

"I think he's great—nothing he says is scripted, and I love that he brings out different things every time. He shows remorse and he is articulate."

When she watches Trevor educating people about America's national shame, particularly when it comes to the treatment of youth, she is amazed at the direction her life took after she mailed a letter to him.

At that time, five years ago, Loraine planned to pursue a degree in psychology due to a long-time fascination with mental health issues that led children to commit violent acts.

After reading about Trevor's case, she decided to add him to her list of prison pen pals across the United States.

"I just try to keep my mind open," she says. "I write to inmates to learn who they are today. I don't ask about their crime and if they want to talk about it, we talk about it. I am writing them as a person, not because of what they did."

When Trevor got her letter, he was suspicious. He assumed Loraine was a college student who had heard him speak as part of the Inside-Out program. He was not allowed to engage with participants, so he wanted her to respect that boundary.

"It was the first time I'd ever had anyone write me who I didn't know—I had never put my name out there on one of the pen pal sites," he says.

Trevor's return letter was brief and demanded to know how Loraine had gotten his contact information.

"I was like, 'What have I gotten myself into?'" she remembers. "That first letter was pretty guarded. It was very like, 'Give me an answer,' and then asked how I felt about restorative justice."

She decided to reach out a second time to provide Trevor with some background information about herself and an assurance that she had never been among his audience.

"We just started corresponding," she says. "I had no intention of meeting him face-to-face. I just wanted to know about him as a whole."

Trevor made it plain that, due to his circumstances, he was not interested in anything beyond a friendship. Loraine readily agreed to that stipulation since she had no intention of getting romantically involved with someone in prison.

For the next year, they wrote regularly, and then Loraine had a near-death experience that she declined to talk about during this interview.

She said that incident made her realize that meeting Trevor was one line she wanted to cross off her bucket list.

It was only a one-hour trip from Eugene, where Loraine lived, to the penitentiary, so she asked Trevor to put her on his approved visitor list.

"In my mind, it was like, 'Why not? We've been writing for a year,'" she says.

Trevor agreed to the visit with some hesitation. He had been dating someone at the time of his arrest, and she had faded out of his life as time went on. He was not interested in the possibility of another painful separation if he came to care about Loraine more than he already did.

"I had a very healthy respect for the stress prison puts on a relationship," says Trevor. "I didn't want to connect in a way that couldn't be broken off."

The divorce rate for people locked up for more than one year is 80 percent. Trevor had seen the trauma that inmates endured when a relationship ended, especially if the ex was his only link to the free world.

"I wanted to be friends with Loraine. I enjoyed our conversations and the opportunity to get to know her. I was just not willing to go farther," he says.

Picking something to wear that would pass muster with prison authorities, but still be attractive, was a real challenge, said Loraine.

The DOC website advised that clothes be conservative and she not show even a hint of cleavage. She couldn't wear sweatshirts or T-shirts with messages emblazoned on them and her skirts could not be too long or too short. Denim and anything blue were prohibited because that was the color residents wear.

She would pass through a metal detector, so an underwire bra was out, and she needed to select jewelry that would not set off the alarm bell. There were a lot of other rules, and as she came to learn later, guards sometimes came up with new ones that were not posted.

"It's not an easy thing to go through," she says of the visiting process.

Loraine and Trevor had a great face-to-face chat and quickly fell into the routine of regular visits. Later, other prisoners would tell Trevor that they could tell he was hooked long before he admitted it by the way he interacted with Loraine.

"Everyone was convinced we were together long before we were," he says.

Loraine came to love his calm assurances and the way he looked at a problem she was having with logic and reasoned out a solution.

"I feel like he balances me out," she says.

Trevor said an incarcerated man feels very powerless and frustrated when something goes wrong in the lives of the people he cares about on the outside.

"Maintaining calm and balance was something that I could do for Loraine," he says.

What she brought him was acceptance of who he had been, as well as who he was.

"I was always very open, honest, and transparent with her, and I really appreciated that kind of engagement," says Trevor.

Little by little, their relationship moved from friendship to romantic, although they both tried hard not to acknowledge it.

Looking back, Loraine said the advantage of being with someone in prison is that the situation necessitates good communication, so you can quickly get to know that person at a deeper level.

Then Trevor did the unexpected. He asked her to be his date at a banquet put on by one of the eleven prison clubs and open to guests on the approved list.

The photographer at the event captured their first kiss.

"After that, I was down. I was 'Oh yeah, you hooked me,'" says Loraine.

When they first connected, Trevor didn't know that he could be a candidate for Second Look, a program available to juveniles convicted as adults that provides the possibility of release after half of their sentence has been served.

When Trevor learned he was a candidate for Second Look, a future with Loraine suddenly had all kinds of wonderful possibilities.

"He seemed pretty well adapted, all things considered," says Loraine of the day that Trevor came home to her (they lived with his mother for a time).

In one area they aren't as compatible. He doesn't share Loraine's interest in prison films and documentaries, but then he's looking at them from the inside out.

"It's something I've lived, so I don't get the shock and awe that other people do," he says.

He has found that having one-on-one time with her family and others helps break down barriers about how they view someone who has killed or served time.

"I hope for an opportunity to engage with people, so they can make an educated decision about who I am before judgment is passed," he says.

Loraine said the cost of maintaining a prison relationship is a hardship for loved ones and family members. An email through the company that provides communication services for OSP, is 25 cents and a video visit is $7.50. A phone call runs $4.80.

Although Trevor had a job to help defray expenses, she says there is not enough work for everyone inside and some paychecks are so small there isn't extra money for communication. That means lower-income families might not be able to connect regularly, which makes it more difficult for the inmate to succeed.

The Prison Policy Initiative, a Massachusetts think tank, estimates that mass incarceration is a thriving business in America. It is a $181-billion-per-year industry when all costs from the time of arrests are added in plus the cost paid by families to maintain connections.

Loraine says getting involved with someone in prison is not for the faint of heart when it comes to dealing with people in the free world.

"It's tough to navigate through the prejudice and stress of having an inside relationship—I've lost friendships because of it—but it's worth it if you really love someone."

"Finding the Word" by Jorge Cabrera

||||||||||||||||||||||||||||||||||||||||||||||||||||||||||||||||||||||||

# GAME Etiquette 101

*Game: Any form of play, any specific amusement or sport involving competition under rules, with penalties; a business, a job, etc...*

*Ghetto definition: The life, the streets, criminal activities, a sideline, a hustle, slanging, the paper game, pimping, macking, hoing, boosting, running drag or pop 'n' con, etc...*

*Etiquette: The form, manners, respect; the conventionally acceptable or required in society, a profession, etc...*

*Ghetto definition: Keeping it 100, being a man of your word, honor, loyalty, and respect, NO SNITCHING AND NO BITCHING! If you're infected with the snitch or bitch gene, you can't hang with us, slang with us, bang with us, DO A DAMN THANG WITH US! REAL NIGGAS DON'T SMOKE WITH SNITCH NIGGAS OR BITCH NIGGAS!*

*(I'm not a gangbanger. I'm a game banger, GAME.)*

The first rule is what's been lacking in the game and that's REACH ONE, TEACH ONE—without this it's havoc! Us OG niggas need to pass it down. My first choice is for you to stay in school and go to college.

The second rule is that everything has consequences. Don't do the crime if you can't do the time. If you ain't built for this shit, stay your ass in school, get a job, and live your life! If you're not prepared to lose your friends and families (because it really is "out of sight, out of mind").

I didn't put you there—you made the stupid choice, not your friends or your family. They are out there, living their lives, and no matter how much it hurts, part of being a man is accepting responsibility for your actions!

The third rule is SHUT THE FUCK UP! You have the right to remain silent; anything you say can and will be used against you or someone else. Ask for an attorney, then SHUT THE FUCK UP! If you're scared, go to church!

*The fourth rule is* KILL ALL THE DUMBSHIT, BUMSHIT, AND BULLSHIT! *This shit is not a game—them streets is playing for keeps. Them courts is playing for keeps! I'm doing life-without, twenty-five to life and forty-eight more years in this hellhole! I* HAVE LOST EVERYTHING! *I didn't see three members of my family before they died, and what hurts most of all is the fact that I won't see my own mother before she passes away. In thirteen years, I've only seen two of my sisters, just two of my family members! None of my friends; my wife is my ex-wife, and my ex is just that, my ex! Black people have the lowest attendance in the visiting room that I have seen. I'm from northern California, and Mexicans from southern California outnumber us in the visiting room five to one easily! You do the math!*

*Look for part two of GAME Etiquette in the near future. Meanwhile and in between time, stay safe out there, and remember, you can learn a lot from a dummy. Buckle up!*

Travell "Paycheck" Holmes
A man in a cage

III

# "Get Even" Mindset
# Fails On All Fronts

Americans can incarcerate more people than anywhere else in the world because it is an affluent nation, surmises Jack Morris, who has spent thirty-two years as a criminal defense attorney.

"It's really, really easy for politicians in this country to be tough on crime. They can throw out their chest and talk a good talk on criminal justice issues. All they have to say is 'Lock 'em up' and people applaud."

Reforming the system is tough, says Morris, because millions of people profit from jobs in prison, or provision of services, so they aren't supportive of change.

That is a big obstacle to overcome but not the biggest as he sees it.

There needs to be a huge cultural shift from "getting even" when someone commits a crime toward treating prisoners like people who are still worthy of mercy and compassion.

"Decisions made with a revenge mindset are counterproductive," says Morris.

He is the lead defense contractor for Hood River and Wasco Counties in Oregon and has witnessed how stripping judges of discretion in sentencing has led to offenders being treated as a collective instead of as individuals.

"Prisoners are a diverse group like any other human beings. Some are pretty decent people, and some you wouldn't want to turn your back on—but you can say that about any group of people."

Even prisoners deemed "monsters" by society should be treated like human beings when they are put behind bars, says Morris. To do otherwise is to fail as a culture on moral and ethical grounds.

"When you talk about taking care of them, I don't think it makes a damn bit of difference what kind of person they are. You've just got to take care of them."

Early in his career, Morris spent six years in Portland, Oregon, as a public defender. He also served as counsel for the Senate Judiciary Committee in the Oregon Legislature for two years.

Those experiences allowed him to observe the callous mindset of elected and appointed leaders when it came to dispensing justice.

"I'm at a loss to understand the things that go on today," he admits. "Right now, I'm having a hard time having any optimism about change."

He said most Americans, unless and until they end up with someone behind bars, are unaware of the high level of brutality that occurs in prisons.

An average of about a dozen inmates die each day in prisons across the US, according to the Justice Department. The leading cause of death is suicide, accounting for about one-third of deaths, followed by cancer and heart disease, conditions that are often untreated. There is a high degree of violence in prisons, although Morris suspects that most incidents go unreported.

To make matters worse, more than half of all prisoners, especially those serving long sentences, have no outside support. There's little chance of finding support in prison, where inmates must be concerned with gaining respect and avoiding fights in the hope of finding safety.

With all of those factors in play, prisons are psychologically damaging and full of despair. It is a place of trauma that actively teaches racism, hate, and a disregard for life.

The longer a person stays under the influence of this broken system, the greater the odds he or she emerges with the calloused and angry philosophy of his peers, says Morris.

People can make positive changes in prison, he says, but that becomes more difficult if they are on their own.

"We treat animals better in this country than we do prisoners. Warehousing people is a complete waste of time and money, and yet we continue to do it."

Having a justice system stacked against defendants produces truly heartbreaking results, says Morris, especially when people who are innocent end up pleading guilty to something they didn't do out of fear of the consequences.

"That's what keeps you up at night," he acknowledges.

An example of the heavy-handed tactics used by prosecutors was a case where one of his clients, a woman in her late teens, was charged with first-degree assault, a felony, for giving another kid, this one underage, a homemade tattoo upon his request.

"That's disgusting, but is it really criminal?" asks Morris.

He said the legal definition of first-degree assault is "intentionally causes serious physical injury to others by means of a deadly or dangerous weapon."

The state said the woman had done that by "disfiguring" the victim.

"That's not what the law was intended to cover," says Morris. "At the end of the day, my client was not convicted, but she should never had been charged like that in the first place."

His representation of Kathleen Blankenship, who was convicted of murder in 2003, also taught Morris about how justice could be skewed by a system that collectively works against a defendant.

Her conversation with detectives was not recorded, and both men presented different views of what had been said.

"Their stories were completely different, and that could have been taken care of if they had a recorder on," he said.

Once Blankenship admitted that she had killed Walter Blankenship, her husband, Morris said investigators appeared to have no interest in finding out what her motivation was.

"They had their suspect and that was enough," he said. "No one was listening to Kat, no one believed her."

Morris said defense teams have a major responsibility to clients and Blankenship's case shows the injustice that can happen when that job isn't done well.

In recent years, he has done a lot of research while traveling to learn how other nations run prisons.

"I think we could learn a lot from other countries, but people have to have the interest to find out," he says.

The European models have provided Morris with examples of more humane treatment of incarcerated people. He contends that it would behoove Americans to follow some of these practices because they produce better results.

Even in South American prisons, which can have harsh living conditions, Morris says conjugal visits are allowed out of recognition that marriages and relationships are already under tremendous stress and those bonds need to be kept strong.

Ironically, says Morris, the Department of Corrections in every state will claim to work toward strengthening family connections because that is key to success when prisoners emerge. And then they will make it impossible to maintain any sort of intimacy because deprivation is another way to inflict suffering.

Another hypocrisy to the state's claim is that no effort is made to locate prisoners near their support system, says Morris.

Prisoners are lodged where there is an opening and moved only for behavioral or security concerns.

"In Oregon, they didn't even consider the well-being of inmates when they built prisons," he argues. "If maintaining family relationships had been a priority, they would have built most of our prisons in the Willamette Valley, where most offenders come from, instead of in outlying communities that accepted them because they would profit from jobs and the money spent by families coming for visits."

Knowing how badly the system works and seeing decades go by with little change can wear you down emotionally, says Morris. "You just do the best you can; you try to do a good job."

Some of his clients stay in touch after they are incarcerated and even after they are released. From them he has learned of the atrocities that go on behind bars and is deeply saddened by that knowledge.

"I don't know if the public is ever going to be sympathetic to prisoners, but that's what it's going to take to truly change things," he says.

||||||||||||||||||||||||||||||||||||||||||||||||||||||||||||||||||||

# Part II
# Kevin: Coming To
# Terms With Life

*It is easy to become institutionalized; if one stops liv-*
*ing, fighting for freedom, or striving for better, then*
*they will succumb to their surroundings. To me, this*
*place will never be home—I reside here, it is a place*
*I lay my head down at night, but my mind is free. I*
*live wherever it takes me.*

—Kevin Young

There are many ways to cope with being in prison, says Kevin Young,
fifty-six, serving life without the possibility of parole at Oregon State
Penitentiary, but it is easy to get lost in the dark places of your mind

and overwhelmed by a sense of hopelessness if you don't rein in your thoughts and emotions.

"Being sentenced to a slow death is hard on a weak mind. Me, I know there is more to life than simply waking up with a phony smile on your face. There is more to life than just shucking and jiving. I am not satisfied with being here. However, I am adapting and making the best life I can while fighting for my freedom."

He and other lifers have meticulously developed routines based upon careful choices that allow them to preserve balance in their days behind bars. They strive to avoid trouble and keep emotions level, full of neither expectations nor disappointments.

Unlike inmates serving a finite sentence, lifers have come to terms with the many deprivations of prison because it is where they will spend the rest of their days unless the political will of the country changes. And that adjustment, says Kevin, is an arduous process that scours the soul.

"When the gavel went down, and I was sentenced to life-without, my trust in God, family, lovers, the system, and the ability of others to understand the truth was gone.

"I did not want to hear anything from anyone. I started taking everything with a grain of salt. A person can't come to me now with a sad sob story and have me automatically feel compassion anymore. I never had trust issues before, but now I don't have many people to place my trust in. My fight, my struggle, my determination, and my dedication are to, yes, gain my freedom but, most importantly, to maintain and preserve my sanity."

The first years in prison were full of mental and emotional turmoil, says Kevin, as he grappled with being separated from his two infant sons and widowed mother.

"How was my family going to survive? Would my children even know I existed? My mother's health, how was my incarceration going to affect her?" were some of the questions that ran in an endless loop through his mind.

In 1992, when he first entered prison at the age of twenty-seven, Kevin said technology had not yet advanced, so email communication was not available, and the price of a phone call was double what it is now, and it is still expensive.

Gradually, over time, unable to do anything about what was happening with his family in the free world, Kevin learned a tough lesson: he had to release the anxiety about what others were doing to avoid being swamped with negative emotions.

"I don't fight, I don't struggle," he says. "I accept life as it comes and deal with stressful situations as they arise. I don't sit around pondering the what-ifs. I express myself, letting it all out in a positive manner. Sure, I get mad at times and in need of an outlet, but over the years, I have learned to cope, release, and move on.

"I never allow things to fester, to spread poison in me. Music and my case are my safety nets. By focusing on those, I know nothing else is going to hold me back. It's me against me and Kevin Duane Young is going to win."

He is thankful to have learned those harsh lessons because there is now a harmony to his days.

"Serving a life sentence will make or break you. A prisoner must prioritize or get swept away in the tide of another's misfortunes," he said. "I'm not trying to be callous, but I cannot afford to care about things I have no control over."

After entering prison, Kevin had to fight to earn the respect that would allow him to move around with some semblance of security. A big man (although he is the smallest of his four brothers) at six feet, four inches tall and about 275 pounds, he had inmates challenge him to show they were fearless.

"When I first fell, a few old heads took me under their wings. My street reputation preceded me. Guys were lined up to fight, get revenge, or make a name for themselves. So I fought. Being scared had nothing to do with it. I had to prove my worthiness.

"Afterwards, the old heads sat me down and we talked. I hung with them because they are respected and accepted me as a man," he says.

Kevin says nowadays, there is heightened gang activity in prisons and more inmates coming in with mental health issues that lead to behavioral problems.

"Things have gotten worse. With mandatory minimums, kids are coming into the system with twenty-five to thirty years and no good time, and they simply don't care who they harass, betray, steal from, or attack."

He says the continual drama wears on the spirits of lifers who seek peace and solitude.

Studies have shown there are fewer disciplinary issues among this population group in prisons because they tend to develop mature coping skills.

However, there is not as much cohesion among lifers as there was a couple of decades ago, says Kevin.

"Now, I am the old head. However, things have changed. There are too many followers, not enough leaders. Life is not that simple anymore. Now, I don't hang with anyone. On a needed basis, I will have a conversation or answer a question. Other than that, I keep it moving. I don't have time to get caught up in another man's drama."

Keeping in touch with those on the outside remains important to him, so he spends time every day writing letters, emailing, calling, or scheduling video visits with family and friends.

In a world that can become dangerous in a heartbeat, Kevin doesn't ever let down his guard.

"I don't dare," he says. "I am kind and willing to help others but am never vulnerable. People prey on the weak. I am no dummy, and my kindness should never be confused with weakness. I help because it is in my nature to do so, not because I must. Many will take advantage of another, then walk around like he has done something really slick until that brick meets his skull."

He said it is essential for all inmates to stay on point.

"One never knows when someone will snap. In here, you have no clue who is on what or who they have pissed off or disrespected. Just being around the wrong guy can get your ticket punched."

Although reserved and watchful, Kevin claims "no filter" on his emotions.

"I wear them on my sleeve, they are my badge of honor," he said. "To be honest with others, they must be able to see and feel my sincerity. I don't leave any doubts. That goes for those I trust and like as well as those who are full of crap. Regardless, they get the message."

There is danger in prison, but there are also regular acts of compassion, says Kevin, who performs five random acts of kindness each week, mostly cleaning the cells of older prisoners.

"Some will take time out each day to make sure an elderly person gets to the yard or showers. Some will sit and read a book, play checkers or cards, or simply have a conversation."

His appeal of a sentence without end was denied, but Kevin is still working on a couple of other legal challenges that could one day bring the freedom he craves. That hope is vital on dark days when all else seems to fail.

To keep his spirits strong for the fight, Kevin has internalized four valuable lessons:

- You must free your mind to free your body. Reading, music, and fantasizing allow him to travel beyond the walls.
- Never follow a fool or chase someone who doesn't want to be caught. He listens to his intuition about others now and usually follows its prompting.
- Hold yourself accountable. Coming to terms with the good, bad, and ugly in yourself is important.
- Believe in the unknown. Miracles happen every day, so keeping hope alive is important.

Although he knows that society and its laws have judged him as unredeemable, Kevin doesn't accept that verdict.

"I pay society no mind," he said. "I don't care what another person thinks of me. No one other than me is doing this time. I and I alone must deal with the banging of steel, being told what to do, hearing the ringing of bells day and night. It is my ass they want to look at while being strip-searched. So when society wants to step up and endure all that I do, I will start caring.

"Society is just a bunch of people who claim to care or want change, yet they are willing to sit back and assume the worst about a lifer. But what happens when that wonderful person in society has a family member who catches a case and must serve time—do their opinions change then?

"Regardless of my situation, I am still human, a man. My mind is free, my life is not over. I have love in my heart, and I possess the ability to care. I still have a choice—I refuse to be played with or talked down to. I have a future. Change is coming and I'm going to be ready."

Untitled by Jorge Cabrera

||||||||||||||||||||||||||||||||||||||||||||||||||||||||||||||||||||||||||

# The Grass Isn't Always Greener

*My name is Robert Maher, and I'm thirty-nine years old and a California resident convicted for marijuana sales in Nevada. I was sentenced two to five years and I've served two as of now.*

*A brief history leading to my incarceration…*

*I own and operate a licensed medical marijuana dispensary in California. The name of the business is ACME Weed Inc. We're on Facebook under that name. We opened in 2011 and have several thousand followers and more than fifty positive online reviews from multiple states.*

*Nevada legalized marijuana for medical use several years ago, but storefront dispensaries didn't get state licenses to open until January 1, 2016.*

*For many years prior to 2016, it was legal, but nobody had a source. I took advantage of a huge market with no supply.*

*I was successful for several years, selling only to people with valid, verifiable prescriptions for marijuana. I love to help people; our products have improved the quality of life for many people of all ages.*

*The permits for Las Vegas got sold for $300K each, and the way to guarantee one was a donation to city hall and the police department. I didn't get one.*

*To sum up my case, I sold to an undercover police "patient" three times, each transaction $100 cash over a two-month period.*

*I got followed home without my knowledge, and soon a SWAT team arrived. The experience of a SWAT team raiding my house has left me with PTSD. I am currently on medication for it.*

*In the raid, I lost $250K of inventory and a $250K home—and my freedom. Three months later, marijuana was legalized for recreational* use and my offense, unlicensed sales, became a fine and not a felony with a prison sentence. No retroactive consideration either.

Nevada wants tax money from the sales, hence the fine for unlicensed sales, but it's costing the state $75K per year to keep me in prison. To me, that's counterproductive. It's why voters made marijuana legal.

That was injustice on the street. The real injustice started when I was in jail with a private lawyer retained to fight for me.

Nevada law allows medical marijuana patients to share and exchange their product with each other. Technically, I'm a patient helping another patient. But in the police report, the undercover officers clearly wrote that they provided me with "fraudulent documents."

My lawyer was all over this! The law breaking the law! My goal in a court trial with a jury was to show the officer had obtained a valid prescription under false pretenses. I then sold to another patient. No jury would send me to prison.

When the district attorney was notified we were going to put the officer on the stand, she had a fit! And she pulled a card from her sleeve, saying there were over forty-five cases with the narc officers using this shady tactic, and if I exposed it, I'd ruin all the other cases.

So to prevent this, the DA told my lawyer that if we put the officer on the stand, she'd have my case turned over to the feds. She has lunch with a federal prosecutor weekly, and she said he'd file charges in federal court because marijuana is illegal federally, period. I'd be looking at fifteen to twenty years in a federal prison if I wanted to go to trial with the state.

The DA had a bargain; I keep quiet about the officer, and she'd keep quiet to the feds and drop eleven to twelve felonies. I would have to agree to serve two to five years in state prison.

Where do I sign?

Fast-forward two years.

I'm sitting in a Nevada prison and I come up for my first parole hearing. I'm excited, ready to go home to my wife and kids in Stockton, California, and to my dog. I have a German shepherd service dog that helps me walk and do other tasks.

In 2004, I went to prison in California for nine months for printing and cashing fake checks. Seems like long ago and forgotten…

*Well, I get my parole hearing decision papers back: "Denied parole." The specific reason: "Prior prison term did not deter future criminal acts." Wow! Haven't I already served my time? I feel punished all over again for something that happened years ago. Also, it's a totally different type of offense.*

*I feel helpless and trapped in this (in)justice system. Six more months and I'm eligible to see the parole board again. Isn't marijuana legal? Wish me luck.*

*My worst experience in prison has been getting into a fight with two other guys in my six-foot-by-nine-foot cell; it was unexpected and was over using the phone.*

*After the fight, I packed up my belonging and told the guards I wanted to move buildings. First was a trip to the infirmary for ice packs and pain pills. Next step,* the hole. *My whole world turned upside down.*

*The next morning, I went to a meeting with the prison administration. I requested a transfer to another prison, which was approved. I was told it'd be a few weeks. Hurry up and wait in the hole. The story of my life.*

*The few weeks turned into a five-month wait. There are many psychological changes from being in a box 24/7, except for a ten-minute shower every third day. Your senses become heightened; your mind learns each sound and what it is. I learned to tell time by the sounds—when guards counted, when they changed shifts, when meals were coming, and who was having a nervous breakdown.*

*Some guys broke down sooner than others. A mental health counselor would come by and do a survey each month we were in the hole, asking us if we felt like hurting ourselves or were hearing voices. A lot of guys started hearing voices and a few attempted suicides.*

*Me, I had a cockroach come in my cell. Ever since, I have a phobia of roaches. I started to think there were bugs on the walls or I'd wake up thinking my bed was full of bugs.*

*The building had serious pest problems. Most bugs would come through the water drains in the showers. I came to realize that my fear was multiplied due to too much time to dwell on it. I kept talking myself out of mentioning my hallucinations to the psychiatrist.*

*I think I remained sane because I love to read, and my family always sends books from Amazon to me. I literally read for ten hours a day in the hole and tried to sleep for twelve. I wrote letters daily.*

*I was limited to a fifteen-minute phone call once a week. Many guys have nobody on the outside to call, which is really sad, but after finding out they've victimized their family and friends continuously for years, it's no wonder they are cut off.*

*I knew my time in the hole wasn't forever, though the weeks turned to months. I knew I was getting closer to my release date and I was physically safe—and learning to be my own best friend! A lot of self-examination time.*

*So my day to transfer comes and I'm excited but anxious because I'm going to a new prison, sort of like a kid going to a new school but with ten times more anxiety.*

*I go from the Las Vegas area eight hours north to the Reno area. The bus ride sucks; your arms are chained to your waist, and your ankles are shackled. A hard-plastic seat and no windows. Armed guards in front and back. I survived.*

*Each facility has different schedules. Going from 24/7 cell time to this new facility was night and day. Now my door automatically opens at 6:00 a.m. and closes at 10:30 p.m. There are different activities to get involved in.*

*A lot of guys go to adult high school or have prison jobs. Myself, I'm a high school graduate, so I'm only able to attend college classes at night. A local community college offers classes at this facility. We pay tuition ourselves or get a scholarship. They award thirty to forty-five per semester to the prison. I was lucky enough to get one.*

*I have filed many formal complaints against the system; my latest endeavor is a federal lawsuit for Americans with Disabilities Act violations. I have a physical disability that prevents me from holding a prison job and those who work get time off their sentence. This is a form of discrimination. A lot of prisoners are affected the same way I am but don't fight it.*

*Sadly, I'll be released before anything comes of the complaint. But I hope it will help change the broken system and benefit disabled guys still stuck here.*

*Overall, in this Nevada system, there are minimal programs and training to help us succeed upon release. This facility I'm currently in has six hundred guys, with about five hundred participating in programs and training. That's a high percentage. The prisons by Las Vegas have about seven thousand inmates and programs available for only one thousand. And the worst part is that if you don't participate in something, the prison adds ten days to your sentence each month you are idle.*

*Everyone is willing to participate, but good luck getting a spot in a class with only room for 10 percent of the prison population. So 90 percent don't get the tools they need to make it. They go right back to what they know; they have no other choices available. Then reoffend, and the cycle starts again.*

*When I was in the 90 percent idle, I filed a formal complaint about never being able to get a seat in a class. The response was that my reoffense risk score was too low to be enrolled. High-risk offenders had priority.*

*I'm not "criminal enough," but I'm a convicted felon. Nobody ever asks, "What do you need help with to be successful?"*

*Low-level offenders don't need to be in prison. In California, it's impossible to go to prison for drugs. Any drugs (except marijuana), an ounce or less is a ticket, resulting in a fine and classes. The same ounce of meth in Nevada carries a ten-year to life sentence in prison.*

*I'm less than one hundred miles from the California border and that one hundred miles means a ticket versus a ten-year prison sentence. There needs to be a universal law. There needs to be change. Nevada needs to learn from other states.*

*Problems were solved in California ten years ago. Can't someone see that? Get with the program. Look next door. The grass is definitely greener—in several ways!*

*As for inmates who have no support from the outside, they have only limited options for luxury of amenities in prison—no commissary, no Nike shoes or Levi's pants, no ice cream or soda. No TV, no radio, no mail or phone calls. There's a lot of guys who literally beg, borrow, or steal; some will borrow too much and can't pay. They then tell the guards they are in "fear for their safety" and get transferred.*

*Some guys are artistic or crafty and draw or make things out of discarded items and barter for items they want. Some guys get paid $20–*

$50 per month from a prison job. It's not much, but it's a lot when you have nothing or nobody.

Prison movies (from Hollywood) always show a lot of violence and sexual abuse, Yes, it does happen but not like the movies portray. I've witnessed stabbings and slicing with razors. The majority of it is because of gangs, not one versus the other but internal issues where one gang member has failed to live according to the code of conduct.

The sexual abuse that happens isn't aggressive gang rape. Yes, there are sexual predators, but what I've witnessed is a lot of mutual homosexuality. One guy might be an older homosexual who seeks out younger guys who have homosexual tendencies. That person is slowly taken advantage of, usually starting with illegal drug use, creating a "bond" or "trust" with the other guy, as well as lowering his inhibitions and creating a sense of obligation to do something to repay the person who supplied the drugs.

Everything is mutual until the relationship goes sour, then sexual harassment or abuse might be reported, and the guys get moved to other prisons. Drugs have a major contributing factor to sexual abuse in prison.

I am a member of a local and national organization that fights to change the system. The websites are Nevadacure.org and curenational. org. Please look them up. We need support and help!

# Love Doesn't End At Gates

When the man you love goes to prison, you don't back away, because that's when he needs you the most, says Jana, who has been with her inmate for thirteen years and engaged for three.

"When Ron first went in, I had a friend come live with me because I couldn't be alone—I needed a distraction to help me cope with depression and anxiety," she says. "I was so heartbroken that I could hardly get off the couch."

The years have been tough, both emotionally and financially, says Jana, but there have also been many valuable learning lessons that have made her a better person.

"I grew up in a conservative family and was married to a dairy farmer for twenty-five years, so there have been times when I can't believe I'm doing this," she says. "But I'm the only friend who's stood by Ron, and I look at how he believes in God, how he understands the need to forgive the people who falsely accused him—he's a good man and I am crazy about him."

Jana requested that only Ron's first name be used for this book due to the nature of his conviction, which makes a prison stay more difficult, and her firm belief in his innocence. The author chose to also protect her privacy.

She and Ron met in the spring of 2003 when she was managing an ice cream store for a nonprofit organization in Oregon that serves developmentally disabled adults.

Ron worked part-time for the janitorial crew that maintained the facility. He was also a part-time salesperson for the industrial supply company that provided cleaning products.

"He would stop in to see what I needed," remembers Jana.

They were attracted to each other right away, but when she found out that Ron had recently separated from his wife and a nasty custody dispute was brewing over their two small children, she drew a boundary.

"I was divorced and had a hard-and-fast rule: do not get mixed up with married men," says Jana.

More than a year later, as the legal wrangling for Ron's divorce continued, Jana decided to make an exception to her rule. The way she saw it, Ron would have been single if his ex didn't keep throwing up roadblocks.

"I just felt an electric pull toward him," she says.

Ron and Jana started dating in 2004 and went on a three-week vacation together. She was ecstatic about finding a man who seemed like the perfect fit.

Jana was unaware of the nightmare unfolding in Ron's life. Later, he would tell her that he was afraid to share the truth because it might mean losing her.

Jana did notice that Ron had lost weight and seemed more stressed, which she attributed to the ugliness of his divorce negotiations.

"One day Ron called and said he was at the courthouse. He said, 'You may not see me for a while because if things don't go well today, I may have to go to prison for a few years,'" Jana recalls. "I said, '*What!*' And he finally told me what was going on."

Jana learned that Ron's estranged wife, who was seventeen years younger, had accused him of molesting her daughter from a previous marriage.

"They hatched a plan to have him put in prison so she could get all their assets," says Jana.

Because the ex had been abused when she was younger, Jana said the story told by her daughter was convincing and made Ron look like a "monster."

"The mother knew exactly what to say because it was what she had lived through," says Jana.

Throughout the shocking phone call when Ron revealed what was happening, he kept telling Jana not to worry because the truth would win the day. He said friends and family were praying for him and he remained optimistic about the future.

He implored her not to walk away.

Jana was home that afternoon preparing for a later dinner and couldn't absorb what she was hearing.

"It was just like my life had stopped," she remembers. "He had no idea how crazy I was about him."

Ron ended his last conversation in the free world by telling Jana that he was headed into court for an uncertain outcome.

"He said, 'If you don't hear from me before 4:00 p.m., things went wrong,'" Jana recounts.

She waited for several hours after that deadline and then reached out to Ron's supervisor at work, who told her that he had been sentenced to fourteen years in prison.

Jana later learned that Ron's attorney had advised him to plead no contest to two counts of sodomy, a lesser sentence, because the chances of prevailing before a jury in an emotionally charged case were "slim to none."

In a no-contest plea, the defendant does not dispute the charge, but neither does he admit guilt. This plea allows a defendant insistent upon his innocence to settle a case outside of a trial if he determines the risk of a longer sentence is too great.

"I was just grief-stricken. It was like someone hit me upside the head with a two-by-four," says Jana. "I liked him and he liked me. We hadn't even said 'I love you' yet."

It would be five months before Jana saw Ron again at an Oregon prison about four hours from her home.

When he had completed the intake process and gotten settled into his "home" prison, Ron called to schedule a visit. Jana says he was still in a state of denial about his situation, insisting that the truth would be revealed.

"As soon as he went to prison, the divorce went through and she cleaned him out," says Jana.

She learned a harsh lesson about standing by your man after people in her life found out she had chosen to continue her relationship with Ron.

"I had a long-time friend who had been sexually abused and she would not accept it," Jana says.

She was ostracized by family members who didn't believe Ron could be innocent if he had been convicted.

His ex-wife left nasty letters at her home.

"There were a lot of losses and a lot of problems, but I loved him, and walking away just wasn't something I could do," says Jana.

She set up a schedule to see Ron once or twice a month and learned how to navigate the intimidating visitation system.

When he was transferred to another facility closer to her home, Jana began visiting once a week and has faithfully continued to do so.

Ron works inside for $3 a day, so Jana puts $150–$200 on his books each month to ensure he has the things he needs and some of the commissary foods that can bring a little joy into a bleak existence.

When his father died in 2018, she paid hundreds of dollars for him to be escorted to the hospital to say goodbye.

"I had gone to see his dad, who was eighty-nine, and he was doing so poorly that I thought Ron needed to get there soon," she remembers. "His father died twenty-eight hours after their visit—he made it just in time."

Men convicted of sex offenses don't normally fare well in prison, says Jana, but Ron has managed to hold his own.

"He's not inhibited. He has street smarts. He has been told to pay money or get shanked, and he tells them, 'Do what you have to do.' They want easy pickings, so they leave him alone."

Despite the obstacles they have faced over the years, and being physically separated by formidable barriers, Jana says their love has grown.

"Sex for us is when I take my shoe off in the visiting room and run my foot up his pant leg," she says, laughing.

That behavior is a violation of visiting rules but one that Jana is willing to risk now and then.

"It's been difficult to see women you know move on in their lives and you are waiting, always waiting," she says.

Along the way, Jana has met other wives and girlfriends who, like her, remain faithful to their men. Although society labels these women as "desperate" or somehow "damaged," Jana argues that people don't get it.

"Until you have someone you love inside, you really can't know how you will act or what you will do," she says. "Just because someone goes to prison does not mean that they don't deserve love. Just because you love someone in prison doesn't mean something is wrong with you. In fact, you have more of an opportunity to learn the meaning of unconditional love."

Jana says it has been a long and hard road for Ron to forgive his ex and her daughter, but he is getting there.

What makes forgiveness difficult isn't just all the years behind bars but what comes next. Ron will have to register for life as a sex offender after he is released in a few months. With that stigma, he will have trouble finding a job, which will be a requirement of parole.

Ron will also be subjected to a lie detector test at the whim of his parole officer to ensure he is not becoming predatory, and he will have to pay for being monitored.

He will have to remain in Marion County for six months because the law requires that felons return to the location where the crime was committed. Jana owns a home in another area of the state.

She is unsure what retirement for Ron will look if he is unable to collect social security.

"I have always believed him," Jana says. "He credits God with getting him through this, keeping him sane. We know that God will get us through what comes next, too."

Having Ron work for slave wages on custom-made furniture that the state profits from is only one of the inequities they have encountered in the prison system, says Jana.

To add insult to injury, she said the cost of purchases in prison far exceeds what the items could be bought for on the outside because the state runs the commissary.

"An eight-ounce bag of coffee is almost $11," says Jana. "A box of graham crackers is $5. There's a whole quiet economy built around prisons and it is a monopoly—who else are you going to be able to buy from?"

From the start of his case, Jana says Ron was judged guilty by the media and general public before the facts were even known.

She said apathetic defense attorneys failed to fully inform him of all options, so he missed opportunities in the appeals process.

"Something is very wrong when a false accusation can ruin someone's life for the rest of their life. This system is all so out of control, I don't really even know how you would start to change it."

III

# Part II
# The Row: High Cost Of Death

Good and bad lawyers decide who lives and dies in the US, so it should come as no surprise that most of the inmates on death row are from poorer families who cannot afford exorbitant legal bills, and a disproportionate number are minorities.

A study done by Columbia University found that 68 percent of all death penalty cases were reversed on appeal, with inadequate defense as one of the main reasons for reversal.

The Death Penalty Information Center, a nonprofit that disseminates studies and reports to the media and public, backs up the poverty background of many condemned prisoners with these figures: Slightly more than 12 percent of adults in the US have not completed high school or earned a GED, yet the rate on death row is 69.75 percent, indicating difficulties in life.

"If we replaced the death penalty with life in prison without possibility of parole, we could save millions to invest in support of the families of murder victims, education, substance abuse treatment, mental health, and public safety," says Ron Steiner, a board member of Oregonians for Alternatives to the Death Penalty. "We need more teachers in the classroom, not more lawyers in the courtroom."

**Racial Inequities**

Whether a defendant receives a death sentence depends on the color of his or her skin and the ethnicity of the victim.

The Pew Research Center, a fact tank in Washington, DC, lists sixty people on federal death row and more than three thousand awaiting execution in state prisons across the country.

DPIC reports that 56 percent of death row inmates are black or Hispanic. However, although racial minorities comprise half of all murder victims nationwide, 77 percent of the victims in capital convictions were white.

For a four-year period in America's history, from 1972 to 1976, the US Supreme Court suspended executions due to the fact the death penalty was applied with unconstitutional racial bias. Capital punishment resumed after the high court deemed that several new laws restored equality.

DPIC contends that racial inequities have never been corrected. For example, in Kentucky, one thousand African Americans have been murdered since the reinstitution of the death penalty. However, by the spring of 1999, all death row inmates in that state were sentenced for murdering white victims, none for homicides with a black victim.

DPIC sees the continuing racial disparity as a clear violation of civil rights guaranteed by the Sixth and Fourteenth Amendments.

Since the death penalty was reinstated by the high court, there have been 1,512 executions in the US. The highest yearly number was 98 in 1999.

Texas holds the top spot in executions, with 563 since 1976, more than the next six states combined.

Since 1973, 166 condemned prisoners have been exonerated because of evidence proving their innocence, according to the DPIC, which is based in Washington, DC.

Given the overrepresentation of black and Hispanic prisoners on death row, Steiner contends that it is hardly surprising that a large majority of those found innocent have been of color. The ratio of exonerations stands roughly at one for every nine executions.

"Think about how many of those executed could have been innocent," says Steiner.

**Unsustainable System**

In addition to the troubling social justice aspect of executions, Steiner says more and more states are acknowledging that they simply can't afford to keep channeling money into death penalty cases, a tiny percentage of criminal justice matters.

He said only 2 percent of people convicted of aggravated murder get the death penalty. However, America ranks among the top ten nations in the world for executions, and the price tag for state-sanctioned killings is exorbitant.

These cases cost at least 50 percent more to adjudicate and may be up to five times as much as imposing a life without parole sentence.

Not only do states spend huge sums to win death penalty verdicts but there is the expense of a costly second trial to determine sentencing, which involves new witnesses and long jury selections. Plus keeping condemned prisoners on death row requires extra security and maintenance expenditures.

There is also a fifteen- to twenty-year appeals process, which is vitally important because society must do everything possible to avoid killing someone who has been wrongfully accused, says Steiner.

The ACLU of Northern California reports that simply housing prisoners on death row costs taxpayers in that state an additional $90,000 per prisoner each year above what it would cost to house them with the general prison population.

According to DPIC, keeping inmates on death row in Florida costs taxpayers $51 million a year more than holding them for life without parole.

Steiner says Oregon spends $29 million each year to prosecute and defend capital crime defendants. And that doesn't include costs for local police, county jails, state police, and incarceration.

There are currently thirty-four condemned prisoners on death row in Oregon, thirty-three men and one woman.

Lewis & Clark Law School and Seattle University recently teamed up for a study of 374 aggravated murder cases between 1984 and 2013. They found after analyzing data that 61 death sentence cases in Oregon cost taxpayers an average of $2.3 million compared with $1.4 million from the 313 cases that resulted in lesser punishments.

Excluding state prison costs, the difference was even more glaring: $1.1 million for death sentence cases and $315,159 for non-death aggravated murder cases.

## Executions Don't Work

If the economic toll of supporting the death penalty doesn't cause public support to wane, Steiner said the fact that executions do not improve public safety should give them pause.

The National Research Council reviewed more than three decades of research and found no credible evidence that the death penalty deters crime. In fact, a survey conducted by the *New York Times* found that states without the death penalty have lower homicide rates than states with capital punishment.

"Most crimes are crimes of passion that are done in situations involving intense excitement or concern," said Dr. Jonathan Groner, who researched the deterrent effect of capital punishment for Ohio State University College of Medicine and Public Health.

"People who commit these crimes are not in a normal state of mind—they do not consider the consequences in a logical way."

These facts, and many more, are presented regularly by Steiner and other abolitionists intent on educating the public and legislators about the need for change.

In Oregon, as in Colorado and Pennsylvania, there is a moratorium on executions, and Steiner wants to see full repeal happen.

He was part of a successful movement that got the death penalty abolished in New Mexico in 2009. There are now nineteen states and the District of Columbia that have wiped capital punishment laws off the books.

Steiner points out that more than half of Oregon's thirty-six counties have never filed a capital case and 70 percent are tried in the five most populated counties.

Three counties—Marion, Multnomah, and Lane—prosecute 74 percent of all death row inmates' cases.

"Taxpayers statewide are helping to pay for these counties more aggressive pursuit of the top punishment available," says Steiner.

DPIC maintains that the disparity of resources across the nation means that the likelihood of a death sentence for identical crimes in different states and even in different counties within states fluctuates greatly, often for no other reason than the attitudes of the local prosecutors.

There is a basic unfairness in being sentenced to the death penalty because you live in the "wrong" location, says Steiner.

## Moral Dilemma

He sees it as hopeful that more and more Americans are pondering the societal question: "Do we have the right to kill?"

That question is made more important by a report from Mental Health America, a leading group in support and advocacy, that 5 to 10 percent of death row inmates have been diagnosed with severe mental illness. Experts argue that some of these inmates did not fully understand the consequences of their actions at the time of the crime, or they did not know exactly what was going to happen to them after a conviction, or they signed a false confession.

Some were forcibly medicated to make them competent enough to be executed. Amnesty International and the National Association on Mental Illness argue that one out of every ten condemned prisoners executed in the US since 1977 has been mentally ill.

While the Supreme Court has decreed that people with "mental retardation" may not be put to death, Oregon and other states have not passed laws banning the execution of the mentally ill.

## Raising Awareness

It is not about trying to help people avoid accountability for the harm they do, says Steiner. Abolishing the death penalty is about the moral fabric of society and the values it stands for.

He said the current situation does not help families of murder victims overcome severe trauma and loss that no one should minimize. The extended process prolongs the agony of these families and executions do not help them heal.

"Families of murder victims would benefit more if funds used to support the death penalty were diverted to counseling and other assistance," said Steiner.

Today, 117 countries—most nations—have turned their backs on the death penalty in law or in practice because their people have decided it is inhumane.

The US is one of the tiny minority of nations to continue with executions.

"We are keeping company with Iraq, Iran, and China, notorious human rights abusers," says Steiner. "There are so many reasons that we should abolish the death penalty that is it time for a serious look at why Oregon and other states still allow it.

"I think if more people were really aware of all these issues, they would not support what we are doing in this country, so it becomes a matter of education."

"Always With Me" by Toshio Takanobu

||||||||||||||||||||||||||||||||||||||||||||||||||||||||||||||||||||||||||||

# Prison Is The Same As
# Life On The Streets

*My life since I was young has been chaotic. I was born and raised in the
Bay Area of California. My father was a pimp and my mother a ho.
Even though it was a highly dysfunctional situation, it seemed glamorous
growing up in that lifestyle. It was everyday life to me despite the police
who took my mom and dad to jail.*

*Once I got old enough to start getting the things I wanted for myself,
I felt that I had two choices: continue with the family business or sell
dope. I went with the latter because I had seen a lot of bad things happen
to my mother, and I couldn't see myself putting another person through
what she went through.*

*But selling dope comes with a certain "party" lifestyle, i.e., drink-
ing, money, getting high, numerous women, guns, and so on. And the
more successful you get within that life, the more things intensify. You go
from a local drug dealer to a state-to-state trafficker. Here I am.*

*What scared me about prison was being away from my family. I
wanted to "break the cycle" of a criminal lifestyle. By coming to prison, I
increased the chances of that not happening.*

*What scares me now is getting out, looking for a job or career, not
being able to obtain or sustain one and coming back. I fear the odds.*

*The worst part of this experience is watching my kids grow up
through pictures and losing time that can never be replaced.*

*I believe I won't notice psychological effects of prison until I come
home, because I've adapted to my current thought process, but I'm sure
there is some damage that has been done due to isolation.*

*A typical day is waking up and waiting for my cellie to do his
morning routine (brush teeth, wash face, make bed, and then get dressed*

*for chow). After that, I do the same. I come back from chow, make coffee, do laundry in our sink, clean the cell, read, then lock up for count. After count, I work out on the yard, come back to the unit, and lock up for count, and after count, I go eat chow and come back and try to occupy myself until it's time to lock up for the night. Then repeat. That's if everything runs smooth that day (no fights, stabbing, or nonsense happens).*

*The reason the recidivism rate is so high is because prison isn't a punishment for us; it's a part of the only lifestyle that we know. How are we supposed to change if we don't know anything else? Make us take programs that are truly beneficial for us and don't just sound good on paper.*

*There is a positive side to my incarceration. I call it the filtration process. I was so caught up in the fast life that I was spending all my time and resources with people who really didn't give a damn about me. I was looking at a life sentence and didn't get one letter from my so-called friends.*

*Now, I only have the people in life who really care about me and my well-being.*

*Being locked up hasn't changed me but has helped me grow and prioritize my life.*

*Laws should change to be less harsh for drug crimes. You've got first-time offenders serving life for a handful of drugs; it's excessive, to say the least.*

Skyler Latigue, thirty-three, serving time for drug trafficking, Warm Springs Correctional Center, Nevada.

# Prisoners Are People, Too

Leann Bertsch, director of North Dakota's Department of Corrections and Rehabilitation, is challenging the status quo of US prison systems by using a more humanitarian approach to the treatment of inmates under her watch.

North Dakota's penal system is the first in the country to adopt some of the protocols used in the successful Norway prison model.

First and foremost, all corrections personnel are expected to treat prisoners with courtesy and respect, says Bertsch.

Second, there is more of a focus on teaching inmates to have empathy for others and to help them maintain family relationships crucial to their reintegration success.

"In order to do things differently, you must view things differently," says Bertsch, who went to Norway in 2015 on a field trip sponsored by Prison Law Office, a California-based public-interest law firm.

The group uses the legal fees it wins in lawsuits against prisons to send state corrections chiefs, judges, and legislators on field trips to Norway and Germany.

"I now have the opportunity to see things through a different lens," says Bertsch of that experience. "How did we, as a nation, think it was okay to put human beings in cages?"

Although North Dakota was already making changes to its system, seeing how well things were working in Norway made Bertsch even more determined to do things differently.

It hasn't been easy to restructure an entire program, she contends, because change is hard to accept in an American culture that is very unforgiving of people who commit crimes.

"It can be a heavy lift. Some people think we aren't holding them accountable. But our prisoners are still doing their time—we just think they can do that while being treated as human beings and that they can change as well."

The legislature in North Dakota has approved bills to expand sentence reductions and reduce mandatory minimums, among other changes. Each county has to offer alternatives to physical custody, such as drug and alcohol treatment plans and home detention.

When challenged, Bertsch tells people that 95 percent of inmates will get out of prison one day. "And then I ask, 'How do you want them returning?'"

Instead of always focusing on negative behavior, which is a standard operating procedure in prisons, Bertsch says her corrections officers are also required to acknowledge what inmates are doing right.

Every correctional officer must note positive actions in a daily report, and lately, Bertsch says inmates have begun submitting their own reports on good work done by officers.

"Incarcerated people recognize what we're doing. It's really, really wonderful to see positive behavior being reinforced."

Officers must spend a certain amount of time interacting with those under their watch, especially if the individual is in solitary confinement, which is used only to stop an inmate from endangering others.

"At one time we had one hundred people in the hole, and now it's in the teens," says Bertsch.

The infractions that can land an inmate in what is now called the Behavior Intervention Unit have been restricted to ten of the most serious, such as murder or possession of a weapon. Time in isolation is spent in treatment sessions to change behavior or classes to earn a GED diploma. Each inmate is issued a report card and an improvement plan that includes specific skills they need to gain to return to the general population.

Most are released within the first twenty-four hours, and no one stays in the hole longer than a few months. The recidivism rate hovers at 21 percent.

"When prisoners are in there, officers are expected to have meaningful interactions with them," points out Bertsch. "That's one of the most successful things we've done."

In North Dakota, lifers who will never leave the prison are also given purpose. "Quality of life is a big deal," she says.

The following values have been instituted under her watch to drive operations at four prisons and one juvenile detention facility, all run by the state:

- Respect: Every person has equal value and needs to be treated with value. Everyone, inmates and officers, is expected to follow the golden rule.
- Professionalism: All prison personnel are to place service above self and show compassion and patience. They are to maintain impartiality and objectivity on the job.
- Teamwork: By working together, common goals can be met and excellent service provided.
- Integrity: The highest standards of behavior are to be followed. Personnel are to be firm, fair, and consistent in their interactions with inmates.
- Innovation: Listening and being willing to embrace and capitalize on change allows for integrated knowledge that can lead to systemic improvements.

The goal behind making incarceration more proactive, Bertsch tells officers, is to help inmates develop a sense of purpose that will give their lives greater meaning.

"You get respect with respect," she says. "We want people in prison to have more empathy for others. I tell my officers they have to model those characteristics and they have to be genuine."

The new philosophy of restorative justice in North Dakota is explained during the hiring process, and Bertsch says applicants who seem drawn to the profession because they want to wield power over others are quickly weeded out.

"No one who's changed their behavior has ever said it came about strictly because of a program. It's that connection with another human being," she maintains.

Officers already on staff who approach their duties with a military mindset are expected to make the mental shift to do things differently or they risk losing their job.

"We don't want officers who are resistant to this change. Some go on their own, and some need a push out the door," says Bertsch. "If they have the wrong belief system, you are not going to train that out of them, and they become like a cancer [that infects the system]."

Despite the heightened focus on humanitarianism, Bertsch's top priority remains workplace safety. She also has a tough stance on crime, believing those who harm others need to be held accountable for their actions.

She served twenty-one years in the National Guard (retiring as a major) and spent eight years as a state prosecutor. She holds a juris doctor degree from the University of North Dakota School of Law and a bachelor of science degree from North Dakota State University.

In addition to running prisons, Bertsch serves as president of the Association of State Correctional Administrators.

In December 2016, she was honored by the association with the Tom Clements Innovation Award for "exemplifying the virtues of vision and innovation" in her industry.

"I always say that this kind of work is not for the faint of heart. It's difficult, it's very emotional," Bertsch says.

There are lessons to be learned from prisoners that can be humbling.

"Whenever I visit the women's prison, I am surprised by how upbeat and positive the inmates are despite their circumstances," she says.

North Dakota now allows inmates to pool hygiene products so those who are indigent can get the things they need, and Bertsch says there is a high degree of generosity in that program.

In most prisons across the US, passing items is viewed as "contraband" and inmates caught doing it are subjected to disciplinary action. Although that prohibition was put in place as an efficient way to stop drugs from being smuggled into the system, Bertsch says it prevents inmates from practicing kindness and meeting the needs of people who are going without.

Inmates are also encouraged to undertake fundraisers that support an outside charitable cause.

"I think the direction we're heading is a good way to go," says Bertsch.

To ready about 1,800 male and female inmates for a return to the free world, she wants environments in North Dakota's prisons as "normalized" as possible.

Chores are part of every able-bodied inmate's daily routine and color has been added to walls so that the environment is not the usual "drab and dreary."

Community groups and people living near the prisons are encouraged to volunteer time, hold art shows, bring in choirs and other forms of cultural enrichment, or conduct educational and personal development programs. This involvement boosts the morale of inmates and provides food for thought.

"We want communities to be more exposed to prisoners so they are more accepting when they return to the free world," says Bertsch.

Parents who are behind bars now get family days when the yard is closed off for barbecues, ball games, and other activities. There is the occasional movie night for parents and their children. "We recognize the importance of that family connection."

Bertsch thought the general population might resent losing time outdoors during these events but quickly found that other inmates were supportive of the program.

Prisoners in classes are sometimes taken on field trips, which Bertsch says are greatly enjoyed and a good incentive to perform well.

"Prisons are very, very negative places that damage and they always will be," she claims. "But you can try to make them less harmful by doing some of these things."

In Norway, she says there is one prisoner to a room, which is not possible in the US because of the sheer number of people behind bars.

However, she said North Dakota has sited modular housing units on some prison grounds for 186 minimum-security inmates who are in for lesser crimes or soon to be released. They are allowed work release and then sign a lease and pay rent in exchange for being given a private room. There is a shared kitchen where they can cook, and a bathroom in between two rooms that is shared by another tenant.

"It gives them solitary time to do some self-reflection," says Bertsch of the housing arrangement.

Inmates who have served long sentences and are soon to be set free are escorted into nearby communities and taught how to use an ATM and enjoy lunch in a diner to get a feel of the outside world.

"A lot of times, people in prison forget how to even have a social conversation," says Bertsch.

Sustaining prison reform efforts in North Dakota is reliant upon being able to recruit enough people who see the value of changes and the new programs showing results, she acknowledges.

Since 2018, there has been a 6.5 percent drop in the state's penitentiary population due to reforms in the criminal justice system. Bertsch says the drop in numbers is due to a number of factors, including admissions, releases, and length of sentence.

"I think it is easier to affect change here because we have a small and nimble system. I would say that some systems in other states struggle to even meet their constitutional requirements, so it will be much harder for them."

North Dakota has a population of 762,062, so inmate numbers are much less than in other states, Bertsch says, and there are not a lot of race-based gangs in prison.

Even though the challenges are much greater in higher population areas, she believes similar changes need to be undertaken throughout America.

"I think every system can do this, but for some, it's a bit easier."

Her decision to pursue reforms followed a rise in crime associated with North Dakota's fracking boom, which led legislators to pass several "tough on crime" measures that began to fill the state-run prisons.

Bertsch was set to ship excess prisoners to a private facility in Colorado when she made the trip to Norway. There she learned that the farther a prisoner is removed from his community, the less likely he is to have visitors. And that sets the inmate up for failure because there is no support system to rely upon when he or she goes home.

That's when Bertsch decided to ease the overcrowding situation with the modular housing units.

In her quest to explore new ways of operating prisons or learn what doesn't work, Bertsch is part of a warden exchange program through Prison Fellowship, the world's largest Christian ministry to inmates. The group was founded by former president Richard Nixon's aide, the late Charles Colson, who served time in a federal facility for Watergate crimes.

One of the tours Bertsch participated in took her to Folsom Prison in California, an aging facility once known for its harsh conditions that is now medium security and houses nearly three thousand inmates, about five hundred more than it was built for.

She contrasts that experience with touring Halden, a maximum-security facility in Norway that *Time Magazine* dubbed "the world's most humane prison" because of its peaceful environment.

There is no barbed wire, guard towers, or electric fences at Halden, which is situated in a remote forest and surrounded by a single wall.

Prisoners and guards play games and sports together and even share meals. Violence is rare at Halden, and assaults on guards are extremely rare. Solitary confinement is almost never used.

Bertsch was deeply affected emotionally by that visit and has become even more determined to change the US mindset that finds its treatment of prisons acceptable.

She says the winds of change are sweeping the country, but it could be a long while before true reform breaks through cultural barriers.

The things she has instituted do not cost more, says Bertsch, who has a $120 million annual budget to spread between prisons, parole/probation, and juvenile services.

She holds regular conversations with legislators to update them on how things are working in the state system and what the next area of change will be.

The recidivism rate in North Dakota—about 40 percent—is calculated on the percentage of prisoners who recommit crimes within three years of incarceration. Bertsch expects the rate to fall as the state embraces a more humanitarian approach in its criminal justice system.

"There's this grassroots movement in North Dakota and citizens are coming forward with no involvement in DOC to ask, 'How can I help?'" she says. "I'm very grateful to have been able to see how things are being done differently [in Norway] and to incorporate some of those practices here."

# Part III
# Kat: A Hard-Won
# New Start In Life

*I'm able to hold my boundaries compassionately but firmly. I take my "temperature" every day and make decisions to be present and look for the blessings I'm given.*

—Kathleen Blankenship

Spending ten years in "a gated community" gave Kathleen "Kat" Blankenship plenty of time to figure out why she had made bad relationship choices and to develop a game plan for starting a new life.

"I now have my independent foundation and I don't have the need to be validated by anyone," she says. "I have an awareness of past patterns of behavior, and I have promised myself that I will never ignore my gut instinct again."

When she walked out the doors of Coffee Creek Correctional Facility in January 2011, Kat was forty-eight years old and determined to make up for the childhood years lost with her sons, who were adults.

Her mother had died while Kat was incarcerated, and she still grieved the loss of a woman who had stood strong with her through a nightmare that seemed endless.

In 2003, Kat was convicted of killing Walter Blankenship, her abusive ex-husband, who was a cop, but that case was later tossed by an appeals court because she had not been allowed to plead self-defense. Kat then pleaded guilty to manslaughter instead of going through another trial because she had already served the mandatory sentence for that crime and wanted to return home to her family.

Her ex-husband had raised the boys after the death of her mother, and she was grateful for his support, coming to a place of forgiveness for his abuse during their twelve-year marriage.

"He and I are peaceful. At this point, I would tentatively say we have a friendship," says Kat.

At one point, there had been speculation in the media that she had killed Walter, along with her ex and her father who had died years earlier, to collect benefits from their life insurance policies. She was informed of that rumor by her attorney during a prison visit right after her ex had been there.

"You better run out and tell him he's dead because he thinks he's alive," Kat recalls.

After "crucifixion" by the media, she was unsure what life would look like in the free world.

"There was more to the story, but the media never asked, 'Why would a thirty-eight-year-old mom snap one day and decide to kill her husband?'" says Kat.

She had learned after being the object of public judgment and censor not to get caught up in the bitterness of unforgiveness.

"I choose to be a giver, not a taker," she says. "I want to build people up with encouragement, not tear them down with harsh words, choices or actions.'"

With the "good ole boy" system still strong in Umatilla County, Oregon where the shooting took place, Kat decided to relocate away from officers who had worked with Walter and defended his actions long after the truth about his depravity emerged.

Walter was found to have accessed over five thousand different child porn sites on their home computer during the investigation that followed his death, says Kat. Yet people in the community still insisted he was a model citizen and could not be guilty of molesting her sons.

"I can forgive those who caused us harm, but I will never forget," she says.

Kat has worked hard in the last ten years to establish a new career as a bookkeeper and set up firm boundaries with people.

She is fierce about guarding her privacy, and only those she trusts, and they are few, get anywhere near her family.

Her relationship with her sons is now good, and she cherishes time with her five grandchildren.

"I look for the miracle in life every single day. I have learned that the greatest treasure is within the smallest gift—the freedom to live life, not simply exist in the shadows. I have emerged from this experience a stronger woman," she says.

Above all else, Kat heeds red flags that point to instability in people's mental or emotional health.

In her world, nothing is taken at face value; trust is earned, and it doesn't come easily.

"I have a close circle of friends but I'm very selective," she says. "I am pretty friendly to everyone, but I don't invite them to my home."

Kat is willing to brave the public eye to advocate for women who are incarcerated because of domestic violence situations. "There are a lot of good people in prison who should not be there."

She has taken the podium at Portland State University and spoken at other forums. She champions Louise Bauschard, founder of Voices Set Free, an advocacy group for incarcerated abuse survivors.

"People ask, 'Why didn't you just leave?' but that is simplistic," explains Kat. "Most victims of abuse don't know how to stay out of that type of relationship. It's familiar and they know how to cope."

Emotional brokenness and low-self-esteem lead many women to crave approval enough that they become obsessed about making bad relationships work, says Kat.

"You don't have to go to prison to be imprisoned. There are people in the free world in a worse prison that I was in."

Kat's parents divorced when she was thirteen, and she believes trauma from the shattering of her family played a role in her desperation to find a forever love. She has worked hard to fix the brokenness inside herself.

Letting go of the past, she found, required her to discipline where her mind wandered.

"Stop thinking about it. Quit talking about it. Quit reliving every negative experience," she advises. "There is a proper time to grieve the loss of dreams, but at some point, you need to pick yourself up, dust yourself off, and put on a fresh attitude. You can't change what has been; you must let go of the old."

What message would Kat give other women who are victims of abuse?

"That's a tough question to answer," she says. "I want them to know they don't have to get lost in the abuse cycle but getting them to realize there are other choices is the tough part. Sometimes they aren't strong enough, or they're not ready."

People are born as social creatures, to have a mate and to be a family, said Kat, and that drive compels many women to stay in relationships even when they are in pain.

"We tell ourselves 'I must have earned it' when we are abused or 'If I love him enough, I can fix him.'"

Only you can't, says Kat. And in the process, you will lose yourself.

"I want a woman to have hope, to use her inner strength to change. You have to choose to live, I can't do that for you."

It is no small feat to leave an unstable person and the fear of retaliation is what often keeps women in violent relationships.

"Leaving a volatile man is not like other breakups," says Kat. "You must plan and extract yourself carefully, gingerly, and then, even if you do everything right, you can still end up being harmed."

She said the criminal justice system often does not take domestic violence complaints as seriously as it should. Giving an abuser a slap on the hand instead of truly holding him accountable has resulted in domestic violence becoming an epidemic around the world.

Some 1.3 million women are assaulted in the US by intimate partners each year, and one in every four women will experience domestic violence in her lifetime. Nearly a third of female homicide victims are killed by their intimate partner, according to federal statistics.

Kat said the economic costs are staggering as well—an estimated $37 billion is spent in this country each year on medical treatment for victims.

The problem is even worse in law enforcement families, where 40 percent of police officers in two separate national studies self-reported that they had used violence against their domestic partners within the last year.

During her darkest hours, Kat said there was always a little spark deep inside her that wanted to survive, that wanted something better.

It takes a lot of courage to admit that you have character flaws and weaknesses that are the underlying influences of the choices you make, she says. But self-evaluation is an essential part of healing.

So is finding a purpose that gives life meaning because people need hope to cope and inspire change.

"Without purpose, life is motion without meaning, activity without direction and events without reason," she says. "Without purpose, life is trivial, petty, and pointless."

Out of our greatest rejection can come the greatest direction, says Kat.

"Keep working at it and you will have more in the future than you have lost in the past. Don't let good enough be good enough. Get your dreams back. Get your fire back. Speak into existence your good fortune."

She says the internal messages that women give to themselves are powerful and can bring life or death to their spirit.

"Seeds can be planted negatively or positively, depending on your thoughts, words, and choices. How do you see your life? A circus? A minefield? A rollercoaster? A puzzle? A symphony? A journey? A dance? A carousel?"

Kat says women need to stop making life decisions based on fear, which may be the result of a traumatic experience, unrealistic expectations, growing up in a controlling home, or even a genetic predisposition.

If she wants it bad enough and is willing to work for it, Kat believes any woman can turn her life around. "The only person that can protect you is you."

Untitled by Allen Howard

# Twins Grapple With Their Violent Past

"In order to fully understand the situation my brother and I faced, you had to know that he and I are two-fifths of what the press dubbed the Oregon Five in the early 1990s. All of us were under the age of seventeen when we committed our crimes and all of us were prosecuted for aggravated murder," wrote Lydell White in *66 With the Possible: Looking Through the Eyes of Twins.*

That book title reflects sentences for Lydell and Laycelle White of aggravated murder plus eight hundred months—sixty-six years—and the possibility that they could be paroled in 2050 and 2048, respectively, with good time.

"As children, we were tried, convicted, sentenced, and punished as if we were fully mature adults," says Lydell. "We are serving a longer sentence because of our age than an adult given the same amount of time."

The twins were fifteen when they broke into the home of Richard and Grace Remy of Salem, both in their eighties, and beat and strangled them during the commission of a car theft.

Lydell and Laycelle were juveniles, so they were spared the mandatory minimum sentence imposed on adults. Instead, they were given life with the possibility of parole, although there was no rule on the books to determine when they would be eligible for release.

That made their sentences much harsher than the time given to adults, who are eligible for a parole hearing after thirty years. The state called the disparity a "legal glitch," and the Board of Parole came up with a new set of rules to address the issue in 1999 that were tougher than those for adults.

Under those rules, juveniles had to serve as many as forty years before they could be considered for release. Even that was just a hearing to see if the inmate was a candidate for rehabilitation.

The Whites filed a legal challenge outlining that their treatment as a separate class of inmates constituted "cruel and unusual punishment," a violation of their constitutional rights. They have been unsuccessful, to date, in obtaining early release.

"When the judge handed down the sentence, I honestly didn't fully understand how much time I had gotten. However, my mom did, because she couldn't stop crying, and seeing her cry made me cry," wrote Laycelle in their book. "I had no kind of conscience, just like the courts had said. I never showed any true remorse for my actions. Oh, I said I was sorry, but you could tell that what I was really sorry for was getting caught."

Lydell, now forty-five, is older than Laycelle by one minute but considers himself the elder brother. He takes the lead in the book, penning the prologue and his thoughts in the first half.

"We decided to write the autobiography to ask people not to throw away our humanity because we committed a heinous crime as a child," he says. "We further ask the reader not to define us by our past but the men we are today. We, like all people, are a work in progress.

"We made a very big mistake and will pay for it for the rest of our lives. However, I won't allow my crime to define who I want to become. This is why I strive to be better today than I was yesterday. I now understand the true meaning of life. I've also come to understand my own worth through all of the programs I have taken, and I will continue to touch and change people's lives as long as I'm on this earth."

Laycelle is hopeful their book will open people's eyes to the plight of prisoners and how they must fight to survive, not just physically but emotionally and mentally.

"I refuse to become what this broken system wants to make me be," he wrote. "Everything I've learned and gained is because I want to, and must be, better than what I was before."

Their self-published book can be found on LuLu.com and picks up two years before the twins decided to steal a car in Oregon to get to California so they could be present for their incarcerated father's next court appearance.

"Looking back, I realize how much Lydell and I fed off of one another," stated Laycelle. "With no real male role model to learn from or look up to, we tended to look at each other, and usually what one said, the other went along with."

Throughout the book is woven the struggle of the twins to deal with their father's abandonment. When James White was released from prison in 1991 after doing five years for robbery, Lydell shares how, at the age of thirteen, he was excited to finally be like his peers with a father at their football games.

Laycelle and their brother Anson, six years younger, were just as excited about the future with a family made whole.

"We would sit around for hours telling each other what kinds of things we would do with him. How we would go hiking or camping or simply go out in the yard for a game of catch. I can't say that I was more excited than my brothers for our dad's return, but I sure felt like I was," wrote Lydell.

The hope of the boys died when Robert came home only long enough to make plans to get to Los Angeles, where the family had come from, to see old friends. It took five days for their father to make travel arrangements from their home in Salem, and Lydell held onto hope that they would all be going with him.

"Dad left without any of us," recalls Lydell. "I was devastated. He hadn't even gone to one of Laycelle and my games. I told everybody I knew that my dad was going to be there to see me play football and track, that he would be so proud of me each time I scored or won a race.

"Now I would have to face those same friends, tell them that my dad would not come, that he didn't want to come, that his business in LA was more important than his children."

After all the bragging he had done, Lydell wrote that he could not face the shame of abandonment, so he told his friends that his father had gone back to California to get everything set up for the entire family to move.

One week after Robert left, he called home to tell the boys and their mother that he was locked up again, although he did not say why. Despite that bad news, Lydell deluded himself into believing that his father was just running into small problems and still intended to reunite with them.

As the weeks and months rolled by without their father, the twins began to act out and get into fights that were an outlet for their emotional pain.

"The more pain I gave to someone in a fight, the less pain I felt in my heart, at least for a while," remembers Lydell.

Sexuality had been an outlet for his emotions since the age of nine, and Lydell began pursuing as many random hookups as he could.

In 1992, he and Laycelle began running away to party, fight and get drunk with fellow members of the Westside Mafia, a Crip gang on the south side of town.

The twins' exploits eventually landed them in foster care and juvenile detention.

"Mom was heartbroken. All she had ever done was bless bro and me with a home, food, clothes, and love," wrote Laycelle. "And in return, we had run away from it all. Looking back on that time, I think it was my desire to be grown, coupled with the need for my father in my life, that made me so willing to hurt the one person who tried so hard to show me true love, devotion, loyalty, and trust."

On August 16, 1993, the twins learned from a phone call to their father's girlfriend that he had a court appearance coming soon. They promised to be there but didn't have money for the bus trip— so they decided to steal a car in the neighborhood.

"There just happened to be a nice white Impala right around the corner, so we planned to get it that night. Neither of us could hot-wire it, so we figured we'd get the keys somehow and drive off," remembers Laycelle.

Their plan was to take a baseball bat to the house, knock on the door, and hit whoever answered to immobilize him or her so they could grab the keys and drive off.

When no one answered their knock, the twins found another way into the house, and both say they can only remember bits and pieces of what happened that night.

They were arrested before they got out of town. Lydell would become a father while behind bars, but it would be many years before he developed a relationship with his daughter. He said the decades in prison have brought plenty of hardship but also a lot of self-growth.

"During this time, I have worked so hard to correct the part of my character that allowed me to think that the course I had taken was the only one I could take," wrote Lydell.

He and Laycelle were fighters when they went into prison and earned respect in a predatory world with their fists. Because of their aggression when together, they have frequently been housed in different facilities or units of the same prison.

Since 2006, they have both been incarcerated at Oregon State Penitentiary in Salem.

In the book, the twins repeatedly talk of their mother's unconditional love for them, despite the pain they inflicted on her.

At an unsuccessful parole hearing in 2015, Lydell noted, "Mom came to the podium and began to talk. As she did, I could feel my throat tightening up. I had to look away. Here we were, twenty-two years after that one fateful night, and this was the only woman who had never let me down. Yet she was also the one person in my life that I had hurt the most. And she was speaking on my behalf.

"I could hear her crying softly, for all the pain I had caused, and she was begging the board for mercy for her son. With that, the tears started running down my face. I was so ashamed that I had put her in this position.

"At that moment, I reiterated a promise I had made so long ago, that if I was released, I would do good, that I would help others and not hurt them, and that I would try to change the lives of others."

Toward that end, Lydell helped established a restorative justice program at OSP that aimed to increase understanding between guards and inmates. He was also involved with the Inside-Out program that brought college students into the prison to meet with inmates who were also taking classes.

As he has aged, Lydell has pondered why he ran from his mother to pursue the parent running from him.

He and Laycelle have come to understand that the anger, bitterness, and deep emotional wounds of their father's callous and neglectful treatment led them into destructive life patterns.

In prison he could have gotten worse, says Lydell, but he chose to finally heed his mother's wisdom to grow as a person every day, something he has tried to pass on to his daughter.

"I have seen much more bad than good, yet I still choose to be good," he says.

In prison, he contends the nice guy is the one who is always getting pushed to his limit, getting worked on.

"It's crazy, but for the most part, people in prison respect you more if they know you'll whoop ass. If they question that, you'll be getting tested all the time. For my first few years, it was like that everywhere I went. I was always the youngest, so most people didn't take me as being for real. They tested me and I got in a lot of fights."

Lydell then notes, "After I made some changes, I found that I didn't want to fight anymore. I wanted to look for other ways to work out my issues because my thinking was now about how I would deal with a given issue if I was out there with my daughter looking up to me and my family standing by me."

In 2008, Lydell and Laycelle decided that, as part of their healing process, they would change their last name from White to King. Lydell changed his middle name to Eemuh, which in Portuguese means "I am a," so his full name translates to "Lydell I Am a King."

Their name change, while legal, will not be official until they are released.

The twins were denied parole several years ago. That denial was based largely on a psychological report that they suffered from a severe emotional disturbance that constituted a public safety danger. However, despite that grim news, their lives each took an unexpectedly positive turn.

Both men have married; Lydell to a childhood friend named Kesha, and Laycelle to Shannon, a pen pal who won his heart.

Finding love behind bars is exceptionally difficult, they said, because inmates get "left to die" by people who professed to be there forever, and after a while, it becomes very difficult to trust and open their hearts.

"Being married while in prison is a very tough thing to deal with, and in spite of my fears, I believe we have a very real chance of beating the odds against us," wrote Laycelle. "I know the statistics and I refuse to be one more tick on that statistical line. Shannon and I are going to make this marriage last."

With greater societal understanding that the teenage brain is still in development, so child killers should not be held to the same standards as adults, the Whites are hopeful of being paroled in 2025, the year of their next scheduled hearing.

"To all of you out there, this is my challenge to you—challenge yourself to open your minds and hearts, to use your own experiences to grow and overcome your obstacles, to learn from them and become a better person. Believe me, if you think that is too complicated, read and learn from my experiences," advises Laycelle to close the book.

# Crisis Within A Soul-Stripper Career

When you walk into the "belly of the beast," otherwise known as the Intensive Management Unit of a prison, anyone who moves grabs your attention because a life-and-death situation can unfold in the blink of an eye.

"At first it feels like being thrown into the wilderness. There's no place for complacency because people can die. You can't be afraid, you have to be fearless," says Michael Morgan, an Army veteran who spent twenty-five years in the field of corrections, more than twelve at the IMU at Oregon State Penitentiary.

The IMU is a twenty-three-hour-a-day lockdown unit for violent offenders and the mentally ill who cannot function within the general population. These are the criminals that no one else wants to be around, says Morgan.

"You actually have to drag inmates down there. They don't want to go into that building. When you are on duty in there, all your senses are heightened. You are listening for calls for help, looking for anything out of the norm."

Living on the edge day after day, year after year, takes such a psychological toll on officers that many began to self-medicate to cope with the stress; others lose their sense of purpose and succumb to the despair and hopelessness by taking their own life.

"Corrections is a soul stripper—it's so dark," says Morgan. "You see things that other people can't imagine and it changes you. All that is good and innocent in the world seems to be a fantasy because you know the reality."

The suicide rate among corrections officials is twice as high as that of both police and the general public, so it is beyond time for the issue to be looked at in the cold light of day, says Morgan.

Adding to the daily stress is the continual labor shortage that leads to officers working massive amounts of overtime to cover for personnel who have been assaulted or otherwise injured.

"Physically or mentally, everyone gets hurt and it changes a person," Morgan says.

The challenge with getting officers to talk about the problems they are having is the stigma associated with being anything less than macho.

"Having PTSD isn't a weakness, it is a reaction to overwhelming stress, and no one should have to pretend like they are fine when they are not," he argues.

According to Morgan, when corrections officials do exhibit problems, it is a very real possibility that their career will be derailed like his was after a breakdown and an honest appeal for help.

By 2008, Morgan had become so concerned about the mental state of many peers that he began advocating for wellness programs. Eventually, he compiled an "untimely death" report that he presented to administrators with the intent of motivating them into action.

"There were seventy-two deaths in that report, either suicide, cancer or murder—deaths that were under unusual circumstances and somehow tied to someone in the family working at the prison," he says.

"I took what I had to the administration because I wanted them to know that what was going on at work was the 'frogs in boiling water' scenario. Many officers did not know they were in trouble until it was too late—the water had heated slowly enough around them that they did not understand what was happening."

Morgan began focusing on trauma-related problems among prison workers after undergoing surgery in 2005 to remove a pituitary tumor the size of an egg that was growing on his brain.

"I had surgery, and five weeks later, I was released to go back to work in the IMU," he recalls. "But my life started changing. I had anger, depression, lethargy, and anxiety—I was on three different antianxiety meds."

He said the pituitary gland serves as the master regulator of the human endocrine system, producing vital hormones unless something goes awry.

Neurological scientists have discovered that battlefield explosions can damage soldiers' pituitary glands in ways that cause lasting health problems that mirror PTSD.

Morgan says damage to the pituitary can also be caused by a violent blow, which is a workplace danger when corrections officials are dealing with explosive inmates. He also believes a high degree of trauma plays a role in the development of tumors.

When he learned that three other corrections officers he worked with also had been diagnosed with tumors, Morgan became convinced the medical condition was directly tied to their line of work.

"The internal chemical makeup is so beautiful because we are fearfully and wonderfully made, that if it's not managed, then weird and strange things can happen to an individual—making them mentally impaired," he says. "I think all first responders should take specific labs to have their internal chemicals monitored."

In 2008, he was assaulted by an inmate during a cell extraction, which dislocated his skull from his spinal vertebrae.

"God put me in a time out," says Morgan of the incident.

The skull injury resulted in nerve damage to his neck and shoulder, so the prison's insurance carrier decided he should no longer be directly interacting with inmates. Instead, he was retrained to cover a desk job.

Then, in 2009, Morgan compounded his health problems by rolling his truck in an accident while on his way to the doctor to discuss a neck fusion for his prison-related injury.

"I broke my neck—but it did fix my nerve damage," he says of the irony.

He was placed in the mail room at OSP during his recovery, but administrators wanted him back in IMU as soon as he was fit for that duty.

By that time, Morgan had lost his ability to cope with a work environment filled with high tension and negativity, so he made the decision to work in the gun tower keeping watch over the yard to avoid any real battles with inmates for the remainder of his career.

But Morgan couldn't avoid the internal drama playing out with destructive patterns in his own life. He felt the nickname Mad Dog, given him by coworkers, was appropriate for his mental and emotional struggles.

"In September 2010, I was pulled over for a DUII and entered rehab to deal with the anger issues that were adversely affecting my life and the lives of those around me," he says.

He continued to spiral downward psychologically and spent eight days in the psych ward at Oregon State Hospital in February 2011. While there, he was diagnosed with bipolar disorder and manic psychosis associated with PTSD.

"After a brief absence, I was again released to full duty as a corrections officer," says Morgan. "I didn't have a driver's license, but I never missed a day because coworkers were willing to make sure I got there."

In June 2011, he was informed that DOC had undertaken a review of his work history to determine if he should be allowed to keep certifications that allowed him to work as a guard.

"Everything I did as a corrections officer was against my will and nature, but it is what I was paid to do and I performed my duties while always treating the inmates with dignity and respect," he says.

As the bureaucracy began rolling toward his dismissal, Morgan reminded human resource staff that he had been diagnosed with PTSD and requested a disability placement as allowed by federal law.

By March 2013, he was decertified as a corrections officer but given the job of processing visitor applications for all Oregon prisons.

"I was grateful to have the position even though it was a 20 percent reduction in pay—it was still a job," says Morgan.

In 2016, he retired and filed a Social Security disability claim before making recovery his full-time job.

He is now on a quest to get DOC officials to care not only about the suicide rate among employees, but the fact they have an elevated rate of divorce, alcoholism, and drug abuse. They also have higher health risks, such as high blood pressure, high cholesterol, and increased risk of a heart attack.

"Prison is a pressure cooker," says Morgan. "The administration knows what it does to us, but they won't talk about it because they need plausible deniability."

He is irate that bureaucrats are unwilling to have an honest discussion about the great psychological harm being done to brave men and women every day in a dysfunctional system.

Morgan entered corrections with eight years of active-duty Army service as a crash recovery specialist. He also served six years in the Army National Guard as a combat engineer.

The transition into prison work was seamless, says Morgan, because that system, like the military, operates with a "suck it up, buttercup" mentality that prohibits any acknowledgment of fears or problems.

Looking back, Morgan sees it as absolutely ridiculous for the system to expect people to be in full battle mode for an entire career. At least in the military, he says deployments are spaced out so that times of hypervigilance and "fight or flight" adrenaline rushes don't happen every day.

In corrections, Morgan says officers are vastly outnumbered by inmates, and any little conflict can quickly erupt into violence, which always has them on edge.

"We are trained to do the unthinkable—whatever it takes in a stressful environment—you never know what can happen," he says. "You might have a guard tower over you, but sometimes you have to be the bullet."

The IMU ratchets up tensions even higher, contends Morgan, because the prisoners in that unit are so out of control, they pose an additional threat.

"When you walk through the gate, your armor kicks in, your shoulder blades lock into place, and you are in battle mode."

An inmate arriving at IMU can expect to be verbally harassed by men locked up too many hours out of the day, says Morgan, which makes the environment even tenser.

"They have to work their energy out so there is a lot of screaming and yelling. They tell the new guy to 'kill yourself' because they are testing him. Anytime someone breaks down and begins to cry or otherwise shows weakness, they are taunted and told to die."

Each day, IMU prisoners get thirty minutes in the yard and thirty minutes to shower and work out, and then it's back to a solitary cell. It is commonplace for fights to break out whenever inmates are together, sometimes as payback for something that happened in the general population and sometimes from mental instability or just to stir things up, says Morgan.

"Some of them want to stay in their cell because they are safer, nobody can get to them."

Moving inmates in and out of IMU is a time of high risk, he says. The individual being extracted might refuse to leave the cell, so officers are forced to enter and restrain him, not knowing if he has some type of makeshift weapon to use against them.

Sometimes human feces is the weapon of choice, and officers are pelted with foul-smelling "bullets."

"There would be times when you smelt like shit the whole rest of your shift—you couldn't wash the smell away," he recounts.

Caged for years in this environment, he says some inmates choose to end their lives, and the most common method of suicide is hanging by a toilet paper rope.

Sometimes, during moments outside the cell, the inmate finds a more surefire way to die; Morgan remembers one throwing himself off the top tier of a housing unit.

"You are expected to leave 'eight at the gate,' but you go home every day carrying all that with you and it significantly affects your life and relationships outside," says Morgan, who was recently divorced from a sixteen-year marriage.

One of his grim memories is the execution of two death row inmates in the late 1990s. There were candlelight vigils going on outside, and the tiers in the prison were eerily quiet with the temperature inside seeming colder than usual.

"It's like all the oxygen was taken out of the air, there was no life in the entire building," he says.

Morgan recalls looking at the crowd outside and thinking: "There are some people who are just evil. You know when you are looking at something that evil because there is nothing in their eyes.

If those people knew the animal we were getting ready to execute like the COs did, they wouldn't have been out there."

He has learned to manage those memories in a way that does not impair his skill to function in the real world, but that ability was won after many soul-wearing mental battles.

Morgan is optimistic that there is enough research being done on the plight of corrections officers that bureaucrats will soon be unable to justify the status quo.

He points to a 2011 study by Caterina Spinaris, a clinical researcher and founder of Desert Waters Correctional Outreach, a nonprofit based in Colorado.

Spinaris did an anonymous survey of corrections officers, testing them for indications of PTSD, and found that twice as many had the condition as military veterans.

Morgan says DOC hardliners have tried to paint him as crazy to take away the credibility of his message, but it becomes difficult to do that with research like Spinaris's to back him up.

He has been sober for more than ten years and feels restored enough in body and soul to fight for corrections workers still in the system and those struggling in their retirement years.

"What my recovery boiled down to was 'To thine own self be true,'" says Morgan. "And now I am at peace with myself."

He said people defending the system may malign him, but he is on a mission and won't be stopped.

There are about four thousand seven hundred corrections officers in Oregon and roughly five hundred thousand across the US, and they deserve support, he says.

Toward that end, Morgan has taken special suicide prevention training to be able to work with people at a high level of despair. He has advocated on behalf of officers who are struggling with addictions or other self-destructive behavior.

"We are called to be our brother's keeper," he says. "Security is not convenient, and we have an obligation to take care of those who provide it. It's a form of respect—we need to honor them."

# Part III
# Keith: The Aftermath
# Of Addiction

*To be addicted to drugs is sad, but the thing is, when you are on them, you're happy. The feeling is like you don't have any worries—when I was high, I didn't care about anything.*

—Keith Ward

The evil of addiction, says Keith Ward, sixty-four, who has spent more than thirty years in prison, is that drugs become your first love and scoring the next high is all you care about.

"I first started out smoking weed every day when I was fourteen," he recalls. "By the time I was seventeen, I was using cocaine and then a guy at work introduced me to heroin. I didn't know that it was going to cause so much devastation. I was invincible, nobody was going to touch me."

His habit grew to $400 a day, and he found that working as a chef in a five-star restaurant didn't provide enough cash to cover that $12,000 monthly bill.

So Keith fell into a life of crime that began with a variety of scams and then graduated into robberies that left his victims terrorized.

"I could function when I snorted cocaine, but I would nod off on the heroin, and I got fired from my job because I was standing over the grill doing that," he remembers.

Although he was unable to hold down a job, Keith remained proud of the fact that he never used a needle to get high and that he always had a place to live and a vehicle, instead of ending up in a crack house.

"Looking back, I was a monster," he says. "I was doing things I had no business doing."

The women he hooked up with were users, too, and those relationships never lasted longer than a few months.

"Basically, my relationship was someone getting high with me," he says.

Keith ended up with a daughter and a son by two of the women he became involved with, but he couldn't focus on his parenting responsibilities and eventually became estranged from them.

His family support dissipated when he went to prison for the second and final time. Several years ago, his mother died and there was no acknowledgment that she even had a son in the obituary written by his sister, who was adopted when he was fifteen.

"That really hurt. My mother always loved me, and she wouldn't have liked to see that," he says.

Keith is one of the astonishing number of inmates incarcerated for drug-related charges.

About 80 percent of the 2.3 million inmates currently serving time in prison have a history of alcohol or drug dependency, according to the National Center on Addiction and Substance Abuse.

Limited funding makes it difficult for these inmates to get adequate treatment to overcome addiction. Only one-fifth of drug-addicted prisoners will receive treatment, even though the cost of providing help would be much less than the long-term costs associated with addicted repeat offenders.

A report from the Addiction Blog, which tracks current trends in recovery across the US, said that if all inmates who needed treatment received it and remained sober, crime-free, and employed, the nation would reap an annual economic benefit of $90,953 per prisoner.

Keith hit rock bottom when he received life in 2001 for being a societal predator. He was ready to get clean and turn things around. "I still loved the drug, I will always love it, but I wanted to find myself again."

Because he has always been a strong individual, Keith chose to quit heroin cold turkey.

He was prescribed methadone to make the painful withdrawal bearable. Over a period of several days in the infirmary, Keith experienced nausea, severe pains and cramps, vomiting, chills, and cold sweats, among other symptoms.

"Basically, overcoming the addiction is a psychological thing. You have to stop thinking you need that drug," he explains.

But getting clean isn't just about beating the opioid; it's about doing an assessment of what led you to use in the first place, says Keith. "There had to be a void in my life for me to get into drugs."

Raised as an only child in Philadelphia, Pennsylvania, Keith always had some type of job to ensure he had pocket change. His mother worked for a federal agency, and although his biological father was out of the picture, he had a stepfather who was a good provider but could be mean when drunk.

His parents worked hard during the week, remembers Keith, and then partied on the weekend. His family denomination was Baptist, and although his parents didn't attend church regularly, his aunt made sure he got there every week.

Keith fondly remembers his grandmother cooking pancakes every Saturday for a small horde of cousins, a happy and noisy affair.

His parents were not involved in criminal activity and Keith was expected to fulfill his responsibilities.

One time he began skipping high school to work in a sandwich shop, a career that ended when his mother walked in and saw him behind the counter.

When he was seventeen, Keith signed up for culinary classes to pursue his interest in becoming a chef. He was also preparing for fatherhood because his girlfriend was pregnant.

That relationship ended with betrayal; the best friend he asked to look out for his new wife while he was in jail ended up in a romantic relationship with her.

From that point on, things went downhill as Keith moved to Las Vegas for the nightlife that drew him deeper and deeper into the shadowy world of addiction.

"By the time I fell, I was on my own," he says. "The only one who looked out for me was my aunt. She stood by me and sent packages when I needed something."

An elderly inmate invited Keith to church shortly after he returned to prison, but he rejected the invitation.

"I told him that I didn't need church, that God hadn't done anything for me," he recalls.

Then about nine years ago, he had a change of heart. It was time to return to his spiritual roots.

"It was like God was talking to me, letting me know that I needed to live his life," says Keith, who now studies his Bible and prays early every morning when the prison is quiet and as peaceful as it is going to get. "He told me that I am here for a reason, that I could have died out there."

His life sentence carries the possibility of parole in 2023, and Keith is keeping his eye on the gate. He wants to help troubled youth avoid the long dark road he has traveled if he is released.

"Would I live that lifestyle again? Absolutely not. If I can help anyone else not go there, I'm going to do everything I can."

Untitled by Allen Howard

III

# Slow Death Penalty

*Look up in the sky, it's a bird, it's a plane—*
*no, it's my spirit! I'm a man in a cage,*
*see me soar no more, like I'm shackled, cuffed, ball and chain.*
*Life Without the Possibility of Parole. LWOP, isn't that just quaint.*
*LWOP—LIFE WITHOUT POSSIBILITIES, NO POSSIBILITIES*
*No possibilities for living—I'm alive but this is not living.*
*For education—a mind is a terrible thing to waste!*
*For rehabilitation—what's the motivation?*
*For hope—just give me dope!*
*For change—that's just another thang!*
*For love—I'm so done!*
*For peace—this ain't the Middle East!*
*For better health care—a $5 copay and then who cares?*
*For better dental care—where's my dentures?*
*For better mental health care/treatment—a razor,*
*and a blazer, pepper spray, bullets, not Tasers.*
*For better trauma care/treatment—they offer none!*
*For better meals—they'll never come!*
*For a better phone system that allows us to keep contacts*
*in our communities without extortionist prices—CDCR*
*gets a kick-back so the prices are "righteous."*
*For better placement and transfers to areas where we're from*
*so that we can maintain family ties. I'm from the Bay Area*
*and they housed me in San Diego—I haven't seen a family*
*member in two years, the cost of a vacation to visit me here.*
*For fair prices for canteen and packages, they'll*
*bleed a turnip until no blood spills.*

*For CDCR to abide by its own rules and the letter of the*
*law—hold up, give me a minute, I'm laughing too hard.*
*For more just laws—a moment of silence, a political pause.*
*For some disinfectant and a toilet brush—now that's*
*some funny shit, you want your lunch?*
*For a clean shower to use—dude, you must thrive on bad news.*
*It's true, I can take college courses and harbor more useless*
*knowledge. I even taught myself how to read and write. I should*
*have taught myself to fight as I just got hit with a left and a right.*
*You may find this hard to believe, but I fought the death*
*penalty and was rewarded by Life Without the Possibility*
*to Parole, the so-called more humane choice of the two.*
*If you believe that, I have a bone to pick with you.*
*I'm thinking about petitioning the court for a reversal of choice*
*because, after 16 years of this Life Without shit, I find that I'd rather*
*be at San Quentin on death row waiting for a lethal injection!*
*LWOP—the slow death sentence.*
*LWOP—Life Without the Possibility.*
*There is no life without possibilities.*

Travell "Paycheck" Holmes
A man in a cage

# Unmasking The Ugly
# Face Of Power

Attorney Gregory Kafoury has spent more than forty years trying to bring authority figures that abuse power to justice and has found the prison system to be a tough foe.

He recalls a case where a mentally impaired inmate known to spend hours each day proselytizing for Jesus was put into a cell with a devil-worshipping murderer.

"He wrote kites [a form of communication with prison staff] saying, 'This guy is going to kill me,' and didn't get any response," says Kafoury. "He was predictably beat to death, and we couldn't even get in front of a jury with that civil rights case. The federal court refused to let it go forward, and that is a continuing problem."

He believes that corrupt guards sometimes deliberately pit unarmed inmates against each other as a perverse form of entertainment. He said investigations of this practice have been done in California and other states, although it is rare that guards are held accountable.

The reason it is difficult to move prison cases forward, says Kafoury, is that society is largely apathetic about the treatment of inmates and sympathetic to guards instead of holding them to the highest standard of conduct.

Their ongoing battle to stop prison and law enforcement corruption has earned Kafoury and his partner, Mark McDougal, a reputation as the top civil trial court attorneys in Portland, Oregon. Kafoury's son, Jason, has also joined the practice and the battle for social justice.

Five years ago, Kafoury & McDougal won the largest sum by a jury for a police brutality case in the history of the city. Their client, Jason Cox, was a forty-year-old man who was viciously punched in the head and Tased by officers as they arrested him on suspicion of drunk driving in June 2011.

Cox, an ironworker, received every dollar he asked for—$562,129—after jurors viewed surveillance camera footage of the assault by police.

"The officers did not know their actions were being recorded. They just thought they could get away with whatever they wanted to do to him," says Kafoury.

The problem began when Cox caught the attention of Officer Jeffrey Elias while behind the wheel of his 1969 Chevy pickup.

Elias testified that he had followed Cox for about ten blocks and pulled in behind him at a nightclub on the east side of Portland to confront him about driving aggressively.

Arriving at the scene moments later were Officers Robert Bruders and Sarah Kerwin.

The situation escalated when Cox began arguing that his truck was too old to go as fast as he was accused of driving. The officers first had Cox put his hands behind his back and patted him down.

They then decided to take him to the ground, where he was given six to eight blows to the head and shocked four times with a Taser.

Police would later justify that their actions were necessary to restrain Cox.

Kafoury says footage from the motion-activated camera in the parking lot of the club showed that Cox had not resisted, as officers claimed.

Cox was charged with DUII, reckless driving, disorderly conduct, and resisting arrest.

A fire department medic called to the scene to remove the Taser probes was so troubled by what he saw, and the lack of a reasonable explanation, that he shared his observations in the official incident report. That man later testified in court against the defendants, says Kafoury.

He says Cox pleaded with the officers handling him to go easy on his left shoulder, which had undergone surgery one year earlier, but the video appears to show police intentionally jerking and pulling on that shoulder, which led to a posterior tear in his labrum.

Having the shoulder reinjured forced Cox to leave his career as an ironworker, which paid $33 per hour plus benefits.

Kafoury says Cox wanted to avoid jail time, so he pleaded guilty to DUII even though his blood alcohol level was .078, below the .08 legal limit in Oregon.

Because Oregon is a zero-tolerance state, a person can still be convicted even if they are below the legal limit.

In the civil case that followed, the jury awarded $33,138 to Cox for medical expenses, $128,991 for economic damages, and $400,000 for pain and suffering.

Although his firm was able to shine a spotlight on one incident of police brutality, Kafoury says the system attempted to protect itself instead of holding the three officers accountable.

After the Cox incident aired in the media, Kafoury says the Portland Police Bureau's Internal Affairs division launched an investigation. The Independent Police Review committee also looked into the matter.

Neither the division nor the committee found that the officers had violated policy, and none of them was disciplined. Police administrators said the case would be revisited following the jury verdict in favor of Cox.

"If civilians had inflicted a beating like this on someone, they would have faced Measure 11 criminal charges," says Kafoury.

He wants to see mandatory body cameras on all police to help prevent future abuse.

"Police can't be a law unto themselves," he insists. "Everything about the police is going in the wrong direction. They are being militarized when they ought to be business professionals in a suit with a badge. They should have to live in the neighborhoods they serve— they need to be part of the community. If they go to church with you and their kids go to school with yours, it's a different world."

The reason that matters, he says, is that police tactics are filling US jails and prisons with people who will end up being mistreated and become more hardened and bitter.

When new police recruits come into the system and question the status quo, Kafoury contends they are viewed as a threat by their fellow officers.

"A friend of mine had a son who became a policeman. He was highly intellectual and a broad thinker, meaning he was capable of analysis and depth," he says. "He was immediately distrusted and, early on in his career, taken into a room where a prisoner was sitting on a stool. He was told to beat the prisoner to show that he had what it takes—and he did."

Once behind bars for any length of time, Kafoury says inmates adapt psychologically to the dangerous environment by incorporating apathetic and dependent thinking that is referred to as institutionalization.

When the inmate is reprogrammed, he or she may be more compliant, but self-determination is destroyed, and it becomes difficult for that individual to reenter society, says Kafoury.

"I had a client whose name was Frenchie Deschand, and he had an identical twin brother. Frenchie and another man were vying for the affection of a woman and it became one-upmanship; they each tried to outdo the other," he recalls one case.

The challenge became robbing convenience stores.

"Frenchie robbed about seventeen stores. He was caught and charged with armed robbery. In one incident, he put the gun on the counter and said, 'You know what this is, don't you?' The clerk said, 'Yes, I do.' Then Frenchie said, 'Put the money in the bag for me,' and the clerk did. Frenchie asked the clerk if he would get in trouble, and the young man replied, 'No, they will understand because you had a gun.'

"Well, a cop pulls up and ends up putting a bullet hole in the door of Frenchie's car. Frenchie tossed his gun out the window. Yet Frenchie was concerned about everyone else at the scene except himself. He was worried that the cop would get in trouble for shooting his car.

"He was in his early forties and had been in and out of prison most of his life. I asked him, 'Do you think at some level you want to go back?' He said, 'I think so, I am institutionalized.' Then he said the saddest thing I've ever heard: 'Maybe one day, my brother and I will be able to serve together.' There was this flicker of recognition and descending sadness as what he was saying sunk in."

Kafoury says the late Michael Marcus, a district court judge in Multnomah County that incorporates Portland, was a tireless advocate of evidence-based sentencing, which he called smart sentencing.

Marcus spoke out against widespread incarceration with diminishing returns. He sought to change the "harsher is better" mindset of Americans through a social justice campaign.

"He knew that the prevailing 'just deserts' sentences might have created uniformity, but there was insufficient data to tell what type of programming really worked—were drug programs really keeping people off drugs?" Kafoury says. "There are a thousand facts about each offender that should be known before a sentence is handed down if we really want to help that person succeed."

Trying to change the law enforcement and penal systems is not a battle for the faint of heart, he said.

"As a general principle, you never know the nature of an organization until you get into a fight with it. When you challenge it, you will see the ugly face of power."

Kafoury remembers a woman in her early twenties being sentenced to more than two decades behind bars in federal court because she had fallen into crime after hanging out with a drug dealer because she thought he was fun to be around.

"The judge told the young woman that she had gotten a long sentence because she was a 'party girl.' How does that make any sense?" he asks.

As he is a child of the '60s, there is still enough idealism in Kafoury to believe that meaningful change is possible in a world he learned long ago is filled with a ruling class that often misuses its power.

"What it's going to take is a grassroots political movement and the scholarship that gives you structural reform," he says. "Right now, authority figures know that they can pretty much do whatever they want."

II

# Part III
# Trevor: The Other Side
# Of A Dark Journey

*You have to humble yourself and start over. You need to realize that you have a long road ahead of you, but you can be more than your past.*

—Trevor Walraven

People presume that someone who kills when he was a teenager must have been horribly abused as a child, but that is not always the case, says Trevor Walraven, who was sentenced for aggravated murder at the age of fourteen.

"I had a very tight family," he says.

Trevor, now thirty-four, and his half-brother, Josh Cain, who is four years older, were homeschooled.

Their parents, Karen Cain and Doug Walraven, had settled their family behind locked gates on fifty-two acres of forest and farmland in southern Oregon.

The property was surrounded by Bureau of Land Management holdings on three sides, so it was isolated, with the nearest neighbor about one-half mile away.

"My mom and dad came to Oregon to get away from Los Angeles, the rat race of the big city," says Trevor.

Kerosene lamps were used for light and a woodstove for heat.

"I feel like we were very middle class and you wouldn't know we were hillbillies if you didn't see how we lived," says Trevor.

The family worked on the new residence—2,500 square feet of cinderblock that resembled a bunker—as money became available for construction.

"Dad didn't believe in debt, so we built as we could afford it," says Trevor.

Because they had grown up with no television or internet, Trevor and Josh did not miss the connection to social media that their peers viewed as a necessity.

When the new house was able to be lived in, Doug and Karen moved in and the boys, then teens, remained in the cabin.

The family went to Grants Pass to do their laundry and load up on groceries. They would sometimes take in a movie, and Trevor joined his father in a love of the action-packed flicks.

"I was really drawn to the 'shoot 'em up, bang, bang' lifestyle," he says.

Josh and Trevor were inseparable. They helped in the family business, which was selling antique gas station paraphernalia and Raggedy Ann collectibles at swap meets about twenty times per year.

"Our neighbors made moonshine and wine," says Trevor. "I didn't know any different, so it was normal to me."

The boys did odd jobs for people in their community and were generally regarded as good kids. People who knew them expressed shock when Trevor and Josh were arrested in 1998 for fatally shooting a local business owner to steal his car.

Trevor has always maintained that Josh is innocent of the crime and was wrongfully sentenced to twenty-five years in prison.

During a search of their cabin following the boys' arrests, investigators seized drug paraphernalia and music with violent lyrics.

Trevor says he was doing drugs and drinking, as well as driving, by the age of twelve.

His father, who is deceased, served two years in a Minnesota prison on a marijuana-related conviction.

"I was nine at that time," recalls Trevor. "That made Mom the breadwinner, and she had to keep things going while Dad was in prison."

His mother took a cleaning job so she could gain access to a phone and the internet to keep in contact with her husband.

When Josh decided to go to Glendale High School, Trevor followed and enrolled in eighth grade, where he failed Spanish but did well socially.

He had only one brush with the law prior to the murder; he got caught driving a dirt bike that wasn't street legal on Interstate 5. He was thirteen at the time and given ten hours of community service for the offense.

Although he was not under the influence on the day of the shooting, Trevor believes abuse of illicit substances adversely affected his mental state.

"Looking back, I don't think we were raised to necessarily follow the rules," he says. "I also think we were desensitized—the family dogs had to be put down after they tore up the neighbor's dog. Dad decided it would be better than chaining them up and, thereby, restricting freedom."

The boys always had access to guns, including the one Trevor used to kill Bill Hull on August 1, 1998.

An autopsy revealed the victim had been shot once in the top of the head with a copper-jacketed, hollow-point .38 special bullet.

He has been described as "evil" in some media reports, but Trevor said he did not act out of malice or rage; that his motive was pathetically simple.

"I wanted to impress my brother's friends by having a car. I was going to do whatever it took to fit in, and no one was going to question my place," he says.

Although he wanted to steal a car, Trevor didn't want the consequences of that action.

"In my mind, the way you did that was not to have a witness."

Josh, who was eighteen when arrested, will be released from prison in 2023. Because he was a juvenile, Trevor qualified for a program that allowed him to be released halfway through his thirty-year minimum sentence.

Trevor shared a cell with Josh at Oregon State Penitentiary and said they now talk every week, although they are not as close as they once were.

"We are very different people than we were, and we've grown in very different ways," he says.

Like Trevor, Josh is concentrating on personal growth and recently completed his bachelor's in the humanities.

"In large part because we grew up around adults and didn't have contact with peers early on, we're able to be respectful and hold our own," says Trevor of their "inside" life.

Most prisoners do not have the resources to prepare for a return to society, and there are not enough effective programs available for those who do.

"Most of these residents are going back into the community at some point, so they need education that can help them succeed and not end up back inside," says Trevor.

Prisoners who join gangs inside do it for support. Many have no one on the outside who values them and that makes their odds of building a better life more difficult.

"If people even receive one visit in prison, there is a 25 percent reduction in recidivism," says Trevor.

He felt fortunate to earn better than minimum wage at his first job in the free world, which he thought was an "amazing" achievement. He counts each day of freedom as a blessing.

"It's all perspective," he says.

Trevor will soon begin studying criminal justice and psychology at Lane Community College. He currently works full-time in data management at Criminal Defense Support Services in Eugene and lives in Salem with his fiancée, Loraine McLeod.

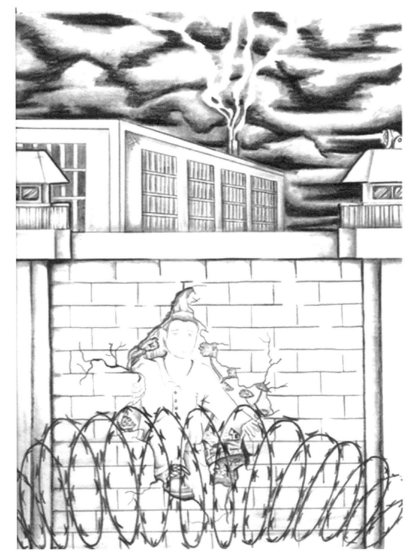

"Hope" by Toshio Takanobu

II

# Real Change Is A Mindset

*My name is Michael Butler, and I am sixty years old. I was convicted of aggravated murder and kidnapping in Oregon and second-degree murder in Washington. I was sentenced to twenty years for the kidnapping, consecutive to a life sentence with a twenty-year minimum for the aggravated murder.*

*I have been incarcerated since August 1980.*

*What led to my committing these crimes was my thinking and inability to manage my emotions. I thought of myself as unattractive, undesirable, incompetent, cowardly, and weak.*

*The emotions that usually motivated me to act were fear and anger. I gave myself permission to commit crimes because I saw myself as a victim. I was at war with the world—everyone was my enemy. No one was to be trusted. Whatever I thought I could do to get by was permissible.*

*What scared me about prison to begin with was dealing with the violence of other inmates. What scares me now is contemplating growing old, reaching the point where I am unable to care for myself and, finally, dying bedridden in the infirmary.*

*The worst part of my prison experience has been a combination of dealing with remorse and shame and not being out in the community to help my lifelong friend as she succumbs to dementia caused by early-onset Alzheimer's.*

*Being locked away in a cell, I feel safe from the violence of other inmates and from the anxiety of unwanted social interactions. On the other hand, I feel sad and lonely from not being with the people I love. I enjoy being able to read, write, watch TV, and listen to the radio without interruption. But it is frustrating not to be able to come and go as I please.*

*I've never been abused by guards. Some correctional staff are easier to get along with than others; some are more or less kind, personable, or reasonable. I have always tried to get along with staff and find that for the most part, they respond well to me.*

*There are programs in the institutions of the ODOC (Oregon Department of Corrections) to help people develop job and life skills. Whether those programs are enough to fully prepare a person to go out into the world and succeed depends on the person. For a person who is already motivated to change, is not suffering from debilitating psychological and social deficits, and has sufficient maturity, there are enough resources available to prepare him or her to make a life when he or she gets out.*

*For those who are not motivated, there is very little to bring them to awareness of their need to change or encourage them to do so.*

*For those with debilitating psychological and social deficits, prison life tends to facilitate their dependency on institutional life. For those lacking maturity, there is plenty to keep them entertained until their release, having changed for the worse or not at all.*

*The positive side of my incarceration is that I've been given the opportunity to gain some education, to participate in some self-change programs, and to work in some jobs where I can contribute to my community. I have plenty of reading and learning materials available. There are people with whom I enjoy socializing.*

*The ways that I've changed since being incarcerated are that I've learned to think differently about my relationships with others, realized that I'm not the victim, and recognized the need for compassion toward others as well as myself.*

*I am developing the ability to be motivated by other emotions than fear and anger. I'm learning to value others and myself.*

*Changes in laws make very little difference. Any change that's needed is in the people, in our minds. When we care about one another and care for each other, the law doesn't matter—there's no need for it.*

||||||||||||||||||||||||||||||||||||||||||||||||||||||||||||||||||||||||||

# Hope Lies In The People

"The whole system is set up to help get you convicted. For that reason, more than we need an Innocence Project—the system mostly sorts that out—we need a Guilty Project to deal with all the injustice in our treatment of the guilty," says Edward Jones.

After a long career as a public defender and judge, he has seen it all and has drawn strong conclusions about what works and what doesn't in the world of criminal justice.

Where is the evidence that reforming the system will work? Jones says that isn't the right question. People need to be asking, "Where is the evidence supporting our use of a system that clearly doesn't work?"

Deciding which offenses justify prison sentences is a political rather than a legal decision—how do you compare sex crimes with drug crimes? And even after laws are passed, it isn't always clear how to apply them.

"Judges and lawyers have to figure out what each new law means," says Jones. "It's hard to write laws that can't be misread. And you always have weird situations that make the law problematic. We are constantly struggling to figure out the application of the law to specific cases."

Politicians won't take on the heavy lift of fixing unfair sentences due to the backlash of accusations that they are abandoning crime victims and endangering the public, says Jones.

Therefore, he believes the real power lies with the people, in sentencing reform as in all things in the political realm.

"Until the public wants it to be different, it's not going to be different. The legislature won't fix it until they are sure the public supports it."

If people don't demand change, Jones says politicians will continually be trying to straddle the line between appearing to be tough on crime and pushing for true reform.

An example of the balancing act can be seen in Oregon's death penalty history, he points out.

Oregon's last two governors have imposed a moratorium on the death penalty, but neither followed through to propose a change in the state constitution to make it official.

"If we have the moral conviction that executing someone is wrong, then we need to do something about that. But so far, no one has the courage to take the steps necessary to get it off the table."

The Oregon Legislature enacted life without parole in 1989, says Jones, because citizens were very divided about someone being sentenced to death. However, elected officials effectively amended the constitution for something that should have been decided by the people.

"Prosecutors knew that juries choose life, so putting someone in prison for the rest of their life was a nicer way of getting people to sentence them to death."

Once a prison is built, Jones says it is less expensive to fill it with people than it is to get them educated or in treatment programs that truly change lives.

"Nor do we account for all the external costs, like welfare for their families. When you sentence somebody, you sentence the whole family."

Society pays little heed to the hardships suffered by a prisoner's family, even though we know staying connected to family reduces recidivism, says Jones.

"It's amazing how little we are concerned about the collateral damage of what we do."

He said there will never be a perfect system, but the US could go a long way toward restoring justice if judges could make decisions on a case-by-case basis.

"Jail is fine for the people we are afraid of, it's not for the people we are just mad at," says Jones.

In the past, Jones says the judge imposed a sentence, but the actual time served was determined by the parole board.

"At one time a life sentence imposed by a judge became a ten-year sentence after the parole board reviewed it. The judge had no idea when he sentenced someone how long the defendant would actually serve."

That led to demands for "truth in sentencing," which led to mandatory minimums, says Jones.

When a person does land in prison, the necessary focus of budget-constrained corrections officials is on discipline rather than rehabilitation.

"We train people in prison not to be self-reliant. All the skills that make you a good inmate do not make you a good citizen."

Locking up people who have made bad life choices—or gotten drawn into criminal behavior due to a drug or alcohol addiction—with hardened gang members forces them into survival mode, says Jones.

"We have an obligation when we put people in prison to keep them safe and we really don't do that. There's nothing anyone can do that would justify being in one of our prisons."

If the inmate is forced to fight for his or her life or to avoid being sexually assaulted, they frequently end up in isolation, which is seen as the answer to everything, says Jones.

"They all ought to be in school getting the education and work skills they are going to need to build a new life, but we don't want to pay for that."

Opportunities for job skills are limited, too, and draw resistance from employers because inmate-produced goods are viewed as unfair competition.

He said the system also fails victims because there are not enough services available to help them recover from trauma and move on in life.

"Victims need much more than a ride to the courthouse," says Jones.

And matters get complicated when the victim and defendant come from the same family, such as when an individual kills a relative.

"The DA is working with the victim side of the family to get a conviction, and even though they adamantly oppose the death penalty, that is what the state is seeking," he says. "These are the troublesome little puzzles that come to your mind over the years."

Jones graduated from Lewis & Clark Law School in 1975 and went into private practice as a criminal defense attorney for almost ten years. He then managed Multnomah Defenders for fourteen years.

After that, he spent nearly two decades as a judge in Oregon's most populous county. At the time of his interview, Jones had retired from the bench and was serving as director of a different defender's office, Metropolitan Public Defenders, in downtown Portland, the state's largest city, which has seventy attorneys on staff.

"We would spend less money and have less crime if we went about this differently," he says. "We spend an awful lot of money for no particular payoff."

||||||||||||||||||||||||||||||||||||||||||||||||||||||||||||||||||||||||||||

# Part III
# Kevin: Lessons Behind Barbed Wire

*Men respect men and nothing is given. You must earn all that comes your way. Good or bad, it is earned or deserved.*

—Kevin Young

Kevin Young, fifty-six, was raised with a good work ethic, to stand firm for what he believed was right. Those were important life lessons during the 1960s and 1970s when racial tensions were running high in his hometown of Hot Springs, Arkansas.

He and his siblings were bused to an all-white school as part of a move by the state to desegregate institutions. The hostility that surrounded them made learning much more difficult.

"You were either going to whup someone or get whupped, but you had to stand tall," recalls Kevin.

Although he was very competitive in sports, Kevin found that, as a black athlete, he was treated differently despite never missing a game and being one of the best players in the Babe Ruth league.

"I never made an All-Star team even though I was ten times better than most," he says. "I didn't become bitter. I just became more determined not to let the ugliness of racism deter me."

With three older brothers and numerous cousins to contend with, Kevin learned as a small child that quick thinking—and fast talking—could help him avoid becoming a target, which earned him the nickname Wit.

"There were times when I thought adversity was my middle name," he remembers. "Things happened to me that were lifelong lessons. I learned at an early age that I must pick and choose what was right for me and what path I should take. I didn't always choose right, but I was never a follower.

"My independent nature evolved from not taking to be picked on or toyed with. As the youngest for a while, I was the punching bag, I was the 'Go fetch it' boy. My siblings weren't being mean, just older."

He recalls tailing along when his brothers went to the pool to watch girls. Sometimes they pitched him in lakes or rivers shared by venomous copperheads and water moccasins, which created more than a few terror-filled moments.

"They taught me to swim by throwing me in and walking off. The first couple of times they did end up getting me out, but I didn't like the feeling of being helpless, so I started kicking and flapping my arms. Pretty soon, I had my strokes down," recounts Kevin.

He remembers other lessons that shaped him during childhood.

At age four, Kevin begged his mother for some swimming trunks to wear to the creek because he was tired of being laughed at for showing up in his underwear.

"One day, she came home from shopping and threw me this three-pack of shorts. I was so excited that I stripped down and put on a pair of my new 'swimming trunks.' I went strutting my skinny butt out of the house, parading around like I didn't have any sense," he says.

"I went over to a neighbor's house, so proud of them shorts. The bubble burst when the cutest girl in the room said, 'Look, Ma, his wienie is sticking out.' I looked down, and sure enough, there it was. Everyone started laughing. The whole time I had been prancing around, Li'l Kev had been blowing in the wind. I was so embarrassed I hid behind the sofa until my mother came over to get me. She told me to walk straight, head held high, chest poked out, facing my fears."

Another memorable moment was a visit to his grandparents' farm, about one hundred miles away. The drive turned "interesting" once they left the freeway and had to travel over curvy mountain lanes and country dirt roads.

"My father had a little too much to drink and wanted to drive home," says Kevin. "My mother argued that we should stay the night, but he said no, he wanted to leave. In the end, I watched them go, holding on to the promise that my mother would be back to get me.

"After a week of going to bed at 5:00 p.m., then getting up at 3:00 a.m. to do chores and empty chamber pots, I was tired and wanted to go home. I was a city boy and I didn't like all the strange noises coming through my window at night.

"So one morning I wrote my first letter: 'Ma, come and get me,' and I waited on the mail lady. I gave it to her, and the next Saturday morning, Mom was there... Twenty years later, I ran into the mail lady. I walked up and gave her a hug, and we shared a good laugh. I remembered her kindness to a little boy, her compassion."

There were losses over the years, two of the most devastating happened in Kevin's early adulthood. In 1986, at the age of twenty-two, his twin daughter and son were stillborn, and that tragedy led to a divorce. His father died the next year.

Four years later, Kevin was arrested for murder on the night of a third child's one-month birthday. He took parenting classes in prison and tried to stay involved with that son and another baby boy of about the same age from a different mother. However, his ability to connect and influence their decisions was severely limited by his incarceration. The pain of forced separation and lost years that cannot be reclaimed never goes away.

During his almost thirty years of incarceration at Oregon State Penitentiary, Kevin has had four stints in the hole: the first of seven days for a charge of disrespect, the second of twenty-one days for fighting, the third of six months for racketeering, and the fourth of two months for "refusing to snitch."

On the shorter stays, Kevin enjoyed the privacy, something not available in "mainline," or the general population. However, spending half a year in isolation required a determined effort to keep his mind from playing tricks.

"One can get lost within himself," says Kevin of the experience.

Like all things behind the wall, he said the key to retaining his sanity was to fight despair, recriminations, and any thoughts of victimhood.

"I knew the consequences of my actions," says Kevin. "My mind soared with possibilities as I was taking that walk to segregation. Hearing others cheer me on—'stay strong, my brother, keep your head up'—don't mean a damn when those doors clank behind you. Now it's make-or-break time."

His years of service in the Navy had taught him to deal with the solitude of months at sea, and he relied upon that training to get through long days and even longer nights.

"I found comfort writing letters to family members and friends," recalls Kevin. "I stayed to myself, but I noticed others screaming and hollering while they tried to cope after allowing the loneliness to settle in."

He worked out, read, and reflected on who he was and what he wanted to become as a man and human being. "No meds, no extra meals, and no favors."

Some inmates broke down emotionally and mentally in the hole. Kevin watched those tragedies play out, more determined than ever not to lose his own internal battle.

"The difference between those who overcome and the one who caves in is the make of the person," he says. "If you go in telling yourself, 'This is nothing' and start making plans for the day you step out of the darkness, then you have already lost the battle because you never know what may happen from one minute to the next.

"You may get some bad news during mail call that sends you into the deep end, or someone comes by and shit-bombs you and then you are sitting there feeling violated… The worst I have seen is people trying to find solace in medication. They complain about not being able to sleep, allergies, or some mystery ailment, and the institution doesn't care, so they give them meds to shut them up and have the unit quiet. So the slick one is feeling good, so good, he doesn't realize he's getting hooked. Again, no one cares. The convicts are laughing, and the staff is content."

When that inmate is released back into mainline, Kevin says he is hooked on drugs and walks around like a zombie, which sets him up for problems.

"Now, the predators smell blood and weakness. They are going to feed that habit and have that person do some strange things for some change."

His determination not to let the system defeat him helped Kevin emerge from the hole unscathed. "I didn't leave any parts of me inside. I walked into the sunlight mind free and body strong."

Kevin came into prison with a street reputation for being tough and able to defend himself in any situation. However, he says the danger level can get high enough at times to turn him "white around the mouth."

He has found that common sense acquired through past trials and tribulations helps him navigate through those situations and the complexities of prison politics.

"My past is just that," says Kevin. "The good, the bad, the ugly, it's all part of my history. I am not ashamed of anything, only responsible. There is nothing to hide, embellish, or be proud of, just responsible."

Decades ago, he learned several lessons from a baseball coach that stayed with him, including "Never be afraid to speak your truth, regardless of the consequences."

He lives by that creed.

"The positive side of my incarceration is that I have been able to take a deeper look at myself, and I strive to be a better father, grandfather, son, sibling, uncle, and friend," says Kevin. "Others say, 'Give up.' I say, 'Never.'"

There is one lesson he still grapples with—an internal dialogue tied to the reason he is behind bars today.

"How can you prepare to not care or protect?" he asks of the shooting that he insists was done to save the life of his younger brother. "Looking back, maybe I should have walked away, turned my back, and let the chips fall where they may."

Someday, he hopes to lay that question to rest, hopefully from the other side of the wall.

He believes his one-week murder trial was badly bungled because his court-appointed attorney didn't put out the effort to truly defend him. His second attorney came on board to assist in the case the day the trial began, so they didn't have the opportunity to collaborate.

He had an all-white jury and there were no expert witnesses. He was not afforded a forensic investigator to counter the state's evidence. He believes the lack of effort by his attorney was a violation of his Fifth Amendment rights.

"At that time in Portland, Oregon, you could get a black ham sandwich convicted," he says. "But again, I'm not bitter. I am determined to keep telling my story until someone listens."

Kevin has very firm thoughts about how change can happen in the prison system.

"In order for the judicial system to work for all the people, citizens must start standing up for their rights and fight for those who can't fight for themselves. As one voice, the people must demand to be heard. Our laws must have meaning, they must not just be used as political tools to create injustice. It's time for people to stop sitting around complaining and pointing fingers. They need to get up and be heard."

"Building Our Vision of Heaven" by Jorge Cabrera

# I Choose Positive Change

*My brother gave nearly eighteen years, well over half of his life, to the justice system as a prisoner. He was reevaluated under a Second Look statute for youth convicted as adults and conditionally released. He will spend the rest of his life under supervision and can be sent back to prison at any time for an illegal choice.*

*I struggle on. I grind on from the inside while awaiting my chance to contribute on the outside. I have taken, and continue to take, every available opportunity to improve and reform myself. I've participated in classes, groups, seminars, trainings, and discussions to make me better at every turn of my incarceration.*

*I have a stack of certificates to prove it, but I discovered long ago that I am not doing this for me. I figured out that to truly give back, I have to do it for anyone else I can help or prevent from stumbling in the ways I have.*

*The scariest thing about prison when I first got here was the threat of sexual and physical abuse, but the worst thing has been separation from loved ones, followed by the inability to do as I please in life to a certain extent. I suffer from not being able to provide for or assist those I love and care about.*

*When you are locked away in a cell for hours every day, it feels caged, lonely, and sad—like you have been discarded.*

*There is consistent psychological abuse here. There have been many times I've been belittled by staff, talked down to, disrespected, scoffed at, and treated with a general attitude of "I wear gray and you wear blue, so I will always be better than you in every way."*

*The disclaimer here is that staff who act this way, while consistently hurtful, are in the minority. The remainder range from caring deeply* to being apathetic. Many are just here for the paycheck and want to get through their day with the least amount of stress possible.

The one time I remember physical abuse in the criminal justice system was when I was booked after my arrest, and the officer was very aggressive while fingerprinting me, reciting my Oregon Department of Corrections state identification number, which is 12922504. I have existed as this numerical designation since 1998, when I was convicted of murder and unauthorized use of a vehicle—but I will never allow this number to define me.

My poorest choice does not outweigh the sum of all my life choices. I am Josh Cain, and this is my story.

My little brother, Trevor, was fourteen when he was arrested for aggravated murder. Our family thought this country treated kids like kids, but Trevor was remanded to adult court and convicted as though he were a fully developed man.

I had turned eighteen just eight months before the crime occurred, so no remand hearing was required for me. I was automatically sent to adult court for the crime of conspiracy. Even though I was in bed nursing a motorcycle injury when the crime occurred, I was held accountable for having conversations with my brother about the idea of a carjacking in the weeks leading up to its commission.

A law in multiple states, called felony murder, mandates that if someone is guilty of an underlying felony, such as conspiracy to commit robbery, and if that crime ultimately results in a death, the defendant is to be found guilty of murder. This law disproportionately affects youth, as they generally talk with and involve many of their friends in a crime, especially one that ends up costing a life.

In my mind, it had all been just talk. Trev and I engaged in conversations about hitchhiking to the East Coast and securing passage as stowaways on a cargo ship to Amsterdam, where we waxed poetic about becoming the youngest drug-dealer kingpins. That was just kids talking.

And let's not forget our conversation about commandeering a helicopter with a magnet large enough to lift an armored car high enough in the sky to drop it and dash it open like an oversized piggy bank.

It all seemed as realistic as he fantasizing as kids do about becoming a rock star, professional athlete, or astronaut, which is to say, a pipe dream.

*Even though Trevor and I had grown up fast and been raised mostly around adults, we were still very immature. We would ride our motorcycles from one friend's house to another, hitting swimming holes along the way all through the summer before our arrest.*

*We didn't think of consequences, or responsibilities, or obligations. We acted on impulse, lived for each day, and were careless in most regards.*

*While I may have been old enough to vote, I was far from adult, and Trevor was barely starting puberty. The best description that comes to mind is "youthful."*

*Recent brain research and MRI testing prove what most of us already know: that despite what we may think of ourselves and our maturity levels as teens, the parts of our brains that process consequences and logical reasoning don't actually complete development until we are in our late twenties.*

*It turns out that maybe insurance companies are the ones who have actually figured it out because they don't lower rates until young people pass their twenty-sixth birthday.*

*There is a slow realization of this important distinction between youth and adult thinking that is creeping across the nation. A few states are even making changes to laws that once charged kids as adults.*

*However, there are still far too many people in American prisons, youth detention centers, and on parole who were convicted as adults for crimes they committed as children.*

*The US likes to consider itself an advanced country, but the ways in which we imprison our kids is nothing short of archaic and inhumane.*

*When I was a teen, I thought there was no way my brother or I could possibly ever be sent to prison. But the truth is that our grandfather had served time for his choices as an outlaw biker in his younger days, and our dad had been to federal prison for growing pot in the '90s, the height of the war on drugs. Furthermore, we were lower-middle-class and lived in a rural, impoverished area.*

*These things drastically increased our likelihood of ending up incarcerated, but we didn't know that. We just thought everyone did illegal things, most of all the politicians and police tasked with upholding the law.*

*We were raised to deal with our own issues without involving Johnny Law; we distrusted government and authority and believed that* most of the things that happened in action movies were based in reality and, therefore, possible.

That's not to say that we didn't know wrong from right or that we in any way thought murder was acceptable behavior. We just didn't know logically about the consequences of our actions on ourselves, our victim, or our family. We were selfish and shortsighted, which is to say, like every other young person who has not yet grown into adulthood.

However, unlike most other young people, a man was killed before we recognized the gravity of our choices. We have been coming to understand the consequences of those choices, and our brains have been developing into maturity ever since.

We made some horrific decisions as boys; there is no excuse for our behavior. Our remorse is equaled only by our drive to do all we can to make up for those choices and live right every day while trying to prevent others from following our path into criminal behavior and imprisonment.

Regardless of whether the scales can ever be righted, we're doing our best to give back.

I cope with life here by staying busy. My boss arrives to take me to work about 5:35 a.m., and I spend most of the morning in the laundry, fixing machines, ordering parts and supplies, leading a crew of a dozen or more maintenance personnel, training, assisting, counseling, etc. I take time for breakfast and to spend time in the yard for exercise.

I do electrical work and studies to accrue hours toward the electrical apprenticeship I am working through as part of my laundry job. We currently process nearly two million pounds of soiled linen each month with the help of the many millions of dollars' worth of equipment that I am tasked with maintaining.

I choose to work seven days a week for about seven hours a day, though I remain on call around the clock and have left visits to make repairs. I have also had staff come to my cell and wake me in the middle of the night to ask questions about alarms going off and other concerns.

I am a firm believer in hard work, but I also enjoy frequent visits from loved ones. I am among the fortunate minority in that regard, and I believe that strong outside support has kept me out of trouble in here.

Those with no support frequently tell me they feel as though they have less reason to stay out of trouble or try to better themselves while here. They use illicit substances more frequently, go to the hole, and participate less in educational and cognitive opportunities. They seem to have less purpose and a reduced desire to stay out once released.

In the evenings, I attend club meetings or report to the hobby shop for metal- or woodworking. The projects I work on include building trophies, jewelry, wind chimes, and even a silver-encrusted horse bit and a replica of Thor's hammer from the popular Marvel movies.

I am the meeting facilitator on the executive body of the 7th Step Club, which works to reduce recidivism among the population at Oregon State Penitentiary by providing resources and programs to those incarcerated and post-release.

I am also a member of the Lifers Unlimited Club and the Athletic Club, so I assist with fundraising efforts and activities.

On the weekends, I participate in a think tank called Another Chance at Education. In that group, I help steer the direction of the Inside-Out program that allows those in custody who are students to meet with students from the University of Oregon. We coauthor articles and plan educational opportunities for as many prisoners as we can.

Although there is a pretty diverse array of programs here, space is limited in all of them. Waiting lists can be longer than the sentences of some of the people who need programs the most, and those with longer sentences may be restricted from participation because of having too much time remaining.

Another problem is that there are many people who would participate in potentially life-changing programming, but mandatory minimum sentences prevent them from having the incentive to better themselves that earned good time would provide.

It is my belief that more classes to help prisoners develop their education, cognitive skills, work skills, life skills, recovery from addictions, etc., would make us all better off. Crime is usually the result of unmet needs. The more needs we can meet while people are incarcerated, the lower we can drive recidivism rates.

More importantly, the more people we can divert into classes and resources that fill those needs, the fewer costly prison sentences will be imposed, and ultimately, prisons can be largely eliminated.

*My life before prison lacked direction and purpose. While incarcerated, I have earned college degrees, become civically engaged, developed job skills, and overall, have become a better person. All these things could have happened in freedom and may have, given enough time. But I have come to believe that time is time, this life is what I know to be true, and I don't choose to concern myself with what-ifs. I am grateful for who I am, and the life I have lived, incarceration included, has contributed to me being me. So I learn, I write, I share in the hope that I can someday be as good a person as my little brother, the teen killer, because he is not defined by his worst choice, and neither am I.*

*Being behind bars has changed my appreciation for many things, and I won't ever take small things, like driving and swimming, for granted again.*

*I have chosen not to be bitter over the things I have missed across the decades, which are many. I have more patience and more insight than I ever did in freedom. I choose to be changed for the positive and not allow negativity to dictate who I am or who I will be.*

Josh Cain, thirty-eight, has been imprisoned since August 1, 1998. Oregon's mandatory minimum sentencing laws require that he spend three hundred months in prison, with no good time discount and no early parole. He is scheduled to be released on August 1, 2023.

||||||||||||||||||||||||||||||||||||||||||||||||||||||||||||||||||||||||

# Reform Starts With Healing Brokenness

Prisons are full of broken people who don't understand how their behavior has been defined by trauma, and only by helping them heal will you achieve rehabilitation, says Jacqueline "Jackie" Whitt.

"Heck, most people in prison don't even really know how they got there in the first place—and that's honest and true," she says. "The way prisons are set up is to perpetuate the belief that they are filled with really bad people. But in reality, there is only a small percentage of people in prison who are bad."

Jackie served two prison sentences at a women's prison in Oregon for crimes that stemmed from her untreated trauma and undiagnosed mental health issues, which led to drug and alcohol addictions. She was only able to get clean and sober after receiving mental health help that was incredibly challenging to access inside. In addition, she worked at developing a connection to her Higher Power and getting spiritual support from volunteers who sacrificed thousands of hours to help people in custody.

"Being in prison didn't make me better. I got better in spite of prison, and that is not the norm," she says.

Most people go inside and come out having advanced their criminality due to a lack of accessibility to productive opportunities that heal or rehabilitate the spirit or better one's life, she says.

Before sharing more, Jackie reiterated that she believes people need to be held accountable for wrongdoing. And she acknowledges the need for a method of correction. However, she calls what the system is now doing an "atrocity."

Prisons operate in the most punitive and degrading way possible, she says, so broken people are further traumatized by abuses of power.

According to Jackie, the prison staff culture is designed to condescend and humiliate individuals. It is a regular occurrence to have staff speak disparagingly to your face or wait until you are directly in their vicinity to patronize and provoke a response from you.

"It is a common tactic to bait people and incite a reason to take them to segregation."

Severe overcrowding—sometimes exceeding fire marshal code—leaves absolutely no possibility for solitude, quiet reflection, or any kind of privacy.

"I didn't want to be treated like royalty, just as a human being."

The things guards do in the name of safety and security, says Jackie, feel like a refined form of terrorism. Officers are given freedom to implement their own methods of degrading enforcement and outrageous conduct in the name of implementing policy.

"The Department of Corrections seems to welcome behavior that flaunts the power differential and advertises to people in custody whose really in charge."

Even something as little as having your cell "tossed" in routine searches for contraband becomes an opportunity to leave the few possessions of prisoners in ruins.

Officers who like to terrorize those in custody can do so by tearing open people's paperwork, pencil holders, and unopened food packages. They fumble through liquid items and spill lotion or shampoo on their bedding, books, or clean clothing.

They destroy religious items, such as Native American feathers, and pilfer through sacred medicine bags, says Jackie.

"They even seek out meaningless violations, like repossessing cracker boxes that may have been used to store letters from home or miscellaneous items. And then they give people in-custody consequences, or 'conduct reports' for what they call contraband, for repurposing a cracker box."

Conduct reports carry the additional consequences of you being confined to your cell or on your bunk for eight to forty-eight hours or sometimes even longer, she says.

"There are hundreds of ways that corrections officers can target you if they don't like you or if they are just having a bad day. And they get away with it in the name of 'public safety.'"

Jackie describes it as "torturous" to fall under these types of penalties, especially if it makes you miss the weekly phone call home or even yard time with a friend.

"Things can change at the drop of a dime. The only thing you can count on is to not count on anything."

Body searches could be done with dignity, she says, but self-respect is stripped away during that demeaning process, as it is in so many other dealings with guards.

"Staff doesn't care one bit about the ones who are locked down," she says. "When we get to prison, we can't even get counted right. There are so many Hispanic, Native American, and even Black and Asian people who get listed in the data banks as White or Eastern European."

Once again Jackie reiterates, "I know prison is not supposed to be a delight—it's not supposed to be a cakewalk. It is a consequence of breaking the law. I just want there to be justice in the justice system, and I do not believe that asking our community to strive for restorative justice is too much to ask for."

One of the biggest injustices inside, she says, is the way the grievance process plays out.

"It is a total sham, and I have never witnessed a time where exercising this right has gotten a fair outcome," she says. "Matter of fact, just the opposite. To be frank, there are innumerable risks to utilizing this process, so it is not usually sought as a viable option, except to a newcomer who has absolutely no clue of what really happens in the process."

Like many who came before, Jackie was warned not to use the complaint process. She was told that if a person files a grievance, it goes directly back to the officer or staff personnel that it involves. No way could that be possible, she thought.

"I found it really hard to believe that this process could be so blatantly unjust."

Witnessing numerous people reporting misconduct and then having the grievance backfire with excessive force or other retaliatory behavior from the officer named in the complaint—including undeserved stints in segregation—made her a believer.

The first time Jackie witnessed this scenario, her mind immediately took her back to childhood and the numerous times she couldn't defend or protect herself from harmful and abusive authority figures.

She knew at that moment that nothing about prison was safe. And nothing would address the indecency and trifling conduct of corrections staff. There seemed to rarely be any accountability.

Jackie also knew at that moment that people in prison had no rights. She spent a great deal of time, as did the other women, learning and decoding the different tendencies and personalities of officers. She learned to steer clear of some guards.

"Some COs would make an announcement when coming onto the cell block like 'I'm here for the next eight hours. You don't like me. I don't like you. So don't ask me for shit while I'm here. Matter of fact, don't even look at me or I'm celling you in. If you need something, wait till I leave and ask the next shift.'"

If that isn't bad enough, Jackie says medical staff in prisons "really detest humanity."

"People die every day from preventable conditions and refusal to call for outside emergency services," she claims.

"They rarely even listen to the other people in custody who are saying, 'Something is not right with my cellie!' If the infirmary does eventually come and get that person, they just end up suffering solitude. It's beyond belief that the medical board would allow this gross negligence and malpractice to continue.

"It's kind of like people apply for a job at the Department of Corrections, and they are asked, 'Hey, do you hate people?' and if they say, 'Well, yes, I do,' they are told, 'Good, you are hired.'"

Another major problem with the callous and often brutal treatment by guards, says Jackie, is that most women in prison have been longtime victims of domestic violence—and the system becomes just another form of domestic violence.

"How does it benefit women, or anyone for that matter, to be subjected to degrading and humiliating procedures?" Jackie asks. "It's counterintuitive if people want a better society. The way we run prisons in this country goes against every value that America stands for."

If she was in a "good" prison and still faced daily traumatization, Jackie can't imagine the level of abuse in prisons known to be "bad."

Women at her facility were sexually assaulted by guards, doctors, and other inmates, she says. "Sexual misconduct by staff was rampant at that institution. Procedures are not followed to keep women safe, and there are countless areas in the prison where there are no cameras."

In addition to sexual misconduct, Jackie says there were incidents where women slept with guards on the promise that they would be given a pair of metal tweezers or fast food, both considered contraband.

"It's dangerous for many in there. If you don't know or understand prison culture or get someone to explain it, you are going to be prey. Sometimes, even if you do have someone to explain it to you, a seasoned veteran of that system can smell fear or vulnerability a mile away and they are lying in wait. Waiting to gaslight you, manipulate you into compliance or toy with your sanity and your sensibility. They have practiced for years the methods that they will use to break you and to maneuver you to live outside of your value system."

There was not the same high level of violence as is reported in male prisons, but Jackie saw female inmates bullied, extorted, and forced to concede to the demands of predatory prisoners.

"I'm a strong character and I've got survival skills—I'm willing to fight you—so I didn't have a lot of problems," she says. "But people in there with white-collar crimes, such as embezzling or DUI, are going to have a rough time—and sex offenders are always targets."

Jackie says not to "even get her started" on the way that visitors and volunteers are treated, almost as if they are criminals.

"They get disrespected and treated poorly on a regular basis by officers running the visit," she says.

The future prospects of an inmate to receive even the slightest help they need for true reform is tied to an assessment given when they first arrive at the prison. At that time, they have literally been stripped naked and put through the debasing intake process, says Jackie.

"It's given to the women at the worst possible time, when they can't even think or process what is being said or asked of them. While their whole lives are collapsing around them and toxic stress floods their psyche."

This battery of tests determines the risk level of the inmate, and those rated lower do not get into programs that could help them turn their life around.

"If you don't do the testing, they force you to go to segregation, but if you do take it, you are doing so when your life is in ruins, and you are stressed beyond measure about what is happening with your kids, how you are going to get everything out of your home before the eviction notice arrives, or how you are going to survive this season of your life in prison," says Jackie. "You are absolutely at the worst moment in your life, and that is when decisions are being made that will affect the rest of your life."

If you are able to get a job inside, the abusive treatment continues with you being used as slave labor, said Jackie.

Employment is where brainwashing starts—residents are tricked into believing that $40–$50 a month is a good-paying job.

When Jackie was inside, the best paying job was $69 per month. The prison received about $35,000 per adult in custody from the state and the wage for that individual when contracted out to the state was probably about the same, she says.

For example, she says there was a Department of Motor Vehicles call center at her prison. She looked up the average wage of a DMV worker in Oregon and found it to be $35,000–$69,000 per year. In addition, the person is in a union position, so benefits are good on the outside and nonexistent inside.

People calling the DMV are unlikely to know that they are being assisted by prisoners who are working full-time for $69 per month, says Jackie.

She said residents of prison do most of the work, like cooking, cleaning, canteen, maintenance, yard work, laundry, plumbing, and electrical. "They get paid peanuts, so the system really profits from their exploitation."

She said furniture produced at some federal prisons is sold for a good profit, especially when so little is paid for the labor.

"It's a racket," says Jackie. "They could at least pay us a decent wage so we could pay off restitution to our victims, maybe some of our court fines, or send some money home to our children—or even save up for our release to lessen the burden on society."

She has become an activist for prison reform since getting clean and sober seven years ago and going through dialectical behavioral therapy to turn her weaknesses into strengths.

Jackie is the first to say that she had a lot to work through.

"The reality was that I was in prison before I was in prison," she says of being trapped in a cycle of addiction and domestic violence. "I had self-destructive core beliefs that continually sabotaged my life."

In addition to that, Jackie's life skills were all about survival. She also lived in perpetual crisis due to an inability to set boundaries with people, places, and things.

Raised with a multitude of different caregivers in her life, Jackie lived with her mom's loving adopted parents from time to time while her drug-addicted parent was in prison. Other times, it was with friends and neighbors and even group and foster homes.

She never met her father, who was Native American. His story was very tragic, with both parents being killed when he was young. It seemed as though trauma, grief and loss, alcohol, and prison followed him throughout his life, says Jackie.

She is grateful to know that her father was clean and sober when he passed away at a mission in Utah.

Although she has two older sisters, Jackie says their abusive father convinced a court that their mother had abandoned them and won custody when they were very young. They grew up being told by their father that their mom didn't care about them.

Exposed to epic dysfunction from the time she was born, Jackie was immersed in the world of domestic violence, untreated trauma, drugs and alcohol, and inevitably, criminality.

Her mom had grown up in the '60s and gave that as an excuse for the many bad things that happened in their home, says Jackie.

Sexual abuse from a long line of stepdads and her mom's male friends was prevalent in Jackie's childhood. She began to learn people on a very dark and sinister level. Each had his own fantasy to recreate with her body, and nobody seemed to acknowledge the strangeness of situations, she says.

"I watched them all [adults in her life] do a lot of stupid things, and I didn't want to be one of them. I watched them do despicable things in the spirit of chasing drugs and crime. I said on so many occasions, 'If I ever had kids, I will never do anything to hurt them.'"

Ironically, she ended up making many of the same foolish decisions despite vowing, "It will never be me."

Determined to do crime the "right way," Jackie thought she could operate "moderately" and make just enough money to stop after a while.

"Of course, that never happens when you do crime for a living," she says. "There is always another need, another goal, another crisis, another asset, another project, another business situation you need money for. It never ends until you are arrested."

Jackie recalls how her descent into addiction began.

She and the father of her three kids had been together for about ten years. He had also come from drug-addicted parents but, thankfully, had been adopted by his father's loving parents. His childhood was "okay" until his grandmother passed away from cancer, which had an incredible impact on his life.

Jackie and her boyfriend got together pretty young and tried to do well as a family. Many things got in the way of that, first was trying to sell drugs while raising three babies that came less than a year apart.

"So many things can go wrong for young people who do not have solid guidance and mentorship," says Jackie.

Her partner began dabbling with powder cocaine. Being in that lifestyle also brought promiscuity, says Jackie, and he had another child outside of their relationship. She felt disoriented by all the lies.

"I felt furious, betrayed and confused," she explains. "It went against the set of values I had at that time, as backward as they were. So I gave him an ultimatum, told him that we just couldn't be together anymore."

However, her boyfriend promised to stop using drugs if she would try cocaine with him one time, in the hopes that Jackie wouldn't judge him afterward. Reluctantly, she conceded—and that was truly the beginning of the end.

She was about thirty when she first tried cocaine, which she instantly loved.

"All of our problems just seemed to melt away," she says. "I even fell back in love with my kids' father, and it felt as if our love was renewed."

Eventually, their drug-induced reality began to catch up with them.

"We became paranoid, thought we were being followed by helicopters," she says. "I constantly felt as if we were being followed and investigated."

At that point, she knew that survival meant leaving the relationship.

In an effort to get her life back on track, Jackie moved into one of the houses the couple had acquired for growing marijuana (pot was illegal at that time).

"We were still kinda together but not really," she says.

Then her boyfriend hooked up with a family member, and Jackie was destroyed by the betrayal. The sense of rejection and abandonment sent her into a tailspin.

"I didn't know it at the time, but I was having some sort of mental collapse. All the years of abuse, untreated trauma, toxic stress, gaslighting, and now this—the deepest of betrayals."

It felt as though she had lost everything at once. First, her heart, then her identity, then her assets, then her sanity, and finally, her hope and will to live.

"It's a miracle I made it through those times," she recalls.

Jackie began to drink heavily and sometimes she lost track of reality. Twice she was hospitalized for alcohol poisoning.

"I remember sitting on the couch for almost a year. The world was going on without me. And I would wonder at times why no one in my life was saying anything about the fact that I wasn't showering, I wasn't eating, I wasn't functioning."

She had always been the matriarch of the family, the one everyone came to for help, so it made no sense to Jackie that everyone seemed okay with her devolving right in front of their eyes.

"I just couldn't believe that no one was coming for me, so I just sat there staring at a blank TV screen."

Criminal behavior of one type or another supported the family.

The incident that changed everything for Jackie and led her spirit to scream for help was her daughter climbing on the back of the sofa one day and continually bumping her back.

"I asked her what the hell she was doing and told her to get down," says Jackie. "She started to cry and told me that she was just trying to hang Christmas lights. I was shocked—it had just been the Fourth of July."

Although she apologized to her daughter, Jackie felt dead inside.

"By that time, I didn't care if I lived. I would wake up and say, 'Oh no, another day!'"

Deep in the recesses of her mind, a story emerged about how a man was stranded in a house surrounded by deep floodwaters. He prayed for help and a boat floated by, but the man didn't snag it because he was trusting God to get him out of the predicament.

Twice more he was given access to some type of help, but he turned it down. When his supplies ran out and the man finally died, he approached the pearly gates in anger.

"Why didn't you rescue me?" he demanded of God.

"I tried, I sent you help three times, but you refused to take it," answered the Creator.

For some reason, that story got Jackie moving and she walked outside in what seemed like blinding sunlight to find a way to a treatment center.

"I was hungover, and I could hardly move," she says. "I had to block the sun so I could see—it was like I was pushing through fire."

Her hair was oily and matted, and she looked like death warmed over, but Jackie was suddenly desperate for help.

An old friend who was driving by stopped to inquire about her welfare.

"Are you okay?" he asked, shocked by her appearance.

"I need treatment. Where do I go for treatment?" Jackie implored over and over.

The man steered her toward a bus, and she got on board and asked the driver the same question.

Although he didn't know exactly where the treatment facility was, the driver arranged for Jackie to transfer to another bus that would take her to the nearest St. Vincent DePaul center that helped people in recovery and the homeless.

"People on that bus were genuinely concerned for me, and I'm sure I looked crazy," recalls Jackie.

She began to shake and get nauseous from the absence of alcohol, but she pressed on in her goal to find help.

When she arrived at the center, Jackie begged and pleaded for treatment but was told that she needed to get on a wait list and follow a process to get help. "I told them, 'No, you've got to take me. I can't go back where I was.'"

After sharing heavy parts of her testimony and why she was desperate for help, staffers at the facility to begin making arrangements for her to get inpatient care.

While they were working toward that end, Jackie began to experience nausea, shaking, and both hot flashes and chills from not having alcohol in her system.

She was in a vicious detox and desperate to feel better. She stumbled out into the street, wincing once again at the blaring sun, and then noticed a bar in the distance. When she got inside, she pulled $50 from the wad of several hundred dollars in her pocket.

"I put the money on the bar and said, 'I need a double,'" she recalls.

After she had downed two doubles, the lady behind the bar told her to leave.

Jackie stumbled back onto the street with despair right behind her. She felt pummeled by the rays of sun shining down on her head.

"I just stood there, listing from side to side like an old war-hardened battleship. I felt aimless, desperate."

Relief from alcohol surging through her being led her spirit to resume its cry for help. Tears poured down her cheeks, and she prayed the opportunity to get help hadn't been lost.

Jackie made a beeline for the door of the treatment center and fell through the entrance with a hopeful, "Have you called my name yet?"

Relief flooded her heart when they said, "No, we are still looking. Don't you disappear on us now."

She let out a gasp of gratitude and took her seat by the window. "I'll be right here." She says that moment was one of tears and exhaustion.

For two months, Jackie was in a treatment center—until she was kicked out for aggression and hostility.

"I stood up for a lady who was being bullied, but they said I did it too aggressively," she says.

"I was very angry because I had used my skills. I had used the process they taught me and tried to talk the bully out of it, but she continued with the disrespect."

Her trauma and abandonment issues came roaring to life when she was rejected by the center, says Jackie.

Back on the streets, she immediately hooked up with a smooth-talking man who offered her safety, security, and a place to live.

"He was like a knight in shining armor who had come to save me," she remembers.

She ignored all the red flags of an abuser, including her new boyfriend's possessive and controlling nature.

"I was so desperate and dejected and this person was giving me love and attention."

Soon, she was drinking again to deal with all the abuse and toxic stress of the new relationship. It was too much to bear when she saw her partner smoking crack. Her world crumbled.

"It felt like my knees were going to buckle," she said. "I had just thought he was a regular drug dealer, but he was a user, too. How was this relationship ever going to get better?'

Things went from bad to worse as her relationship became more abusive and their criminal behavior ramped up.

Ten months later, Jackie landed in prison for stealing cars. She was thirty-one and spent thirteen months behind bars.

Constant noise and bad smells are her most prevalent memories of that time.

"You cram all these broken people in a tiny little space, and it is just a horrible experience," she says.

Jackie didn't qualify for programs because she hadn't scored high enough on the intake assessment as a potential threat to others. Plus, she had served some county time and that affected her out date.

"I was in shock, so for thirteen months, I just sat around. I got out of that place without any real treatment or any place to go."

She said recovery programs offered by prisons are inadequate because they do not help the inmate work through the issues that led to addiction—that is, unless you get a bed in a treatment dorm.

Shortly after her release, Jackie returned to prison for twenty-six months, and this time she began to figure some things out.

"I lacked impulse control, and I really needed mental health help," she says. "When you grow up with a lot of trauma, undiagnosed ADHD and PTSD, you don't know why you do the things you do."

She said there is such a stigma on getting treatment that people are reluctant to admit to problems, despite the fact that most families have a loved one with issues. "We need to start calling it mental hygiene."

And while we're at it, argues Jackie, ADHD should be called something like neurodiversity so people don't feel ashamed of that very common condition.

Her faith evolved during incarceration, and Jackie believes that is something missing among prisoners that has the power to lift them to higher levels of thought. She said, with faith, the loneliness of prison becomes a time of solitude and quiet reflection.

"It doesn't have to be Christianity," she says of the need for diverse spiritual services inside.

"My faith played a big part in my healing. It made me feel like I didn't have to prove myself ever again. I don't have to take on everything or every offense."

Continued counseling has helped Jackie, now forty-five, recover not only enough to stay away from drugs and alcohol but to become an advocate for others.

"I have learned that the things people do out of trauma have nothing to do with me and I don't have to react," she says.

Repairing the damage that her problems inflicted on her children is an ongoing process.

"I remember saying that if I had kids, I would never abandon them, I'd never chase alcohol, I'd never chase drugs," she says. "Then I realized that I had done the same thing as my mom—only I was worse because I knew what it was like to have someone in prison and she didn't."

Reentering society after incarceration is very stressful because you feel like an alien in an unknown world.

"When I came home, it was very strange, it didn't feel natural," she says.

To make matters worse, people coming back into society are flooded with problems to deal with because the time they were behind bars did not make their issues go away. They still owe on unpaid utility bills and back rent, and getting a driver's license again is a nightmare.

"When I finally got my license after twenty-seven maneuvers, I thought that's one situation down, another 137 to go," says Jackie.

Many people with a true intent to change their lives end up failing because they can't navigate a hostile world beset with stigmas, so they go back to what they know.

"I think all people should get six months of government assistance when they get out so they have time to adjust," Jackie says.

Society also needs to deal with the fact that prisons are filled with people of color, and the system is racist at heart, she contends.

"I am part Native American, but I look white. When I was young and my four black friends and I got arrested, they believed what I was telling them even though I was the one who gave them a fake name because I was the only white girl. That was how we survived the system when we got into trouble together."

She now advocates on behalf of tribal cultural and spiritual issues in prison and for women who have been incarcerated due to brokenness that led them to make bad choices in men.

Jackie joins Trevor Walraven, a youth offender, and other former prisoners in pushing for overall changes in the criminal justice system.

"I am issuing a compassionate call to action. One way or the other, the prison population is everybody's problem. If we don't start steering this system toward restorative justice, communities will continue to bear the weight of this burden. What are we going to do about it?"

||||||||||||||||||||||||||||||||||||||||||||||||||||||||||||||||||||||

# Part III
# The Row: Traumatization
# Of Juries

It isn't just the families of defendants and victims who have trouble coping with the delivery of a death sentence, juries can also suffer a huge psychological toll, says Janvier Slick, a retired licensed clinical social worker.

She has debriefed and counseled juries since 1999, including those involved in capital murder cases. Over time, Slick has come to see people who serve on these juries as unrecognized victims of the criminal justice system.

She says jurors deciding whether a defendant should be executed have to live with that verdict for the rest of their lives, and many have trouble coping with the choice they made.

Both defense attorneys and prosecutors want jurors to emotionally connect with their side of the case. Witnesses portray the defendant as a son, father, or husband and talk about his achievements and even his life challenges. Photos of the victims and testimony from distraught family members bring that person's presence into the courtroom.

The jury gets to know the victim and the defendant, so the case becomes personal, says Slick.

"I started doing this because a judge identified in one particular case that jurors appeared to be struggling. I think they make a conscientious effort to make the best decision within the constraints of the law and the death penalty ups the ante on the trauma they will experience."

In capital cases, as well as other tough criminal and civil matters, Slick offers jurors an opportunity to share feelings and concerns.

"I just appreciate the difficulty that they recognized what they needed to do but didn't necessarily want to do. I think our jury system is pretty amazing. I am so impressed by how engaged people are in the process."

She spent thirty years in the field of child welfare and underwent specialized training in PTSD that proved valuable when she went to work for Jury Resources Inc. of Salem, Oregon.

"Jurors are unconsidered casualties in death penalty cases. The impact on them in the immediate and long term should be included in any consideration of ending executions," she says.

That same conclusion has been reached by the Capital Jury Project (CJP), a consortium founded in 1991 and supported by the National Science Foundation. The goal of the continuing research program has been to examine the decision-making of juries in death penalty cases within the US to determine if they conform to the constitution.

The findings of CJP determined that jurors may not understand all the legal terms used in trials and may be uncertain about their alternatives in making decisions.

Race also seems to play a factor in verdicts. According to CJP, if the defendant is white, the jury is more likely to evaluate him as mentally unstable than if he were black. Also, the jury is more likely to view the defendant as dangerous if the victim was white.

Some jurors openly admit to racial prejudice, reported CJP, and some unknowingly voice racially prejudiced beliefs.

The race of the victim plays a big role in whether the jury finds mitigating factors that would allow a lesser sentence than the death penalty, say CJP researchers.

Also troubling are findings by CJP that jurors are often confused or misled by the judge's instructions to the jury. People serving on the panel appear to make decisions from personal experience and personal moral guidelines instead of just considering the evidence.

Fifty percent of jurors interviewed by researchers admitted to making death penalty decisions before the penalty phase of the trial had begun, and 45 percent said they did not understand they could consider any mitigating evidence during the penalty phase, not just the factors listed in the judge's instructions.

One researcher from CJP reported that patterns emerging from data reflected that jurors had serious misconceptions about the death penalty process, which appeared to have led to confusion that produced a bias in favor of the death penalty.

The conclusion of CJP was that the jury decision-making process in the US is so flawed that constitutional principles are being violated. The group's research continues.

Slick says jurors have expressed frustration to her about learning in news reports after a trial that they had not been given information in the case that could have changed their decision.

"They are very aware that someone's life is in their hands, and they don't take that lightly."

Slick's observations have made her a strong opponent of the death penalty, in part, because of the effect on juries.

Now on the board of directors for Oregonians for Alternatives to the Death Penalty, she helped compile a booklet to illustrate why reform is necessary.

"This was something I felt needed to be done for educational purposes and I retired five years ago from DHS, so I had the time to do it," she says.

The booklet *Not in Our Name* includes stories from murder victims' families who found that the execution of the killer did not aid in their healing.

Somehow there has been a faulty belief in our vengeance-oriented culture that putting a killer to death brings peace to the family because "justice has been served," writes Sister Helen Prejean, a Roman Catholic nun and leading advocate of abolition.

She is known for her bestselling book *Dead Man Walking* (1993) about her experiences with two convicts on death row for whom she served as a spiritual advisor before their executions.

"If there is a lesson about believing in the sanctity of each life, it is that there are no exceptions. Without a death penalty, there is room for the murderer to fully repent," wrote Prejean.

One of the essays of *Not in Our Name* is penned by Aba Gayle, the mother of a murdered child who struggled with grief, rage, and a desire for revenge.

Twelve years after the death of her nineteen-year-old daughter, Catherine Blount, in 1980, Gayle wrote a letter of forgiveness to the man convicted of her murder, Douglas Mickey, who was on death row in California.

"When I put that letter in the mailbox, all the anger, rage, and deep ugliness that I had carried around in my body for twelve years was instantly gone," wrote Gayle. "In its place I was filled with love and joy and inner peace. I then knew I did not need another human being to be killed by the state so that I could be healed."

Slick says her research for the booklet confirmed that people can forgive even the worst tragedies. "If these families can find in it themselves to do so, then shouldn't we as a society learn from their example?"

*Not in Our Name* can be found on the OADP's website, www. oadp.org.

"My hope is that this booklet gets people's attention and makes them supportive of reform," says Slick. "I'm really starting to see a shift. I'm hopeful. It's crazy what we are doing to people, and it's time to do something different."

Untitled by Allen Howard

||||||||||||||||||||||||||||||||||||||||||||||||||||||||||||||||||||||

# Chasing A Rainbow Is Better Than Reality

*My name is Lee Knoch and I was convicted of aggravated murder and various assault and theft charges. All of my crimes are against one man, twice my age, whom I had known since I was fourteen years old.*

*I was given forty years under M11, followed by five life-without-parole sentences. Jail and house arrest started January 9, 1996, when I was eighteen, and I got to Oregon State Penitentiary in May 1998.*

*What led to my life of incarceration was that I didn't trust anyone. I didn't communicate well, and folks never seemed to listen to my side of things. Because others never seemed to believe me, I lost all expectation that they would.*

*My story takes place between late 1995 and May 1997.*

*I was a very square teenager, working in landscaping, construction, and auto repair with my Dad in the manufactured home transport and setup business. I never smoked and drank or gambled. I never used any form of narcotics. All of my friends were either good kids or working-class men and women. The one exception was my friend, Robert, who fancied himself a militia-type person.*

*I had first met him when I was fourteen and he was twenty-eight. He was a coworker of my nineteen-year-old friend Tara. Robert was reckless and flaunted convention—and that sort of appealed to me. After a couple of years, I met someone and grew out of my friendship with Robert.*

*In the summer of 1995, my Dad was in an accident, ending the better part of my employment. Robert got himself into some kind of trouble and we begin running together again. He was afraid for his life and intent on hiding out. His situation was outrageous and unbelievable.*

Robert tried to draft me for a robbery plot at his former workplace. When I backed out, he was markedly hostile. I was still living at home with Dad and Robert kept hanging around there off and on for weeks in December and January. We had several altercations during that time, but they never amounted to much and we remained on cordial terms. He still demanded my help.

During that time, he obtained $20,000 in cash and gave it to me with instructions to deliver it to his ex-fiancé. I took the money but did not deliver it as I was told, at first intending to return it to Robert's family. I told Robert I had delivered it and nothing bad had happened.

I showed off the money to my friends, pretending it was mine. Eventually, I began to rationalize that no one would be able to prove that it wasn't mine because the transaction must have been illegal anyway.

On January 6, 1996, Robert showed up at Dad's place with extensive injuries. He was back on January 9, demanding money, and I bounced him out. The police picked him up a little while later that day, and he told all about the money and attributed every one of his injuries exclusively to his altercations with me, carefully omitting his role in starting the fight and denying he had ever had trouble with anyone else.

I was completely blindsided by the assault charges, and I never really tried to defend myself. By the time I was convinced I needed to tell my side of things. I was represented by an attorney who insisted that we keep my story secret so the prosecution wouldn't know what we had. But that was only the first stage, and before long, my attorney wanted me to plead guilty without telling my side to one count of assault one with an eight-and-a-half-year prison sentence.

Meanwhile, Dad posted bail using the insurance payoff for his totaled semitruck. My attorney told us that pleading guilty would forfeit the bail money to the victim—who my Dad had hated with a passion from the very first day he met him. I was on house arrest and could only drive back and forth to work.

As a year wore on, my attorney's investigator uncovered a lot about Robert's past. He was a thoroughly bad guy. It made me embarrassed to have been his friend. But as he had been designated the crime victim, none of this was admissible in court.

*Meanwhile, the district attorney was presenting Robert as an inno-*
*cent simpleton who, by no agency of his own, had fallen under my evil*
*teenage genius.*

*I had to notify the county where I was working, and they, in turn,*
*notified Robert. He and his friends started coming around my workplace,*
*threatening me, Kristen (my girlfriend), and Dad, who called the attor-*
*ney. The attorney warned us that any contact with Robert, no matter*
*who initiated it, would likely be the end of my release on bail, and we*
*could lose Dad's money to boot.*

*I broke up with Kristen, my first love, to get her out of harm's way,*
*and the next thing I knew, she and Robert were having an affair. In*
*January 1997, Robert or one of his friends drove up alongside me on my*
*way home from work and opened fire with a handgun. I was wounded*
*and had to go to the hospital, putting me out of work until the trial.*

*The state police detective commented that the gunman was "shoot-*
*ing to kill." I was afraid to tell the investigators about my pending legal*
*issues or my belief that Robert was the shooter because I was afraid the*
*county would revoke bail and confiscate Dad's money.*

*My trial date was set for April 1, 1997. We got a call on the first*
*Friday afternoon in March, telling us my attorney had been removed*
*from the case and replaced with an attorney unknown to us. At the same*
*time, the trial date was moved up to March 18.*

*When we met the new attorney, he warned me that if I did not*
*take the plea agreement, forfeiting Dad's bail money, the court intended*
*to impose the maximum sentence for every charge on the indictment,*
*equaling over forty years in prison.*

*The attorney said he was completely unable to defend the case and*
*considered the long sentence to be a foregone conclusion if I did not forfeit*
*the money.*

*I murdered Robert on March 16 and was arrested ten days later. I*
*did not deny my crime, but I could not take a plea agreement on the aggra-*
*vated murder charge because Dad's bail money was still in contention.*

*The court imposed an insanity defense over my objections at the*
*urging of the court-appointed attorney. The result was that I was found*
*guilty and sentenced to life-without and all of the prison terms for the*
*first case.*

*From the very start, I expected that everyone was against me and determined to do their worst. If I would have trusted that folks would believe me and would treat me fairly, I would have argued strongly about the need to return Dad's bail money and refuted the accusations from the beginning. If I would have been more worldly, I very well may have secured a resolution that did not lead me down the road to murder.*

*What really bothered me about prison was the thought of losing all my friends. I missed them terribly for a long time. But I hated for them to see me and think of me like this. I imagined that they felt guilty for not writing or visiting more. So I tried to disengage as much as I could.*

*When I was in isolation in the Lincoln County Jail for several months, it was particularly bad for me as I was right off the street and unaccustomed to imprisonment and idle time. I have always been mildly claustrophobic, so it took all my willpower to overcome the anxiety in the first days.*

*In prison, I was in isolation in the Disciplinary Segregation Unit (DSU) and then in the Intensive Management Unit (IMU) for almost five years, from March 1, 2001, to November 2005, for escape. Throughout this ordeal, I was told that I would be kept in isolation for the rest of my life. I was only released when the counselor in charge was transferred and replaced.*

*The time in DSU and IMU was so long that it went through many stages. It should be understood that, while the isolation and noise of IMU was unpleasant to me, I was personally able to cope with the conditions and the supposedly perpetual duration of my time there.*

*My distress sprang from my inward doubts and the uncertainty of a life-without sentence rather than the isolation.*

*Deprivation of human contact gradually refocuses the mind inward. Abstract concepts and fantasies become the subject of life. I became zealous for my thoughts and my time thinking, refusing meals, showers, and "recreation" time to focus on the thoughts I was entertaining. For more than three months, I refused any time out of the cell and took meals only when I felt I really had to. I fasted for days at a time and prayed for interminable durations through days and nights.*

*There is a whole other mode of existence and a whole other ideal version of oneself that exist as thought and that is what I explored in the hole.*

*I am told that I am being punished for my crimes and the punishment will never end. A punishment that doesn't end seems absurd to me. My greatest fear is that the punishment really will not end, and I will have no chance to rebuild what I had before.*

*Every moment of this will be worth it if I can get out and find someone and have friends in a home again. But I feel that it would be better to have passed away long ago if this is the way it has to be until the bitter end.*

*By far, the worst part of my prison experience has been the absence of women in my life. I am an only child from a very rural homestead. I am shy and quiet, and as a teen, I was always out of sorts among strangers. Having an intimate partner made up for my shortcomings and eased my doubts and unhappiness in life. She made up for my poor communication and made me feel confident and comfortable in every setting. I really needed that, and I have not felt right without her.*

*Other than that, the isolation from folks I have things in common with has also been a constant stress. I enjoy art and cinema. I am an avid reader of history and philosophy, and I write frequently on these subjects. These subjects are not much appreciated among prisoners, and so I have no one to talk to about the things I enjoy.*

*During my time in prison, I have remembered much clearer what I think about and feel rather than what is going on around me. The days all run together in months and years. Extraordinary events stand out, but the content of each day is inaccessible to my conscious memory. My clearest memories are of my own thoughts.*

*I live in the privileged cell block and have worked in the activities department for almost seven years as the facilitator of a self-help group. My job is to keep current the attendance rosters, purchase orders, contact list, and self-help material for the narcotics anonymous group.*

*We usually have around 250 members in the prison and dozens who have been released but stay in contact.*

*What is life like for inmates who have no support on the outside? This has been a bad one for me. I spent many years with no help on the outside. I was never even on the phone for more than fifteen years. I don't need money. I've never had a craving for junk food or fancy shoes.*

*The $50 I make each month pretty much covers anything I could want in here. But I have wanted to publish my writings for over fifteen years. It is absolutely impossible to do anything from here. I have spent years of my life racking my brain about how I could go about initiating a program that permits prisoners to publish what they're writing, but there is just no way without help from the outside.*

*I cannot imagine a world where there would be enough of the right kinds of programs for prison. The way things are done in our system cost way too much and are devised by people with no experience in the conditions they want to address. The transition from prison to freedom should begin the day someone gets to prison.*

*Currently, a prisoner has zero responsibility all the way up to their release date. Often prisoners do not even have time off for good behavior to lose for irresponsible acts. They remain in this condition of no responsibility until the day they are released, when they are suddenly assigned all the responsibilities of a free citizen and even more than most if you count the post-prison supervision system.*

*If every prisoner earned a major responsibility (meaning that his actions remained a factor in his fortunes), he would be more inclined to develop the habits of a successful person. Moreover, these should more gradually shift to real-world responsibilities rather than converting from bureaucratic programs to real life on the single day that he is released.*

*To my knowledge, very few of Oregon's prisoners reenter the community in graduated steps. Few work release or halfway house programs exist. There are no legislative provisions to convert part of the prison sentence into a reentry program. If the current thinking were to turn itself to this, I fear it would make a mess of it.*

*The number one thing that has to change is no more never-ending sentences. It is a horrible part of my life, facing a completely unknown future every day since the mid-1990s. A life-without sentence is not experienced like any other prison sentence. In moments of fantasy, I imagine that something has changed, and I have an end date to this ordeal. When I think of the upcoming reforms and I imagine that my life actually could change, I think of all the educational opportunities I would immediately seek. I have been down for over twenty years now, and even if the end date were ten or more years away, it would be an instant relief. No number of years is psychologically the same as "Never!"*

*There should be a universal second look or parole for everyone after half of their sentence or every two years after twenty years for longer sentences. I do fear that a second look or a chance for parole would be like chasing a rainbow and I may never get out—but it would be infinitely better than* never.

||||||||||||||||||||||||||||||||||||||||||||||||||||||||||||||||||||||||

# Stigma Makes Reentry Difficult

A woman who had served more than five years behind bars went into a store after she was released to buy hygiene products and had a meltdown because there were too many choices to make.

"She told me she felt stupid. She knew it was ridiculous to break down over something like deodorant, but she couldn't handle all the options," says Hilary Young, vice president of advocacy and philanthropy for Pioneer Human Services, a Seattle-based nonprofit that helps people with reentry.

"When people are incarcerated, they are told when to wake up, when to eat, when to shower—everything is so structured, there is no room for independent decision-making."

The longer a person is inside, the more difficult his or her adjustment to the free world will be, says Young.

If people have been incarcerated for decades, they also struggle to master technological challenges and cope with the fast pace of today's world.

"It can be overwhelming even when you have support, and it's even worse for those who don't," Young says. "You can really feel lost in the world."

In addition, many prisoners have been traumatized by their experiences behind the wall and need time to heal.

Young says cognitive behavioral therapy is a huge component of success on the outside because conflict resolution is vastly different than inside, where most problems are settled on a primal level.

Major contributors to personality changes in prison are lack of privacy, frequent fear, the need to wear a constant mask of invulnerability (to avoid exploitation by others), and the requirement to follow externally imposed rules and routines day by day.

"When you say that people who have been incarcerated need time to heal, people think you are crazy, but the idea that everyone inside is a hardened criminal with no emotions is not true," says Young.

She said the puritanical mindset of American culture makes it difficult for prisoners to reenter the outside world and succeed at building a new life.

"As a society, we don't want to give people with felonies a job, and we don't want them living in our neighborhoods, but we're quick to say, 'Get your act together,'" says Young. "They are discriminated against at every turn, and their crime becomes their defining characteristic. At what point does punishment end? People do not stay the same, we cannot waste human potential by punishing them forever."

Pioneer primarily serves the western side of Washington, which is where the majority of the population lives, but provides a range of services in Spokane, a large city located on the east side of the state.

Even though the organization helps nearly ten thousand people a year find housing and employment, Young says there is not enough funding and manpower to meet the demand for services.

Washington has twelve prisons—ten for men and two for women—so hundreds of people are being released daily with very limited options for help and support, says Young.

"People need somewhere to go, people who will help them," she says.

Pioneer gets some federal and state funds for its job readiness programs, among others, but there are limitations on what public dollars can be used for, says Young.

Helping people write resumes, learn interview skills, or get the clothes they need to work in the business world and providing transportation to jobs are some of the practical needs that Pioneer can meet with other donations.

Due to the scope and scale of client needs, Pioneer partners with other organizations that are working toward the same ends.

If people coming out of prison don't get the help they need, Young says they are more likely to seek out past friendships and fall back into old habits, which will land them in trouble with the law again. So it is vital that someone help them build a proactive new life.

Toward that end, Pioneer successfully worked with other advocacy partners to get a bill approved that allows people to get a certification of rehabilitation on a background check, which will aid them in getting jobs or housing.

"We need society to see former prisoners as people and treat them like people," says Young. "At Pioneer, we believe that people have limitless potential and can change— -we are all more than our worst mistake."

Part of her advocacy role is to lobby for changes in laws that stigmatize people.

There are many old laws that discriminate against felons, such as not allowing anyone who has served time to be a barber, and Young says it is time to get these rules off the books.

"On a societal level, we can come together to change laws— especially laws that don't make sense."

The problem with gaining public support for big changes, such as sentencing reform, says Young, is that most citizens are unaware of what people go through when they are in prison or they believe someone should suffer endlessly for the harm they have done.

With one in three American families having a loved one with a criminal record, she says it should not be as difficult as it is to transform the justice system, but the climb is steep to get any meaningful reforms in place.

"Show me one person who doesn't know someone struggling with mental health or addictions who hasn't had some run-in with the law. If you see that person as someone with value, why can't you show others in prison that same grace? At some point, we have to be willing to give people second chances and not just say it."

Helping former prisoners succeed isn't just a humanitarian cause; it's also a public safety issue when the vast majority of people will one day be released and the odds they will reoffend are high if they return to the only lifestyle they know, says Young.

"We have to attack this on multiple levels. We need help to get more people into programs while the legislature is working on the heavy lifts of policy changes. There's definitely work to do on every front."

Women are the fastest-growing segment of the prison population, and Young says society seems to view them as less "scary" and be more forgiving than they are of males, but there is still a lack of services to help them and their children.

"Most of these women come from backgrounds with a history of neglect and sexual and physical abuse, and many were young mothers—the stories are just so sad," she says.

Pioneer was established in 1963 by Jack Dalton, who served time at Washington State Penitentiary, and is now the largest provider of reentry services in the state.

After graduation from the Roadmap to Success program, former prisoners can apply for open positions within one of Pioneer's enterprises or seek jobs with external employers that Pioneer partners with in the community.

Many choose to apply to Pioneer's sheet metal fabrication facility that manufactures for the aerospace and commercial industries. Boeing, a multinational corporation with large-scale operations in Seattle, is one of its major customers.

Students can also apply for open positions with Pioneer's food services division or aerospace distributions center.

While preparing clients to reenter society, Pioneer teaches them what they need to disclose and what their privacy rights are when an employer or landlord asks questions about their criminal background.

People who have been incarcerated and are interested in reform frequently speak at events to educate people, but they are always told by Pioneer, "You have the right to your story. You don't have to answer any questions that make you uncomfortable."

"Telling their story can retraumatize them as a person over and over again," says Young. "However, some people find it therapeutic and say it gives them confidence, so they just need to feel comfortable about it."

Education is the key to true change, she says. Society appears to be more empathetic about the plight of prisoners now than it was decades ago. There is societal awareness that something needs to change, and documentaries and television shows such as *Orange Is the New Black* help portray people in prison as human beings with introspective thoughts and feelings.

However, Young says in most programs, the past criminal behavior of a character is still a huge part of his or her role.

"I feel like we'll know we have made it when we see people on sitcoms who've been incarcerated and that's not their defining characteristic."

||||||||||||||||||||||||||||||||||||||||||||||||||||||||||||||||||||

# Prison Has A Place, But Not For Everyone

On the shelf behind Stevens County Prosecutor Tim Rasmussen's desk is an unusual piece of art—a Styrofoam cup that has a scenic vista etched into it with a blue ballpoint pen.

The landscape ringing the cup features a snowcapped mountain and a river flowing through a valley. The art captures attention even though the canvas is pretty basic.

The cup was decorated by the defendant in a criminal case that Rasmussen prosecuted long ago. He says the man worked on the piece during his trial, and before he was led away in handcuffs following a conviction, Rasmussen asked him for it, and the man gave it to him.

"It just shows the potential," says Rasmussen, who kept the cup to remind him about the possibilities in the human spirit on tough days when it is difficult to have faith in the ability of people to change.

He has been the elected prosecutor in the rural Washington county for fourteen years but spent five years before that as a deputy prosecutor and fourteen years as a defense attorney in two states. This background gives Rasmussen the ability to look at the issue of prison reform from differing viewpoints.

"The tension that exists between punishment and treatment is what creates the chaos in sentencing," he says. "People who do things wrong must be held accountable, that is punishment. But folks who can't help but do things wrong need treatment. Mistakes made in differentiating between the two is where things can go wrong."

A great deal of sentencing is based on the faulty assumption that people value freedom so much that they can and will modify their behavior, he says. However, someone in the throes of a mental health crisis, or the person whose mind is saturated with drugs, is incapable of modifying his or her behavior even if they want to.

Rasmussen contends that people who have grown up in survival mode on the streets or in the home cannot change their behavior without first understanding its underlying causes.

"All behavior is purposeful—to help people change their behavior you've got to figure out the purpose and the cause."

Helping people realize what drives their impulses so they can retrain their thinking is time-intensive and costly, Rasmussen says, which is something an already over-burdened system often ignores.

A further obstacle to change is that people who serve long prison sentences can become institutionalized and, at the end of their stay, are no longer able to make individual choices.

The best hope for behavior modification, says Rasmussen, is to help people turn things around before they assimilate antisocial or criminal values into a life view or a habitual response.

"Only by addressing the root causes of crime can the numbers in prison be pared down," he says.

Toward that end, he has worked in Stevens County to set up a diversion program for nonviolent crimes. People charged with an offense can choose to participate in the program to avoid a felony on their record. They must agree to perform community service and pay restitution to victims, as well as pay a fee to the court and the cost of any treatment they receive.

Rasmussen worked with county officials to institute the diversion program to relieve the local jail overcrowding situation. He believes giving people a second chance before the hammer falls is also a public safety benefit, given the state's prison three-year recidivism rate of 45–49 percent. However, he is quick to enact penalties if they don't take the second chance seriously.

"If someone fails in a diversion program, the person should rightfully be held accountable for the harm done."

As the state criminal justice system is set up now, Rasmussen says mandatory sentencing laws sometimes extract punishment that is out of proportion to the crime.

For example, several years ago, he dealt with a case where a young man of twenty-four, who had prior juvenile felonies, went on a spree, this time stealing about $200,000 of merchandise, including more than a dozen guns.

Because he was a felon with stolen weapons in his possession, he was subjected to harsh provisions in state law. First off, the "hard time for hard crime" legislation of the late 1990s required sentences for each stolen firearm to run consecutive to the others.

That law followed Washington enacting in 1993 the "three strikes, you're out" law, the first in the nation, to deal with repeat criminals. People with multiple offenses have since been given greatly increased prison sentences, including life without parole.

As a result of these laws, Rasmussen said the young man ended up with a mandatory sentence of somewhere near 120 years. The case was sustained on appeal because there was no error in the process to warrant a new trial. The appellate court ruled it was up to the legislature to ameliorate the harshness of the law that made the punishment mandatory.

"I support judicial discretion in sentencing, but I support discretion down but not up," Rasmussen says. "My reasoning is that it's a protection against community bias, against someone's emotion and society's prejudice against certain offenders.

"Sentencing guidelines are a mechanical, cubbyhole approach to justice. But people aren't pegs, you can stick them in a hole, but if they don't fit, nothing beneficial happens."

Prosecutors have a lot of tools to pursue the right result in cases, he says, but it is simplistic for defense attorneys to say they hold "all the power" because of the immense responsibility that goes with the job.

"We have an obligation that no other participant of the judicial system has—and that is the obligation to do justice," Rasmussen says. "This system only functions well if the prosecutor is willing to uphold that standard." He admits that some prosecutors are not.

It is in murder cases that the state bears the greatest amount of responsibility, he says. The prosecutor stands in the place of the silenced victim, which is a heavy lift that no one else in the courtroom has to bear.

Many decisions about charging suspects come down to the prosecutor's sense of what justice requires for a given crime, says Rasmussen.

There are times when a charging decision does not represent what actually happened and a conviction cannot bring about justice, he says. This may be because there is not enough evidence to proceed with the real charge that should be brought. Or it could be that all the elements of a criminal case exist, but after review, a prosecutor determines it would be wrong to charge someone, as in self-defense matters or where there is sufficient provocation.

Some prosecution offices adopt policies about how certain types of crimes will be charged in response to community pressure, says Rasmussen. For that reason, some crimes may always be taken to trial and not "plea bargained" down to a lesser offense.

If a law-abiding citizen is arrested for making a foolish mistake, he says a prosecutor may decline to pursue a case because the person is unlikely to ever reoffend, so a conviction would be costly to taxpayers and serve little purpose. For example, a fourteen-year-old carelessly killed his brother with a new hunting bow. That case was not prosecuted because the prosecution would not benefit anyone. What lesson could be taught by the punishment?

Charges may also not be filed if the victim doesn't want to cooperate, an individual is deemed not to be a credible witness, or the alleged victim appears motivated by an improper purpose, such as revenge.

If the judge is unlikely to mete out reasonable punishment or accept a plea agreement, Rasmussen says a case might also not be pursued.

Prosecutors have an affirmative duty to correct things. Under a new view of prosecutorial responsibility, a prosecutor may be successful in obtaining a conviction, but if evidence later surfaces that the defendant was actually innocent, then the prosecutor has a responsibility to file motions to get that conviction set aside.

"I have seen prosecutors who would not do that because of their ego, their desire to win, or their alignment with victims or law enforcement," says Rasmussen.

He has learned through the years that attorneys can be honorable or dishonorable on both sides of the aisle.

"I have seen police officers and prosecutors lie, as well as defendants and defense attorneys," he says.

The power to charge is a very serious power, so it is a terrible thing to abuse, says Rasmussen.

He was born and raised in Michigan and earned a master's in social work from the University of Michigan.

His first job in the early 1970s was as one of five program managers at Green Oak Center, a maximum-security juvenile facility near Ann Arbor operated by the Department of Social Services. There were one hundred boys between the ages of fourteen to eighteen incarcerated, many with horrific crimes, such as rape, murder, and arson. The institution was essentially a school with educational and treatment opportunities. Staffed with special education teachers, Green Oak Center could plug boys into whatever grade range they functioned.

The recidivism rate was 80 percent when Rasmussen got there. A treatment program labeled Guide Group Interaction was instituted and a psychiatrist helped with behavioral therapy and helped the staff understand the boys' emotional situations.

Some of the teens increased by five grade levels in education during their stay, which was usually about one year. They also received vocational training and assistance with military enlistment, if possible, to bring a sense of purpose to their lives that would get them on a positive track.

"That was a tough first job, but we had some notable successes," he says. "We were a school but there were barbwire fences."

The recidivism rate had dropped to 60 percent by the time Rasmussen left four years later.

There were also some notable failures during his tenure, says Rasmussen. One of these was Daniel Remeta, who, after being at Green Oak Center, spent time in adult corrections. Following his release, Remeta went on a 1985 killing spree in Kansas, Arkansas, and Florida.

He was ultimately convicted of five murders and executed in Florida on March 31, 1998. Rasmussen regrets to this day that he did not respond to Remeta's request that he visit prior to the execution.

"I should have taken the time," he says.

Rasmussen reinforced his belief that positive intervention could turn things around his next eight years as a social worker for a large medical center in Southern California.

He represented patients who had been injured and sought institutional changes when needed.

After a divorce, Rasmussen found himself unemployed and living in rural North Carolina. A friend influenced him to apply to law school, and he earned his juris doctor in 1988 from Georgia State University in Atlanta.

He then began working as a private attorney and handled appointed cases as a public defender in North Carolina. He was involved with several death penalty cases.

In 2001, Rasmussen moved to Washington State to be near family and, a year later, became a deputy prosecutor in Spokane County, a job he held for five years.

"After fifteen years in defense work, I wanted to experience the other side of the aisle," he says.

In 2006, Rasmussen ran for his first public office and was elected prosecutor for Stevens County, a job he holds today.

What he noticed after moving to Washington was the drastic difference in the way criminal law procedure worked.

During his time in North Carolina, Rasmussen said the law was designed to convict the accused, while in Washington the law offers defendants more protection and functions more to set the accused free, not focusing on victim's rights.

For example, in North Carolina, any witness could be impeached by their criminal record. The jury was informed about any crime the witness had committed in the last ten years that carried a jail sentence of more than thirty days. In Washington, you can't ask about a prior conviction except in very limited circumstances, says Rasmussen.

In North Carolina, if a person submitted to one breathalyzer test but refused the second, the evidence of the first was admissible and could be used against them. In Washington, if someone doesn't provide the second breath sample, the results of the first breathalyzer test cannot be used in court.

Other differences among states are reflected in how death penalty cases are handled when new evidence emerges that could exonerate a condemned prisoner.

In a United States Supreme Court case, Justice Antonin Scalia stated, "Mere factual innocence is not a bar to an execution based upon a properly obtained state conviction."

Rasmussen believes that viewpoint is morally and ethically wrong, that any time new evidence emerges that exonerates the defendant, it should be a cause for review because a human life is at stake.

"The court based its decision on a state's rights principle," he says. "Finality of judgment is a value that states are constitutionally allowed to incorporate into their criminal justice systems."

Some states have laws in place that allow a reconsideration of new evidence for one year and some set a ten-year limit. Texas had a three-year limit, and new evidence discovered in cases after that time passed were not considered.

With that said, Rasmussen supports the death penalty. He says it is because he believes in the right to self-defense. He reasons that if the person being attacked has the right to defend himself or herself with deadly force and is justified in killing the attacker before the attacker can kill him, then the state has the right, if the people choose, to stand in the place of the victim and take the life of the attacker after the attacker has killed the victim.

"If the victim had the right to do it, and the attacker deserved it before he took the life, then surely he deserves it after," says Rasmussen.

He is troubled by the fact that most death row inmates are poor. "Economic status affects the outcome of the criminal justice process," he says.

Rasmussen also believes there are some people who prey on children and the vulnerable and will always pose a public safety threat, such as violent sexual offenders. They must remain behind bars as soon as they are identified for the protection of society.

"Individuals whose sexual drives become fused with their aggression are not likely to be rehabilitated," he says. "We must protect our children and vulnerable citizens from them. Jails and prisons do not make most people better, but we have to have them to protect ourselves from the violent and dangerous among us who will not or cannot change."

Despite his long years of being exposed to the worst of human nature, Rasmussen still believes people can be rehabilitated if they sincerely want change. On the wall in his office, there is a quote that he clipped from the *Ashville Citizen* newspaper many years ago.

The article titled "No Simple Answers" was written by Amos E. Reed, retired secretary of the Department of Corrections for the State of Washington: "This is not the kind of problem even the best-intentioned people, with unlimited resources, could ever expect to solve… I don't find any simplistic answers, but if there are any at all, they have to do with establishing a healthy living environment for children and adolescents beginning in the home and in the public schools and the community where there is a good self-image and a concern for others…and avoiding this anomie…this… 'I'll do my thing, let everyone else do theirs.' This is the self-serving kind of society we have developed.

"You just have to turn on your television and see the violence and filth and selfishness and glamorizing of drugs and violence. Then people wonder that this can influence their children. To me, it has become an idiocy… We have all these terribly damaged persons, psychopathic personalities, people with problems with drugs and alcohol, and then people think they can send them to prison and change them for the better. That's stupidity…absolute stupidity."

Rasmussen said young people are faced with problems earlier generations never dealt with. Many children growing up today get their values from television and movies and violent media. One of the most popular games portrays the scene from behind a gun as the "player" shoots and kills his enemies. There is plenty of realistic digital gore to accompany the action.

"Adults can see these things and reason that it is simply a depiction and not a real event, but children who are exposed over and over to these scenes lose the ability to distinguish between reality and this virtual world," he said.

"We become what we experience. Children learn from what is around them. We know abused children are much more likely to become abusers. Children who are exposed to violence in the home are much more likely to be violent when they are adults."

Rasmussen agrees with Reed that there are no simple answers when it comes to justice reform, but he also feels strongly that people can turn things around with a lot of determination and a little help.

"I believe in the power of people to change because I have seen it and experienced it," he says. "There is a better way. We can find it if we have the will. We know what does not work. Prison has its place, but it is not a place for everyone.

"We, as a society, need to reexamine our responses to criminal conduct and be willing to find the resources to implement changes that will work."

"The Heavens Declare the Glory of God" by Francisco Hernandez

# A Ray Of Light

*Through the trials and tribulations,*
*I've grown accustomed to the darkness.*
*I live this life, a young innocent heart,*
*battered and shattered into a million blood-drenched pieces.*
*Each piece holds a story untold,*
*each drop of blood my own.*
*In the dark days and nights of my life,*
*the darkness has grown;*
*comforted me, embraced me.*
*You see, it hides all you cannot see,*
*the hurt, the pain, the abuse and neglect.*
*The things I feel when no one's left,*
*and I'm alone in the darkness.*
*I'm lying still, yet my pillow's wet;*
*alone, drowning in my tears.*
*I'm thankful and most grateful for the darkness most of those times.*
*When I pour out my shattered, battered, and tortured heart,*
*Body soul and mind, I contemplate suicide—dare I die?*
*My cries become my prayers and suddenly, and so very unexpectedly,*
*each of my teardrops start to sparkle like a rare*
*diamond in a single ray of light.*
*Hope and love has reached me, touched me, and caressed me,*
*So gently yet so very deeply.*
*I'm amazed that hope and love shine through,*
*My darkness lights—I'm amazed by a ray of light.*

Travell "Paycheck" Holmes
A man in a cage

||||||||||||||||||||||||||||||||||||||||||||||||||||||||||||||||||

# Where Are They Now?

**Trevor Walraven**

Since this project began, Trevor Walraven, now thirty-six, has finally won his freedom but has yet to return to school. However, he has cofounded the Oregon Youth Justice Project under the umbrella of the Oregon Justice Resource Center to reduce the criminalization and incarceration of young people, particularly those from disenfranchised communities. His organization also focuses on restoring rights to families of incarcerated children. Currently, parents are very limited in their ability to make basic decisions regarding their incarcerated son or daughter's health, safety, or development.

Trevor is happy to connect about his work and can be reached at 4unlimitedpotential@gmail.com. His nonprofit's website is https://ojrc.info/youthjusticeproject/.

On the personal side, Trevor has purchased his first home in the Eugene area and grown into a management position within the company he works for. He's given well over one hundred presentations in Oregon and beyond.

**Joshua Cain**

In June 2020, Oregon Gov. Kate Brown granted Joshua Cain's clemency petition, and he was released from prison after serving twenty-two years for a crime he did not commit. His brother, Trevor Walraven, and other family members gave Cain a month off to reintegrate back into the free world, and then he went to school to finish working on his master's degree in business and join his brother in fighting for prison reform.

## Kathleen Blankenship

Kat Blankenship's update is simple, and that is exactly the way she likes it: "Living life in rural Oregon! Remembering every day is a blessing… Enjoying watching my grandkids grow and seeing my sons as fathers!"

## Keith Ward

Keith Ward recently worked with two churches in Colville, Washington, to raise funds to buy medical scrubs for inmates working in the hospice care center at Northern Nevada Correctional Institute. He also recently became a facilitator for NAMI (National Alliance on Mental Illness) to help prisoners with disorders navigate the brutal penal system.

On another front, Keith has tucked a couple of developmentally delayed inmates under his wing to provide them with protection.

While keeping his eye on the gate with a parole hearing in 2023, Keith is applying to the pardons board and is hopeful that they recognize his will to give back to society and grant him early release. His ultimate goal is to work with youth who are heading for trouble in the hope of stopping them from following his dark path. He has also promised to demonstrate his chef skills by making the author the best batch of cinnamon rolls she has ever tasted once he is released!

## Kevin Young

Kevin Young is taking care of older inmates on the inside and working on a legal case with Trevor and the author. His aggravating factor in sentencing is no longer on Oregon's list, and he is also preparing to challenge his life-without parole designation. He believes Americans are understanding more every day that prison reform is necessary, and he could one day realize his longtime hope of being free. When that day comes, he plans to open a used auto repair and detailing business and hire mechanics who received their training inside. He plans to lead a quiet life and spend lots of time with family and friends. He is considering a book to tell his own story, so stay tuned.

## Jacqueline Whitt

Jackie Whitt recently got a bill passed in her city that will assist women in prison with civil legal issues prior to their release. The measure lessens the burden of women reentering society and saves taxpayers thousands in state assistance. She hopes to expand this movement and continually works toward solutions for the prison population.

On the personal side, Jackie is completing a union electrical apprenticeship and continues to be clean and sober. She lives at home with her three grown children and loves learning and volunteering.

## Lydell and Laycelle White

Twin brothers Lydell and Laycelle White, now forty-one, scored a victory in the Oregon Supreme Court this past year—the court tossed the nearly sixty-seven-year sentences given to each man, declaring that they constituted cruel and unusual punishment.

That ruling set a precedent as it was the first time the Oregon court applied a previous federal decision to sentences that aren't true life but essentially add up to life because the number of years given the defendant extends past his normal life expectancy.

The twins will return to Marion County Circuit Court for resentencing, although that date had not yet been set as of publication.

## Frank DePalma

Frank DePalma has been released by the Nevada Department of Corrections and is making his way in a foreign world. He is slated to be the subject of a documentary about reentry into society after more than four decades of incarceration.

The other subjects in this book either continue to fight in the halls of justice for prison reform or are waiting patiently behind bars for America to recognize that they are much more than their crime.

The incarceration numbers published in this book may be somewhat lower at this time because while this work was being formatted for publication, the COVID-19 pandemic hit, and some states were releasing prisoners most at risk.

# Artist Bios

**Jorge Cabrera**

*I am a forty-two-year-old Latin artist. I was raised in Miami, Florida, but moved to Portland, Oregon. Unfortunately, I've made some bad choices in my life. In spite of my circumstance, I remain positive, making the best of my opportunities. Early on I was inspired by Nicolas Gauze. I have been drawing since I was a kid; slowly I created my own style with a hip-hop vibe/culture.*

*I caught the graffiti bug doing pastel pieces. My art is complex and abstract with a 3D flair. I have my own ideas of art, and I am known for my realistic portraits. It is a struggle at times, a challenge to create freely and not be influenced by my surroundings. Art is a beautiful way to express one's emotions.*

Jorge Cabrera provided art for *Shame* on pages 28, 44, 111, 147, 160, and 241. He is incarcerated at Oregon State Penitentiary for manslaughter, burglary, and robbery and is eligible for parole in eighteen months.

**Francisco Hernandez**

*Many of my paintings focus on the beauty of creation, centering on wildlife, landscapes, and portraits. Birds hold a fascination for me, both as creatures of beauty and as symbols of freedom. By using design, light, and color, I bring the viewer in to let them experience what I see.*

*I am a self-taught artist who has been creating art for the last sixteen years. My artwork continues to be influenced by my University of Oregon bachelor's degree in general social science with an emphasis in law, crime, and society. My studies focused on many social problems, including mass incarceration, inequality, poverty, and racial issues. Even though some of these themes are very hard for me to paint because of my past experiences, they are important to express so that others may see some of the injustices present in our society. You can see more of my art at franciscohernandez.org.*

Francisco Hernandez opened *Shame* on page 12 with his illustration *Civil Death*, which is his interpretation of how people see prisoners. He said of that work: *"Being incarcerated puts us outside the consideration of society. To the outside world we who are in prison are at times presumed dead, so the skull face is not about how I see myself, but how others may see me or don't. However, the hands of flesh defiantly declare 'I am alive' to remind the viewer that this person matters and is not dead. The writing in the background is about the effects of warehousing people. With so many resources devoted to prison beds and not enough to programs, such as education, people will earn an ACTTD, or associates of criminal thinking transfer degree. The cage number with the infinity sign represents the millions of people incarcerated and the future millions if nothing changes in our current system."*

Francisco also created *The Heavens Declare the Glory of God* to end the book with a message of hope on page 289. He said of that work: *"God fills all things. God is everywhere, even in prison. What I want this piece to communicate is that the values of Jesus are not held in by walls, institutions, or people. When Jesus said to forgive, to have mercy, to feed the hungry, to have compassion, he was not saying to have it only for those we love or like, but for every single person. The truth is that if Jesus was on earth today, he would be in this prison eating with us, feeding us, forgiving us, restoring us, washing our feet, and showing us his mercy and grace."*

Francisco has paid his debt to society and is building a new life full of purpose and cultural enrichment.

## Toshio Takanobu

Toshio Takanobu drew the art for the front and back covers of *Shame*. His art is also featured on pages 74, 179, and 228. He has been incarcerated at Oregon State Penitentiary since 2007 for manslaughter, robbery, and unlawful use of a weapon. His earliest release date is 2033. You will notice the keyhole to the cell on the front cover is upside down. Toshio drew it that way to symbolize that a prisoner's spirit cannot be locked up.

## Allen Howard

Allen Howard drew the magical pieces on pages 58, 124, 196, 215 and 267. He has been lodged at Oregon State Penitentiary since 2002 for robbery, burglary, and unlawful use of a weapon. His earliest release date is 2042.

## Imani Williams

Imani Williams provided art on page 95 that was drawn during his time in the hole. He is serving life for murder and assault at Oregon State Penitentiary.

||||||||||||||||||||||||||||||||||||||||||||||||||||||||||||||||||||||||

# Acknowledgments

My deepest gratitude to Trevor Walraven, who was both my inspiration and mentor during the process to get this book together. Anytime I called on you for help to find an expert in the field of reform, you came through. Of equal importance was your input about life inside and the topics that should be addressed. I learned much from you and consider you and Loraine to be family.

Keith Ward, Kathleen Blankenship, and Jackie Whitt, you did an excellent job of laying out not only the pain and hardship you have endured but the remarkable ability of the human spirit to rise from the ashes and carve out a bright new path.

Travell Holmes, my gentlest breath of hope comes your way. The despair in your soul has carved a deep path and you can, and must, write your own book. You have the ability to touch hearts in a way that few can. I look forward to helping you with *Man in a Cage*.

To all of the families and professionals who agreed to help me educate America, I am thankful. You have given us a tool to demand change. Let's turn this thing around!

David Marvin volunteered his expertise in graphic arts to help me get the manuscript together and designed the wonderful book cover. I literally could not have done this without you.

Fulton Books is owed much gratitude for helping me polish this work and get it out into the book realm so that people can learn what is happening behind the wall. Pam Hogan, you snared me with your empathy for the cause and your interest in helping me reach others.

Kevin Young, it has been an honor to get to know you as a man and a human being. Your strength of spirit and ability to endure the cruelest sentence of all has inspired me to be a more focused and compassionate human being. You have worn suffering with great dignity and grace. It has become my mission to help you once again walk the streets of the free world. I look forward to that cup of coffee.

||||||||||||||||||||||||||||||||||||||||||||||||||||||||||||||||||||||||

# About the Author

To walk into a prison to visit someone you love is a daunting experience. To walk out after the visit is to breathe freedom and feel a cloud of oppression being lifted from your spirit. To know that a person who is very valuable to you is being abused at the whim of guards and caged like an animal never allows your soul to rest.

That is RaeLynn Ricarte's description of the time she spends behind the wall visiting prisoners she has adopted. Her commitment to provide care and comfort for inmates began six years ago when a young Marine she had adopted suffered a psychotic break after his second deployment to the Middle East and lashed out in violence. Jonny pleaded guilty to two counts of attempted murder and was sentenced to thirteen years in prison with a "good time" discount.

As a journalist, Ricarte was unable to witness Jonny's suffering without challenging the hypocrisy of a society that claims to be all about mercy and compassion but is apathetic about mass incarceration.

*Shame* is not Ricarte's first book. Several years ago, she interviewed twenty-nine warriors and their families about the true meaning of sacrifice for *Living the Oath: Warriors Take It, Families Endure It*, which was published in the fall of 2013 by Black Opal Books.

Ricarte has won state and national awards for stories that give a voice to people without one. Helping America change its punitive mindset to adopt a more restorative model of justice has become her passion and life's work.

CPSIA information can be obtained
at www.ICGtesting.com
Printed in the USA
BVRC091319180921
616964BV00007B/69